LET HIM GO

"I honor the past not by repeating it but by learning from it – by refusing to add pain to pain, grief to grief. That is why we must answer hatred with love, violence with peace, resentment with generosity of spirit and conflict with reconciliation."

(Jonathan Sacks, *The Dignity of Difference*)

In memory of my parents

The Holocaust was so terrible and heinous that one could have had believed in and hoped that it would have been the last genocide in history. But then came Cambodia, the killings of the Iraqi Kurds, Bosnia, Rwanda and Darfur. This book is dedicated to my children and grandchildren in the hope that they may live in a time when this madness will stop.

LET HIM GO

A Danish Child in Ravensbrück and Theresienstadt

IB KATZNELSON

Translated by Robert Maas

VALLENTINE MITCHELL
LONDON • CHICAGO, IL

First published in 2019 by Vallentine Mitchell

Catalyst House,
720 Centennial Court,
Centennial Park, Elstree WD6 3SY, UK

814 N. Franklin Street,
Chicago, Illinois,
IL 60610 USA

www.vmbooks.com

British Library Cataloguing in Publication Data:
An entry can be found on request

ISBN 978 1 912676 08 8 (Paper)
ISBN 978 1 912676 09 5 (Ebook)

Library of Congress Cataloging in Publication Data:
An entry can be found on request

Printed by 4edge Ltd, Hockley, Essex

Contents

Notes on the Book's Sources   *vii*

Foreword: Children in the Hell of the Holocaust   *viii*

1. **Prologue**   1

2. **"Viking Jews" and the "Russian Jews"**   11

3. **The Prelude to the Action against the Danish Jews**   19
    The Cooperation Policy during the Occupation   19
    August and September 1943   21
    Passivity? Or were the Warning Lights Very Dim?   26
    The Telegram of Fate? Best's Telegram of 8 September 1943   29

4. **Betrayed and Detained**   38
    We Went Underground   38
    It was now 4 October – Assembly Point: Syrefabrikken   44
    Helper or Informer?   47
    Infernal Noise, Shouts and Screams – The Gestapo Raid on
        Syrefabrikken   52
    Interrogation in Dagmarhus and a Night in Western Prison   61
    Horserød Camp   62
    The Agreement that Prevented the Danish Jews from
        being Sent by Transport   68
    Perhaps a Brain Tumor: Attempts to get my
        Grandmother Released   71
    We Remain in Horserød Camp   72
    The 23 November – Deportation to Germany   84

5. **Ravensbrück – "Welcome to Hell"**   90
    My Mother and my Five Months in Ravensbrück   93

6. **Sachsenhausen**   **111**
   My Father's Six Weeks in Sachsenhausen   112
   My Father's Ten Days in Berlin   120

7. **Theresienstadt**   **124**
   Transport of No. 9 and 10/XXV/4 to Theresienstadt   124
   Theresienstadt's History   127
   Theresienstadt's Organization   130
   Our Arrival at SS Headquarters   135
   Descriptions of our Arrival at Theresienstadt   139

8. **Arrested Already: 1 October 1943**   **142**
   Why were they at Home? And why did they Open the Door?   142
   Hohenelber Barracks and a Children's Hospital   148
   Glimpses of my Aunt Annie's Daily Life in the
        First Seven Months   154

9. **Red Cross and the Potemkin Façade**   **164**
   The Red Cross Delegation's Visit   164
   Red Cross Food Parcels   171
   Rathausgasse 1   175

10. **A Drawing and the Artist**   **188**

11. **The White Buses – The Myth that is Hard to Knock Down**   **193**

12. **Beginning a New Ordinary Life**   **205**
    Tylösand   205
    After the War   210
    Our Arrival at the Kommandantur   215
    Justice – Not Vengeance   217

13. **Acknowledgements**   **221**

Timeline   223
Bibliography and Archival References   224
Index   228

Notes on the Book's Sources

The historical sections of the chapter "Viking Jews" and the "Russian Jews" are based on various information about shtetler in Belarus. In searching the internet one should be aware that Bobruisk, Lubonichi and Kovchitsy are transcribed in several different ways. The personal accounts of my grandfather are from a tape-recorded interview about his childhood with a woman, who is unknown to me, from September 1982. Only a very few passages are from another interview with the linguist Jan Katlev (1944-2013) whose family was originally also called Katznelson and also came from Lubonichi. The quality of this recording is very poor and was therefore only sparsely used.

Quotes from official announcements and telegrams etc. in "The Cooperation Policy during the Occupation" and the following chapters are from the source collection *October '43. Danske jøders flugt til Sverige eller deportation til Theresienstadt (The Flight of Danish Jews to Sweden or Deportation to Theresienstadt)* with diaries, telegrams, letters, meetings and illegal magazines etc., published by Humanity in Action and edited by Anders Jerichow.

The descriptions in boxes of a number of people and institutions are mainly paraphrasings of the postings from Den Store Danske, Gyldendals åbne encyklopædi (Gyldendal's open encyclopedia) and Wikipedia.

The details in the section "Passivity? Or were the Warning Lights Very Dim?" about the burglary of Arthur Henriques' office are from the explanations given in connection with the trial against Paul Hennig after the war.

My grandmother saved my mother's letters from Horserød Camp as well as the letter from Tylösand written just after the liberation. My mother found them after my grandmother's death. I have given the original letters to the Jewish Museum in Copenhagen.

The information in "We remain in Horserød Camp" about my grandmother's inquiries at Dagmarhus to get us released, is from the interrogations in connection with the trial against Paul Hennig and my grandmother's explanations to the police.

Foreword

Children in the Hell of the Holocaust

By Therkel Straede, Associate Professor of
Contemporary History at the University of
Southern Denmark in Odense

*"Bearing testimony about such extreme experiences is a
courageous step which opens the way for breaking the silence."*[1]

Ib Katznelson and Otto Dov Kulka have two things in common: 1) they were
in German concentration camps as children. Ib as a very young child, as his
second birthday had just been celebrated in the Danish detention camp
Horserød, when he was deported to Germany; 2) how in their maturity they
look back seeking to find out what it was they experienced as children in the
incredibly brutal Nazi camp system. They visit the sites, they dig into their
memories and scrutinize witness testimonies.

Landscapes of the Metropolis of Death is the title Otto Dov Kulka gave to
his book which appeared in Hebrew in 1984 and later in extended versions
in German, English and other languages, and in 2014 also in Danish. Strictly
speaking, Otto got to know two Nazi death camps from the inside:
Theresienstadt and Auschwitz-Birkenau. The book's subtitle, *Reflections on
Memory and Imagination,* sets the tone for the book. Otto, born in 1933 and
raised in a small, provincial Czech town, was deported to Auschwitz-
Birkenau with his mother and other family members from Theresienstadt
in September 1943, and was locked up in camp section BIIb, the so-called
"family camp". When this camp section was liquidated half a year later, he
was an internee at the camp hospital (*Revier*), went unnoticed and survived.
Meanwhile, his mother was deported to the Stutthof concentration camp and
perished there, while Otto stayed in Birkenau with his stepfather. Here, the
now ten-year-old managed to learn how to survive in a system where the
prisoners' knowledge, culture and ethics were constantly being attacked by
the Nazi's totally distorted misanthropic "values" which caused brutalization
to spread, also among the prisoners. While big, strong men perished, Otto

learned to avoid the perpetrators, ducked to avoid the blows when SS men and Capos hit, and hid when a "selection" approached.

The "selections" were used by the SS to sort out prisoners who, in spite of malnutrition and disease still had some working capacity left, from those who were completely "used up" and designated to be murdered as "useless eaters". Otto himself is – from a Nazi point of view – a "useless" character from the first to the last day. He is a child – even a Jewish child – in a slave labor camp where work mostly consists of construction work of the hardest kind. Children almost never escaped the first selection which took place on the ramp when the prisoners arrived by rail transport from many European countries. Here, SS doctors selected strong young men and women for slave labor and sent the others – children and the mothers accompanying them, the elderly, the sick and frail – directly to the camp's crematoria where they were murdered in gas chambers immediately upon arrival. However, the Jews who were sent to Auschwitz from Theresienstadt in September 1943 were – as an exception to the rule – deported to Birkenau as a group and families stayed together, among them Otto's. So began a childhood so radically different from what most people experience, both scary and cruel, as people were being murdered for the smallest of excuses or simply having to give up, because ruthless exploitation had exhausted the last of their strength. Even if men, women and children could still live together in the "family camp", the conditions and the violence were basically the same as in the rest of the Auschwitz camp complex.

Otto had some basic protection from his mother and later on from his stepfather. For the stepfather, saving the boy from hell became an important mission. Thus, throughout his time in the concentration camp universe Otto had an adult helping him from day to day with practical things as well as presenting interpretations for all the extremes that he experienced. The boy learned to "read" the camp, move in the closed and open spaces of the constant confinement, and decode its human – and to a large extent utterly inhuman – relations. The visual impressions, the sounds and smells of Auschwitz coincided with the camp's physical structure and the topography of terror, which later as a grown-up man Otto tried to recall in his book and arrange in a way that made sense.

Otto Dov Kulka from Prague found himself in a Nazi camp in September 1942, at nine years old, for the only reason that, according to the Nazi definition, he was a Jew. It was for the same reason that Ib Katznelson from Copenhagen, one year later, fell into the clutches of the Gestapo. When the German action against the Danish Jews was launched in October 1943, his mother and father with two-year-old Ib attempted to escape to Sweden from Kastrup in the south of Copenhagen, but were arrested along with family members and other Jews. Most were deported to Theresienstadt while Ib, with his parents, was detained in a German internment camp near Elsinore, the *Polizeigefangenenlager Horserød*.

On 23 November 1943 the three of them were deported again, Ib's father to the Sachsenhausen concentration camp in Oranienburg near Berlin, Ib and his mother to Ravensbrück in Fürstenberg between Berlin and Rostock. Here in Nazi Germany's main concentration camp for women, mother and son were separated from each other, and being without one's mother or another adult for protection was something children in concentration camps rarely survived. However, other prisoners took care of little Ib, who was reunited with his mother after some time. When the two of them were transported on to Theresienstadt on 23 April 1944, they were reunited with Ib's father as well as with other members of the family.

Theresienstadt, north of Prague, was another Nazi metropolis of death, albeit with a special character. The Nazis had established a myriad of different camps. The camp as an institution can be said to be a characteristic feature of the twentieth century: the fact that people in large numbers were – voluntarily or by force – removed from farms, households and homes, accommodated collectively and segregated by categories into camps with varying degrees of surveillance and discipline. Nazi Germany utilized the organization and confinement of people by categories, determined by the state, to the extremes: youth camps, state labor service camps, military and POW camps, foreign and forced labor camps in many forms. Different societies – including social and liberal democracies – in the 1930s and 40s used camps as an organizational tool as well, and still do, as in today's refugee camps. Nazism, however, created coercive camp institutions which were unique in their brutality and contempt for human life – concentration camps, extermination camps and ghettos – the last two types developed to exclude Jews from society and eradicate them by means of hunger, disease or poison gas.

The Birkenau part of the Auschwitz camp complex, which Otto Dov Kulka experienced, was primarily an extermination camp, and secondarily a concentration camp, and it was the largest of its kind in both categories. Majdanek near Lublin also combined the two functions but on a smaller scale. In 1941-42, four camps were created for the sole purpose of exterminating Jews: Bełżec, Sobibór and Treblinka with stationary gas chambers, Chełmno with mobile gas vans. Particularly in Eastern Europe, where most Jews lived, they were typically firstly concentrated into ghettos, where inhuman living conditions decimated their numbers, and then after a shorter or longer period of time taken to the extermination camps and murdered. Only a minority of the Jews who came to the camps in 1943, and particularly in 1944, were included into the concentration camps as slave laborers; but forced labor in the special *Zwangsarbeitslager für Juden* and in ghettos generally had the same character and deadly result as in the proper concentration camps.

Theresienstadt was special in the Nazi camp system: a ghetto, strictly controlled by German police despite a certain self governance by the prisoners, led by a "Council of Elders" *(Ältestenrat der Juden),* and externally guarded by Czech gendarmerie. The living conditions for the Jewish inmates were somewhere between the horrible circumstances of the ghettos and the abysmal misery of the concentration camps. Theresienstadt, however, did not have the rigid separation of the sexes that concentration camps had, so in Theresienstadt families could live together, albeit in poverty with very limited space, and with primitive hygiene facilities. If they had any strength and energy left after long hours of forced labor and all their worries, prisoners could even maintain a sex life and participate in cultural activities. But in Theresienstadt, too, the constant threat of death was on every prisoner's mind: Otto Dov Kulka talks about "the immutable law of death, the law of the great Death".

Theresienstadt, in what was then the German Protectorate of Bohemia and Moravia, was located in an old fortress town at the river Eger, a tributary of the Elbe. In one part of the fortress – *Kleine Festung* – an ordinary concentration camp was established for members of the Czech resistance and other, mostly non-Jewish, prisoners. In the second, the much larger part was the special ghetto for Jews dating from November 1941 to May 1945.

The establishment of the ghetto coincided with the beginning of the systematic extermination of German and Western European Jews. The complete physical extermination of the Jews was German policy from the beginning of the "Barbarossa Campaign", that is the attack on the Soviet Union on 22 June 1941. At the beginning it was limited to the Soviet territories which were occupied by Germany and implemented in a quasi-military way with massacres carried out close to where the Jews lived. The mass-killings are carried out by shootings by the so-called *Einsatzgruppen* of the German Security Police and special police battalions, along with units from the ordinary army and supported by collaborationist troops and local anti-Semitic activists. But once total annihilation began, it expanded to the West, as German and Austrian Jews were deported to places in the occupied Soviet areas where the massacres took place and were usually shot immediately upon arrival.

At the same time the German police experimented with the use of poison gas, a technique which had already proved useful for the massacre of ethnic

Germans and Poles who were mentally ill or otherwise disabled. In early December 1941 the first mass killing of Jews in a gas chamber was carried out at Chełmno, and already during spring and summer of 1942, all of the aforementioned extermination camps were operating, and the Polish Jews – which with its three million Jews was the largest Jewish population in the world – were drawn into the murderous process. At the same time Jews from the Netherlands, Belgium, France and other countries were already being deported to the extermination camps.

In order for the total annihilation to run smoothly it was important that the victims be kept unaware of the destiny that awaited them. Therefore, the perpetrators made them believe that the deported were to be relocated and deployed to forced labor. Theresienstadt was given a special function. In addition to serving as the place of concentration of Czech Jews like Otto Dov Kulka and his family for later transportation, the ghetto in the old garrison city gained a crucial role in camouflaging the genocide: while able-bodied younger Jews from the German area were being deported eastwards with their families and shot, the elderly were placed in a special "old peoples' ghetto" in Theresienstadt. Here they would live and were encouraged to exchange letters (censored, of course) with the outside world. This made the cover-up story of forced labor more credible to the Jews, to German society and to foreign countries. Also Jews who for one reason or another could not just disappear were locked up in Theresienstadt: high-ranking war veterans, artists and media people, scientists and other well-known Jews with special qualifications or significant foreign contacts.

Thus, it is logical that the Danish Jews were deported to Theresienstadt, whereas the Norwegian Jews were deported directly to Auschwitz-Birkenau one year earlier and where most of them were murdered on the day of their arrival. In Norway, the Norwegian authorities, ruled by the local Nazis, were responsible for the deportation and carried it out with the utmost zeal. In Denmark, the democratic parties from left to right of the political spectrum made sure that, despite initiatives by the German occupying power, there was no legislation against Jews or discrimination. Even after the government ceased to function on 29 August 1943, the central administration continued to make an honorable – albeit only partially successful – effort to protect the Jews. That it was possible to ensure that the Jews who were deported from Denmark remained in Theresienstadt is an important example of this. Normally, Jews who came to Theresienstadt were sent to the gas chambers in Treblinka or Auschwitz-Birkenau after a few months. By then the requests from relatives, troubled neighbors and others who had not understood the radical nature of Nazi anti-Jewish policies, had normally ceased.

Of the more than 140,000 Jews who were incarcerated in Theresienstadt between 1941 and 1945, almost 90,000 were sent to the extermination camps, while 35,000 died in the camp itself, typically of hunger and epidemics. Even though Theresienstadt did not belong to the concentration camp system management (the *Inspektion der Konzentrationslager* department of the *Reichssicherheitshauptamt*), as did the proper KZs, and even though the regime at Theresienstadt differed from that of other Nazi camps, it was just as much a metropolis of death as concentration camps such as Stutthof, Sachsenhausen and Ravensbrück, and the Auschwitz-Birkenau extermination camp.

What was it like to be a child in such a place? That is what Otto Dov Kulka and Ib Katznelson wish to tell us about, and it is not easy for them. How much can one remember in adulthood of what happened when one was ten to twelve years old, not to mention two to three years old? In the Danish popular magazine *Samvirke* from July 2016, Denmark's then oldest citizen, 110-year-old Ellen Brandenborg from Aarhus (Jutland) says: "I can remember back to when I was five years old. We were going to the photographer, the two youngest of my siblings and I. I wore a white dress with a red silk sash tied in a big bow." The article is illustrated with a photo of the five-year-old with two sisters wearing the dress just as described. Has the picture, maybe paired with older family members' stories about the episode – including details such as the colors which are not apparent from the black and white photograph – over the years become like a personal memory? Or has memory in the course of more than one hundred years really preserved the episode as it is reproduced in the interview? Or could it be that the picture served to keep an authentic piece of early childhood memory alive, while myriads of other episodes from a long life have faded into oblivion?

Both Kulka and Katznelson struggle with this problem: Which parts of what they remember can be considered authentic memory from the camps? After having avoided it for many years, they finally reached the point of being willing to contribute their narratives of what they experienced during the Holocaust and testify. Otto Dov Kulka has done this before in court proceedings against Auschwitz staff in Krakow in 1947 and in Frankfurt am Main in 1964, and has worked a lot with the history of Nazism and anti-Semitism in his scholarly career as a historian. But in the courtroom, he focused on what happened and who committed which concrete criminal acts, not about the deeper layers of the prisoners' experience of the universe in which these occurred. He avoided addressing these layers of consciousness when working as a historian, where he strictly and "objectively" kept his own biography out of his research work. *Landscapes of the Metropolis of Death* is, however, based on the idea that fragments of memory – not least dreams –

represent authentically the reality of the camp which can, therefore, be truthfully represented in despite the time-span.

Ib Katznelson – educated in systematic social sciences – is even more skeptical about his own ability to remember as he was much younger when the events took place. His strategy is to present a careful study where he summarizes what a number of eyewitnesses have told him about his early history, and conscientiously presents and discusses the contradictions in the source material as well as his own reasoning. So his narrative is less inward-looking than Kulka's and it links the meticulous reconstruction of his time in the camp, based on a large number of eyewitness accounts, with a wide range of scholarly literature dealing with the institutional and political background to the events. The result is an analytical account with an unmistakable personal diction.

Everyone who has experienced the Holocaust has a need to express his or her experiences linguistically by integrating these extremes with the ordinary part of their lives. By the use of talking and conversation one can face the trauma and thereby make it seem less threatening. This is widely recognized today; but it was considered differently right after the war. The number of testimonies from camps, ghettos, etc., which appeared in the media, was huge in the first few months and years after the liberation. It shows that the need to talk and testify was urgent, despite the fact that the pain must have been raw as the events were so recent. But the very extreme experiences of the survivors were hard to verbalize, and the outside world apparently had difficulty relating to them. So their stories obstructed the understandable desire to return as soon as possible to a normal life after the war and the crimes of the Nazi period.

In the survivor narratives there was an implicit accusation – or at least, this was how it was felt by many: If what happened in the Nazi camps and torture chambers was that bad, that extreme, shouldn't one have done more to fight that Nazi ideology and its followers? Did the survivor narratives from the Metropolis of Death not pose a categorical imperative that only few felt they had lived up to? Not even the victims went free of self-accusations, for could they not have done something else, done more in order to prevent what happened? Ib Katznelson's story contains painful examples of these self-indictments.

Actually most survivors were soon told to keep quiet and move on with their lives! They felt the discomfort of the people they addressed, and sometimes also received very direct messages to shut up. This was the professional advice of those days to the survivors who struggled hard with their memories: look forward, do not cling to the past! Quite paradoxically, considering the strong reputation of psychoanalysis at the time, psychologists and psychiatrists were in no way reluctant to recommend people – the mentally ill as well as the healthy – to go back in their personal history in order to seek relief and find a basis for personal development and growth. However, they meant only general experiences of early childhood such as the relationship with the father, the mother, emotions and sexuality, while the experiences made in an environment that was in a more or less permanent state of emergency, and characterized by violence and ever-present death, did not really fit into that formula. This extreme environment certainly gave those who lived through it experiences that are impossible to integrate into a social normality and personal continuity, and already difficult, if not impossible, to verbalize. When the outside world showed disinterest or even refused outright to listen to and relate to these narratives, it is understandable that most Holocaust survivors soon chose silence while only a minority insisted on talking about what had happened.

Otto Dov Kulka confesses that he personally was unable to read or even open books about the Holocaust. His way of dealing with what he calls "the immutable law of death, the law of the great Death" was to concentrate on the most rigorously "objectivist" historical research and completely refrain from merging that with biographical elements of his personal experience. He meticulously explored the background of the crimes – in ideology, politics and social dynamics – and their later effects. But he stayed away completely from topics such as life in the ghettos and camps and what it did to the Jewish victims, and decided not to speak of what he had experienced himself in his own body and mind. In this there was strong psychological repression which was apparently beneficial for a time, but in the long run did not do away with the urge to talk, which eventually also provided him with the courage to do so.

Ib Katznelson for his part says that it was only many years after the events that his mother and other close relatives opened up and began talking about their time in the camps. He even chose – despite the fact that the time in the camps had caused him permanent health problems which marked him throughout his childhood, youth and adulthood – to respect his relative's mutual decision to keep quiet. It was only after events outside the family circle – a changed socio-political situation following the fall of the Berlin Wall and the collapse of Communism – changed the global agenda that he felt free as well as obliged to ask questions about his early childhood history, and to tell his story.

An important impulse for Holocaust survivors such as Otto and Ib, to start talking about their terrible experiences, came from the USA. In the 1980s, and even more strongly in the entire Western world in the 1990s, the attitude towards contemporary witnesses, and in particular Holocaust survivor testimonies, changed from negative indifference into positive interest.

In the 1950s and 60s, the influential historian of the Danish resistance movement, Jørgen Hæstrup (Odense), was attacked by fellow historians for partly having based his books about the resistance on interviews with former freedom fighters. In the scholarly journal *Scandia,* from 1968, another influential historian of the German occupation of Denmark, Henning Poulsen (Aarhus), in an article "on contemporary historical interviewing" more or less dismissed oral evidence as a valid historical source, if it was not based on decision-maker's testimonies that could be verified by written documents of preferably government provenance. In the 1980s, however, the international Oral History movement – with swells also into Danish waters – struggled to achieve recognition for scholarly history to also consider seriously the stories and histories of ordinary people, and not put lesser value on oral testimony over the documents that happened to end up in public archives. Historians who, under the impact of the mental and cultural revolutions that took place around 1968, developed a more democratic attitude to history, and found that personal – especially oral – testimony could bring oppressed groups and forgotten stories out and rehabilitate the everyday stories of "ordinary people". And as far as their place in the collective memory of society is concerned, the victims of Nazism – Jews and non-Jews alike – were indeed such a forgotten, oppressed group struggling with their extreme "everyday stories" from a somber universe that had so very little in common with the happenings and sorrows of an ordinary life – and for this reason seemed quite eccentric to most people.

However, the image of the victims of Nazi persecution as a neglected minority changed completely from the 1980s onwards. First, the television series *Holocaust,* which in 1979 emptied streets in many countries when broadcast, gave rise to an interest in and identification with the Jewish victims of persecution in Western societies, and created a new sense of self-assurance among the victims. Then, Claude Lanzmann's mammoth documentary *Shoah* (1983) moved the personal testimony from the periphery of social – and media – discourse into its center, giving the victims a new position of authority, and encouraging them to speak up. Popular initiatives and history projects "from below" started creating forums where it was legitimate and appreciated that the victims tell their stories. When the filmmaker Steven Spielberg, with the profits from his Holocaust feature film *Schindler's List* (1993), established the Survivors of the Shoah Visual History Foundation and in 1994 started a systematic and mass-scale worldwide collection of life-story video interviews with Holocaust victims, eventually even the shyer and more modest survivors were motivated to stand up and testify to their experiences.

While the Shoah Foundation collection of memories was going on, there was a lot of criticism from scholars about its methodology as well as the sheer scale of the project. Would it gain a monopoly status and could it be trusted to represent a true pluralism of voices and narratives? After the vast majority of the today 54,000 plus interviews have been indexed and made available to researchers around the world, and about 2,000 interviews made available to schoolchildren and students via the Iwitness.usc.edu website, broad recognition has come about that the fact that so many Holocaust survivors were given the opportunity to tell their stories in due time, is invaluable. The value for macro as well as micro history and Holocaust studies in general is unchallenged today, for the Shoah Foundation interviews cover almost any place, topic and aspect one can think of, and narratives conducted in the most diverse modes of diction. Furthermore, the large-scale media coverage of the project caused large numbers of survivors to open up and realize the value of their personal contribution in the form of their testimonies. A good example is Ib Katznelson's mother. Her decision to speak with the Shoah Foundation interviewers opened her up to – also in other contexts within the family and in other contexts – talk about what had been so extremely painful and still was: the experience of utmost powerlessness during the years when the small, peaceful country of Denmark was hit by German occupation and targeted within the Nazi attempt to annihilate all the Jews of Europe if not worldwide.

Ib would probably not have been able to tell the interviewers anything even if he had wanted to. For although the early years of childhood are extremely important for the formation of the personality, what a person can consciously remember from the age of 2-3 years is by nature very limited. A life-story interview – which was the Shoah Foundation concept – would soon reach its limit, no matter whether the urge to tell and structure by way of narrating the story the events and emotions that he went through during his childhood years in Nazi camps – was undoubtedly the same for a victim like Ib Katznelson, who was a young child during the Holocaust, as for older survivors.

As mentioned earlier, Otto Dov Kulka, who was already a schoolboy when he came to Theresienstadt, discussed in his book which of the fragments, impressions and memories he has kept can be regarded as authentic, and he is extremely self-critical. Stories of other survivors have filled in holes in his memory, as have the contributions to collective memory by scholars, educators, and the media. Also, throughout the many years after the liberation, imagination has filled in holes even in the narrative of an extremely disciplined, critical observer like Kulka. As he was being asked again and again about his personal camp experiences, and increasingly felt the urge to find out for himself, in the end he decided to find out the up's and down's of his personal story, and make it available to the general public.

Being a *child survivor* is not easy, though. The Nazis did not spare the children – it is one crucial area where their morality and habitus differed fundamentally from what was generally applicable in their – our – culture, and probably in all human societies. The Nazis disregarded the basic need of man to protect his offspring and care for the weak members of the species. They actually aimed their repressive and annihilative measures particularly against the Jewish children. With psychological insight – or instinct - and great cruelty Germany introduced in the 30s a vast number of laws, regulations and rules specifically aimed at making life miserable for Jewish children: They were excluded from schools, sports, playgrounds and like the adult Jews referred to starvation and the extreme scarcity of everything. And when the total extermination drive started, it became apparent - after a short period where the killings was predominantly aimed at skilled men respectively men capable of bearing arms - that it was children and women with small children who were the first to be forced in front of the firing squads or conducted into the gas chambers.

No consideration was shown to either parenthood or the children, on the contrary: by striking at the weakest, the perpetrators felt that they demonstrated their own strength, heroism, and the right to rule while at the same time demoralizing the grown-up Jews and forcing them to face impossible, inhuman dilemmas. Hence the children were the Nazis' favorite victims; but those who survived can hardly testify about what they went through because the victim's story of suffering is – as it always applies to life stories since Goethe – an adult story.

The collection of interviews with victims of Nazi atrocities by the Shoah Foundation – and other smaller, but important interview projects such as the *Zwangsarbeit 1939-1945* and *European Resistance Archive* repositories, not to forget the *Yale University Fortunoff Video Archive for Holocaust Testimonies,* which pioneered the gathering of video interviews – took place while many thousands were still alive, who had experienced the Nazi years as adults or teenagers. Their stories took precedence over what those who had experienced the events as children could tell. But the need to testify was felt equally strong by child survivors, and we as future generations certainly feel the need to hear, see and read their testimonies because without the children's stories we do not really grasp the totality of what the Holocaust meant to the victims, and means to mankind.

Paul Valent, who experienced the ghetto in Budapest as a seven year-old, recalls in his book *Child Survivors. Adults Living with Childhood Trauma*, that the Nazi persecution of Jews, which almost entirely annihilated the Jewish children of Europa, and cost the lives of 1½ million children, was unprecedented and must be considered as the most massive extermination of a specific group of people in history. So, as skeptical as one may be about childhood memories, especially from the earliest childhood years, one must, in order to create as complete a picture of the Holocaust as possible, include the widest possible range of experiences, and thus also recognize the contribution that child survivors can give, as well as their democratic right to speak up and participate in the formation of the collective memory of the Holocaust. Their participation is necessary for therapeutic reasons and because the Holocaust, without involving the children's optics and experiences – as strange as it may sound given the overall view that countless adult testimonies on the unspeakable atrocities and sufferings caused by the Nazis have already portrayed – would come across as "too nice", too mainstream.

When children are involved, the Holocaust becomes even harder to integrate into the general history of mankind, the western, European or German world, and appears as an even deeper, more epochal breach of civilization than what we come to see as a result of the post-war "revolution of witnessing"; the integration of the children's stories render the image of the Holocaust more unbearable – and more truthful.

According to Paul Valent, children who survived the Holocaust were inflicted under the most horrible circumstances by numerous and serious traumata.

Of course, this ultimately applies most extremely to the vast majority of Jewish children who perished – and therefore rarely left any kind of trace. Thus, there is every reason to be grateful to those who defy the traumas and the pain and try to bear some kind of witness to what they experienced. This gratitude must be directed to Otto Dov Kulka, who ends up looking at the dreams he incessantly has for traces of the realities of Auschwitz and Theresienstadt. And it must equally be directed to Ib Katznelson.

Ib Katznelson's strategy to reconstruct what he was exposed to at the age of two to three and a half years is a different one: a careful, reflexive exploration of history, faithful to sources, and using the tools of systematic analysis and critical reflection that he acquired during his professional training in political science and used during his long career as a civil servant in ministry departments and international organizations. That he at the same time demonstrates profound empathy and a certain twist of – Jewish? – humor, only makes his account of his and the family's history during the Holocaust even more readable. It makes us richer in insight into the historically unique crime we call the Holocaust, and into what our civilization and human beings in general are capable of.

Therkel Straede
Copenhagen, July 2016

Note

1.   Geoffrey Hartman, "Video interviews on the Holocaust. Thoughts on the key documents of the 20th century", in Daniel Baranowski (ed.), *Ich bin die Stimme der sechs Millionen* (Stiftung Denkmal für die ermordeten Juden Europas, Berlin: 2009), pp.15-26, p. 18.

1

Prologue

There wasn't a team of crisis psychologists at the quayside in Malmö when the White Red Cross buses brought us safely from the concentration camp Theresienstadt.[1] We had driven through a Germany that was more or less bombed to rubble, via Denmark to Sweden, where we arrived on 18 April 1945. And there weren't any psychologists when, after six weeks in a kind of internment in Sweden, we returned to Denmark. It was not considered necessary, neither professionally nor as a general perception in 1945. Such a "procedure" was not used at that time. The Swedes were, understandably, mostly interested in whether we had brought infectious diseases with us and preferred to keep us in a kind of isolation.

What does one then do to process the trauma that obviously must have prevailed after having been a prisoner for five months in Ravensbrück concentration camp, a couple of months in Sachsenhausen and a year in Theresienstadt?

You get it out. You talk about it, long and intensely. You talk with others in the same situation, try to understand, try to come to terms with the thought that the situation was close to going fatally wrong several times, reconcile yourself with the guilt about why it was you who was saved while millions of others perished in the Nazi's hell.

No! It was not like that in my family. It was not something we talked about. It was not mentioned to others that it had affected us and was in our minds day and night. Nothing was spoken about what had happened. Care was taken not to expose us, to be outspoken or to be seen. And nobody outside of our own close relationships should know that we were Jews. This "creeping into hiding" was commented on by the then Chief Rabbi Marcus Melchior, who in articles after the war opposed this hush-hush policy that the majority of the Jews were prone to.

It is not completely true that in my home we did not talk about what happened to us during the war. My father tried to process the trauma by focusing only on the more amusing stories that, after all, had also occurred during our captivity in Theresienstadt. There was the story about one of his good friends who got into trouble and was punished because he had stolen a girdle for my 15 year-old aunt, with whom he had fallen in love.

There was the story about how my father got into trouble because he called the conductor Peter Deutsch by the name of Ragnhild Hveger, when he was on the podium with his arms outstretched, conducting the orchestra in Theresienstadt. Peter Deutsch was a German refugee in Denmark and Ragnhild Hveger was an Olympic gold medal winner in swimming and closely connected to the Nazis. Peter Deutsch conducted the orchestra that was established during the staged Red Cross delegation's visit to Theresienstadt in June 1944.

You did not expose the fact that you were Jewish. No, we went one step further and hid it. After the war I was still quite weak and was placed in a sanatorium three times, each visit lasting three months. I am still deeply grateful to the forest ranger on Kalø [2] Hans Moes and his nice wife Margrethe that they, despite having their own three children and four forestry students living with them, agreed to take a completely unknown, weak boy from Copenhagen for six weeks' vacation during the summer holidays. I spent the summer in their home, and came back summer after summer. But it was only after the fifth summer, as I approached my thirteenth birthday, that they realized that I was not about to start the usual Christian preparation with a priest in order to be confirmed, that we had to "reveal" that we were Jews. It should be hidden.

Jews have reacted very differently to the Holocaust. Many did as we did, and went into hiding, so to speak. Others were baptized, others changed their names so as to not to flag their Jewish identity.

Religious leaders have struggled with the issue of how the God who in Exodus in the Torah (The Five Books of Moses) says that "... you shall be to Me the most beloved treasure of all peoples ..." could allow six million Jews to be murdered and let the booming Eastern European Jewish culture perish. Many turned their backs on Judaism, although one might think there was every reason to do the opposite as the Jewish theologian Emil Fackenheim puts it: "Jews are commanded to stay Jewish in order to deny Hitler a posthumous victory".

It was not until 50 years after the war, in the spring of 1995, that I heard my mother mention the word Ravensbrück for the first time and my father his internment in Sachsenhausen.

We were invited by the Land Brandenburg's Ministry of Science, Research and Culture to the commemorations in Germany marking the 50th anniversary of the liberation of Ravensbrück and Sachsenhausen, the concentration camps in which we had been prisoners.

My parents were very interested in accepting the invitation. I was hesitant. I was only two years old in 1943 and my repression of the events, that I could not remember anything about, was so strong that I had very little inclination to be confronted with a painful reality. But in the end all three of us accepted the invitation and we decided on our own initiative to continue to Theresienstadt straight after the commemorations in Ravensbrück and Sachsenhausen. However, I could only make it if I could get my two eldest children to accompany me.

The commemoration events were moving. Many former prisoners were still so affected by their past that it was sometimes heart-rending to watch.

My parents' reaction to visiting the camps was somewhat muted. They felt an inner joy and pride that the Germans now welcomed them as free people and as guests in a country that had done a lot to come to terms with the guilt that generations must have felt. They were touched by the great helpfulness from the many young people who were present to assist. And the fact that we were transported around with a motorcycle escort and that on the television in the hotel room the screen read "Welcome Mr. and Mrs. Katznelson".

The visits made things change somewhat for my mother, who until that time had not talked much about the events during the war. My father did not manage to talk much about the events, and he passed away the following year. For myself, there was still a reluctance to ask questions and to get more knowledge.

My parents and my eldest daughter at the commemoration in Germany in April 1995, marking the 50th anniversary of the liberation of Ravensbrück. (Private photo)

More than 7,742 people, mostly Jews, fled from Denmark to Sweden in October 1943. For almost 500 the escape was not successful, and almost all of them were deported to Theresienstadt, the German's so-called "Gift to the Jews", a title that Norbert Troller used as the title of his book about Theresienstadt.

The events of September and October 1943, when the action against the Danish Jews took place, have been quite extensively dealt with in accounts, historical as well as personal, in books and magazines. Beginning with a few in the first years after the war, and then more, they increased in the run up to the 70th anniversary of the Danish Jews' escape to Sweden, the event that led to most Jews being rescued.

So why, then, another book about some others' fate, the ones of myself and my close relatives? Each and every one has their personal story, whether their flight across the Sound to Sweden succeeded or they ended up being deported.

My parents and I were not, like most other Jews who were caught by the Gestapo, immediately deported to Theresienstadt after our arrest. We were interned in the concentration camps Ravensbrück and Sachsenhausen. For my mother and myself it was only after five months that we were deported further on to Theresienstadt. I was two years old when we were deported. My mother was 26 and my father 28.

A passage in Daniel Mendelsohn's excellent and captivating book from 2012, *The Lost: A Search for Six of Six Million,* says that it is easier to understand the meaning of a major historical event through one family's story.

He mentions that Rabbi Richard Elliott Friedman, a professor of Jewish studies at the University of Georgia, writes that in the first chapter of Genesis the specification progressively moves from an image of the heavens and the earth down to the first man and woman. The history's focus continues to narrow from the Universe to the Earth, to mankind to specific areas and peoples into a single family.

In 1994 the International Committee of Ravensbrück issued an appeal which states, among other things, "That we fellow prisoners in Ravensbrück have promised each other to remember, testify and tell also what cannot be described".

Inspired by Daniel Mendelsohn's mindset and in the light of the appeal by the Ravensbrück Committee, I have finally found the courage to embark on trying to find out what really happened to us then, more than 70 years ago.

I have also tried in this book to include some of the major events during the occupation of Denmark as I tell my and my family's story.

For example I touch upon events that preceded our arrest and deportation. The occupation of Denmark in 1940, the politics of cooperation, the dramatic day of 29 August 1943, when the government stopped its cooperation with the occupying forces and what then followed, is the subject of numerous reports.

However, brief accounts of this part of the history are included in this book as a background to our personal story, just to illustrate how significant events can affect an individual's fate.

For a non-Danish reader it might be useful to highlight just a few points about the special situation concerning Denmark when the Germans occupied the country. Without that, it is difficult completely to understand some of the events during the German occupation.

When Germany's military occupied Denmark on 9 April 1940 the Danish government remained in power and Denmark was treated as a neutral country. Germany and Denmark were never formally at war and negotiations went through the ministries of foreign affairs of the two countries. Nazi rule was not put in place in Denmark, and the Danish courts continued to function. The police also continued to function until the autumn of 1944 when the Nazis deported most of the police force to Germany.

In 1994 the famous American film director Steven Spielberg created the Fund "Survivors of the Shoah Visual History Foundation", which aimed to record on video testimony from survivors and other witnesses of the Holocaust. The Foundation has since then collected more than 53,000 video interviews of survivor experiences in 32 different languages in 56 countries. In 1996, my mother talked for the first time to the Shoah project, more coherently than ever before about what happened to us.

After that she gave a number of lectures. In 2003 she talked at the Hvidovre Club for elderly people. In his introduction the head of the club said that about 100 people had signed up for the event versus the normal turnout of only about 40. There was complete silence in the room while my mother spoke and the talk made a deep impression on the audience. I have a film of that event as well as film footage from our visit to Ravensbrück, Sachsenhausen and Theresienstadt in 1995. I also have a couple of other recorded interviews with my mother.

The talk she gave on that occasion tells a lot about my mother's psychological defense mechanisms. Her way of telling the story was a very sober and unsentimental description of the events, and even the most terrible things were told without trepidation in her voice. It was almost as if she was describing another person's experiences. This perspective also applies when interpreting another rather remarkable observation from the talk that mentioned me.

For part of my childhood and youth I lived in Hvidovre [3] and most of the audience would have known me. Nevertheless, my mother did not even once mention my name and she didn't even once say: "my son" but only "the boy". This is probably an illustration that "we" in our story psychologically became "them". It was as if it were a story about somebody else and not us.

My mother's sister, my aunt Annie, was with her husband Viggo on vacation in Prague in 1993 and they decided to visit Theresienstadt, as it is not far from Prague. They had a tape recorder with them and from that recording I have their long conversation about a lot of issues: her and my grandfather's arrest, their transport to Theresienstadt and about their life in the concentration camp.

At some point during the visit my aunt stopped in front of a commemorative plaque in Theresienstadt. Next to her was a German lady of about the same age. Apparently this lady felt a need to apologize by explaining that she was only 15 years old at that time and therefore did not feel any guilt or responsibility for what happened. My aunt responded by saying that she was also 15 at that time and she, not having been guilty of anything, had been imprisoned in the camp for one and a half years.

The woman did not say anything but turned around and left.

Should one avoid those kinds of comments? Does it serve any other purpose than giving oneself a kind of relief? Hardly!

For many years I have been uncomfortable with a remark I made myself which I later regretted. In a part of my professional life I was involved in international cooperation. In that context I have encountered numerous pleasant, interesting and talented German colleagues. At a dinner in the Bundesbank in Germany a number of years ago I was sitting next to an elderly German colleague. In the course of our conversation we touched upon, for one reason or another, something about Berlin, and he asked if I had been to Berlin. Here nature took over from culture and I said "Yes, in November 1943". He did not leave but there was some silence afterwards.

Did my parents make hints in similar ways to people they met? It happened, and one episode is clear in my memory. This is connected with the so-called Bovrup Catalogue.

DNSAP, The Danish National Socialist Party, had its headquarter in the village of Bovrup [4] where the leader of the party Frits Clausen lived. The Party's membership records included about 50,000 names. In 1945 the resistance movement copied the records. For one reason or another the transcript, the so-called Bovrup Catalogue, contained only about 28,000 names. The transcript was printed. It is divided into sections according to where members lived and is arranged alphabetically by name.

In 1946 the Copenhagen City Court issued a verdict that publishing that transcript was covered by the Archives Act which means that one can only get access to the transcript by applying to the National Archives and only professional historians can have access to it.

Immediately after the transcript was published, the names were obviously studied diligently. My parents managed to get a copy of the Catalogue published by the resistance group P6. On the front it said: "May only be sold and traded between members of the Group". The police seized as many copies as they could get hold of. In my home the book had its special hidden place.

Every time my parents met new people after the war, privately or professionally, they checked the Bovrup Catalogue to see if they were registered in it.

At one point, I remember, they found the name of some new acquaintances in the Catalogue. The husband claimed that his kidney disease was caused because he had been beaten up by the Gestapo which his wife, who apparently knew nothing about her husband's past, believed was the truth. My parents decided after much bickering among themselves that they would not risk destroying their new friends' marriage, and came to the conclusion that they would keep their knowledge to themselves and continue the friendship.

Back to the filming of my parent's and my aunt's stories.

Along with the scattered things I've learned over the years, these recordings form the basis of this book, combined with extensive research in the National Archives and the Royal Library. My mother, my aunt and other key players in the story should be allowed to speak for themselves. Therefore there are many quotations, particularly in the chapter about when we went underground. I have tried to tie together what they said and create a context for telling the story.

I have corrected some of the quotes to settle some erroneous dates and points. And for linguistic reasons, as the footage is conversation without a script, I have made some edits in direct quotes, with a gentle hand.

During the course of the events I also follow, in some cases very briefly, some of the people with whom we were arrested and interned.

It is a common observation that it was usually only many years later that survivors of the Holocaust started to talk about what had happened. Memories recounted years after the events risk the story becoming colored for any number of reasons. Holes might be filled in with thoughts about how this or that hung together, thoughts which, as time goes by, are conceived and described as how and why it really happened.

Why would so many years pass before my parents started talking, in a mostly scattered manner, about their experiences during and just after the war? It is difficult to give a clear answer as to why it was like that. Two somewhat contradictory quotes can contribute to understanding. Also there is the completely banal observation that when you reach the final chapters of life, there may be an urge to dive into the past. Both of the quotations contain a part of the truth about the many years of silence.

One quote is in the introduction to Sofie Lene Bak's book *Da Krigen var Forbi* (*When the War was Over*). She writes: *"There is no future without the past"*.

There is a somewhat longer explanation given by the Commonwealth's former Chief Rabbi, Lord Jonathan Sacks, in connection with a message to the British Jewish congregation before the big Jewish holiday of Yom Kippur (the Day of Atonement). He said almost the opposite:

> After the war Holocaust survivors, by and large, didn't talk about their ordeal, deeply traumatic though it was. And only after several decades, in the 1980s and 90s, did they begin to talk about what they'd seen in Auschwitz and Treblinka and Bergen-Belsen.
>
> I think the reason they didn't was that they knew that anger and rage are also forms of imprisonment, ways of being held captive by the past. To be free you have to focus on what you can do to build a better world, not on the sins others have committed against you. To be free you have to let go of the anger and the pain and move on. You have to build a future before you can look back in freedom on the past.

I have been very much in doubt while writing this book about a couple of issues. Should I, in regard to some unclear issues, write what I have been told or what I have found in my research? Or should I keep quiet about it? I ended up deciding to go ahead and also mention unpleasant things about my family as well as other named persons. They are long dead and can no longer defend themselves, which was the reason for my dilemma, but I decided that above all it was important to present the facts as truthfully as possible.

I also decided to discuss the Danish cooperation policy, the events of 29 August 1943, and the different episodes in September and October 1943, which at least indirectly came to play a role in our arrest and subsequent transfer to Ravensbrück and Sachsenhausen and then on to Theresienstadt.

Historians disagree about a number of issues concerning the interpretation of these events. As a non-historian I dare not contribute independent interpretations, but in the description of the events I try to touch upon some of the different interpretations.

To help the reader, persons whose names are encountered in much of the literature about the occupation of Denmark are put in boxes with some factual information about them.

As this is a personal story there are also many names that are not generally known. On this point, to help the reader, they can refer back to this chapter. Here is a box with such names.

It is first and foremost my parents **Karen** and **Max Katznelson**. They were born in Denmark in 1915 and 1917, respectively. My father was always called **Max**, but in a few places he is mentioned by his real first name, **Moses.**

It is my grandparents **Gisse** and **Sjaje Katznelson**, who came from Belarus, and their youngest son, my uncle **Bernhard**. My grandparents were sent to Theresienstadt, while my uncle managed to escape to Sweden after his arrest.

My grandfather **Itzko Kermann**, always called **Isak,** and his youngest daughter, my aunt **Annie**, were also deported to Theresienstadt. My aunt's husband **Viggo** is also mentioned in the book.

My grandmother **Yrsa Kermann**, born Pedersen, remained in Copenhagen throughout the war even though she had converted to Judaism. She was the daughter of boatsman Niels Pedersen and Marie Kristine, born Sørensen. My mother, who was born before my grandmother converted, was therefore born as a non-Jew. She converted when she was nearly three years old together with my grandmother on 18 June 1920. My grandmother married my grandfather on 2 July 1920. The Jewish community's former Rabbi, Professor Simonsen, conducted the ceremony.

My mother's middle sister, **Ida Lea** and her husband, **Børge** are mentioned in my mother's letters from Horserød camp. Their son, my cousin **Jørgen**, is also mentioned in a letter. Ida Lea was baptized and married Børge, who was a Christian. They were never approached by the Germans as Jews married to non-Jews, in principle, were exempt from the Nazi action against the Danish Jews.

The group of people who were deported together with us from Horserød camp on 23 November 1943, and who were with us for a shorter or longer period included **Annie Smaalann, Corrie** and **Sven**

Meyer and their two sons **Peter** and **Olaf, Karen** and **Sven Hoffgaard** and their two daughters **Kate** and **Lillian, Salomon** and **Klara Feldmann, Michael Singerowitz, Carl Suskowitz** and three young men, **Löb, Heller** and **London.**

Hans Michael Diehl, Kaj Ernst Pedersen and **Heinrich Christian Vanselow** had troubling roles in this story. All three were convicted after the war.

And finally, there is **H.** It will be clear in the section "Helper or Informer" why I on this one point, as an exception, chose to keep his name anonymous.

Finally, one comment to end this Prologue. These events have always been very repressed within me. The time spent researching and writing the subject of this book, and having become almost obsessed by it, has taken a significant mental toll. It has been an important defense mechanism for me that the text is not tainted by too many of the emotions that naturally welled up in me. This approach may be an advantage or a disadvantage to the reader. Here is the story, come what may. But before coming to the story of our arrest and what followed, I must establish where my family comes from.

Notes

1   Strictly speaking, Theresienstadt was not a concentration camp. For the prisoners this kind of organizational/linguistic terminology was irrelevant. In short, they experienced Theresienstadt as a concentration camp. In this book the terminology used about Theresienstadt varies partly depending on the context.
2   An estate in Jutland, Denmark.
3   Hvidovre is a suburb of the municipality of Copenhagen.
4   A village in southern Jutland.

2

"Viking Jews" and the "Russian Jews"

"Viking Jews" is what the old Danish Jewish families are sometimes called. They were families that had been in the country for hundreds of years and who were deeply integrated into Danish society. Most of them were not religious and not particularly aware of their Jewish identity. The German Nuremberg Laws from 1935 did not distinguish between people like them and the Jews who came to Denmark at the end of the nineteenth century and the beginning of the twentieth, the so-called "Russian Jews".

My grandparents on my father's side and my grandfather on my mother's side, who were arrested by the Germans in October 1943 and deported to Theresienstadt, belonged to the "Russian Jews" group. When they came to Denmark – my mother's father in 1906 and my father's father in 1912 and my grandmother came a little later – they, like the other Jewish immigrants, settled in the inner city of Copenhagen in the neighborhoods of Prinsensgade, Adelgade and Landemærket. The neighborhoods are well described in Sam Besekow's novel *Fra Majonæsekvarteret til det Kongelige Teater* (*From the Mayonaise Quarter to the Royal Theater*).[1]

My knowledge about their childhood and youth is quite sparse and primarily based on a few tape recordings of my father's father.

My grandparents on my father's side came from Belarus, from two very small villages near Bobruisk in the Minsk district. My grandfather was born on 1 January 1892 in Lubonichi, my grandmother on 20 November 1893 in Kovchitsy.

They both spoke only broken Danish, even after living in Denmark for more than 50 years. When they talked to each other it was often in Yiddish. My grandmother had never been to school, and she never learned to read or write. In many ways, they lived what one might call a normal Danish life. They had Christian friends but the majority of their relationships were with the "Russian Jews".

What kind of area did they come from? From the end of the fourteenth century, Jews were officially allowed to live in Belarus, which was part of Poland-Lithuania. In 1495 the Jews in Belarus were expelled, but were allowed to come back in 1503.

There were many attempts by the Christian community in the sixteenth and seventeenth centuries to deter Jews from settling permanently. They tried to prevent Jews from getting any work and from building synagogues. Christian Russians attacked the Jewish congregations, forced Jews to convert and murdered many of them.

By the end of the eighteenth century Belarus was annexed by Russia. In the period 1792–1917 five provinces were considered Belarusian, including Minsk province, from which my grandparents came. That meant that Jewish life was regulated by the Czarist Russia's laws. Among other things, Jews could not own land, and they could only live in cities or villages.

Towards the end of the nineteenth century the Jewish communities had increased in size, and in 1897 more than 725,000 Jews were registered in Belarus. Many congregations were so big that there was a Jewish majority in some of Belarus's largest cities.

Towards the end of the nineteenth century Zionism began to spread among the Belarussian Jews, and Minsk and Bobruisk were centers of the labor movement part of Zionism. Then pogroms came in waves. The first steps towards organized Jewish self-defense were established by the worker-Zionists in every city in the region, and only a few congregations in Belarus were attacked.

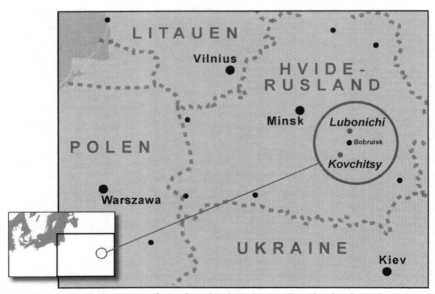

Map of Belarus with the towns of Minsk and Bobruisk as well as the shtetler Lubonichi and Kovschitsy, where my grandfather and grandmother were born.

Lubonichi, my grandfather's birthplace, is located approximately 140 km southeast of Minsk, and was founded in the sixteenth century as a shtetl[2] in the Rehitsa district of Minsk province in Greater Lithuania. In the first half of the seventeenth century it is known that there was a Jewish population in Lubonichi and in 1897, when my grandfather was five years old, there were 506 Jews in the shtetl. Some Christians lived on the outskirts. At the beginning of the twentieth century there was no synagogue, but three prayer houses. Timber, grain, vodka and mushrooms were the main industries for the Jewish population. In 1882 there were 39 wooden houses in the village. In 1909 there were 150.

In 2007 my wife and I visited Lubonichi and Kovchitsy. The villages were undeniably far, far out in the countryside and situated in a very large wooded area. There were practically only wooden houses in the villages. The quality of the timber that was used to build the houses seemed to be so good that the houses from my grandparents' childhood could very well still be there. There were no traces whatsoever of the Jewish communities. During the Nazi advance, if not already before, everything was destroyed. Jews who may have been there at the time would have been murdered.

Unfortunately, we could not communicate with the few people we met. At one place we were invited inside a house. I tried to draw a family tree with

Typical wooden houses in Lubonichi, 2007. (Private photo)

small men to explain why we had come. The young woman wrote something down on the paper in Russian. Of course I was excited to know what she had written. When I returned to London, a Russian colleague translated it for me. The text was not very informative, for she had only written "some strangers came and I do not know why".

My great-grandfather was a mason. In the summer the family, consisting of my great-grandmother and three boys and a girl, could survive economically. It was worse during the winter. I have a few confirmations that he actually was a mason, which seems surprising in an area where there are forests as far as the eye can see.

My grandfather says that a Rabbi who settled in the village was worried about the little boy's lack of Jewish knowledge and he gave them money to attend the teaching in the prayer house. My grandfather proudly says he was one of the most talented, so he got some extra money as a prize. The arrangement gave the boys food and there was heating in the prayer house. His parents lived a traditional Jewish life. He himself says that he was not religious, and his parents would probably also have been more traditional than religious Jews.

Already at the age of ten or eleven, my grandfather became politically conscious and participated in Poal Zion, a Zionist labor movement. They were in favor of emigration to Palestine and sang Zionist songs.

There were pogroms in Lubonichi and the Jews were hardly popular because of their left-wing views. But the Jews defended themselves actively. They had home-made guns and sticks for self-defense.

In 1902, when my grandfather was ten years old, he traveled (probably on foot) from Lubonichi to Bobruisk, which was a big city. The distance between the two cities is about ten kilometers.

The city was Russian in the nineteenth century and had a strong fortress. The building of the fortress and the concentration of the military there was the reason why trade and craft flourished, and the city became a traffic hub. Bobruisk was predominantly Jewish around the turn of the century when my grandfather settled there.

In 1897 there were more than 34,000 inhabitants in Bobruisk, of whom almost 21,000 were Jews.

In Bobruisk he was apprenticed in shoemaking and worked in several places. At the first place he stayed two years. His master's son slept late in the morning, and worked until late in the evening. Therefore, my grandfather had to work in the evening as well. The father on the other hand got up at three in the morning to work, so my grandfather also had to get up and work at that time. It was work around the clock to get food and lodging. After three to four years he became skilled shoemaker.

After the failed revolution in Russia in 1905, the pogroms intensified, and Jews were often afraid and had to hide.

My grandfather said that he was active in the Jewish Marxist-Zionist movement, Poal Zion, and that they were very aware of the risk of getting into the Russian secret police's spotlight. In addition, there was the constant threat of pogroms. "My master had a home-made rifle in the attic", he said. It was important to be able to defend oneself.

Both because of its geographical location and because the city was a traffic hub, Bobruisk came to play a central role in the German advance against the Soviet Union in June 1941. The reckless violence practised by the Nazis against almost everybody, and especially against the Jews in Bobruisk, is ruthlessly described in Dennis Larsen and Therkel Stræde's book from 2014, *En Skole i Vold: Bobruisk 1941-44* (*A School in Violence: Bobruisk 1941-44*). This city that around the turn of the century was strongly influenced by a lively Jewish culture and religion was completely eradicated of its Jews.

When my grandfather was twenty years old in 1912, he was drafted into military service. This meant six to seven years of military service. As he did not like that idea he approached a Jew who could help people out of the country.

My grandmother and grandfather, 1961. (Private photo)

At that time he knew my grandmother. They had talked about getting away together. He was told that for 50 rubles he could go to France or Denmark. As an acquaintance of his had a brother in Copenhagen, who allegedly would help him if he chose to go to Denmark, that became his choice.

There seem not to have been strong emotions about the separation in the family, because when questioned on whether his parents knew that he would leave, he answered in a quite down-to-earth manner: "Well, my mother knew that I would leave".

He went by train to Minsk. He changed there to a train to Warsaw and from there he reached the border with Germany. At the train station, still on the Polish side of the border, he was very scared because there was a lot of police as well as military. He had been told that he should go to the Hotel Metropol.

He spent a couple of days there together with some others in the same situation and then continued the journey on foot – a very long trip – to the border. They met a soldier who had probably been bribed because he helped them over a stream by placing a board over the water. On the other side they were almost crawling in order not to be detected. Later however, they met the German police who were not interested in them. On the German side of the border they came to a small town where they were accommodated in the community house. The whole trip had been very strenuous. He had no money, and there were many times when he was not offered a meal.

After a few days he got a ticket for the rest of the journey. The rest of the trip to Denmark was by train via Berlin to Copenhagen.

In Copenhagen it was not easy to get work and was not at all possible to get a job with the Jews already living there. He got some sense of the Danish language by looking at the signs in the shops but, of course, he could neither read nor write Danish. But this improved over time.

In Socialdemokraten[3] he saw an ad that they needed a shoemaker on Strandvejen 183.[4] He walked all the way out there from Adelgade, where he lived. Despite some difficulties he got the job after a while. He worked in that place for three years and was on very good terms with the master.

My grandmother was pregnant with my father's sister when my grandfather left Bobruisk. He said that he sent for her, and she arrived in Denmark at almost the same time as he got his job.

My grandparents' home was definitely not a religious household. No kosher[5] housekeeping, no mezuzah[6] on the doorpost, and although there were always guests on Jewish holidays, there was never the singing or reading of religious Jewish texts nor, for that matter, the lighting of the Chanukah candles.[7]

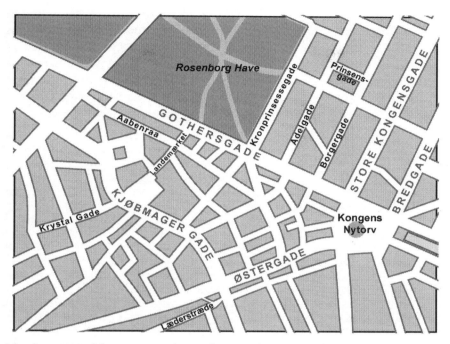

Map from 1910 of the inner city of Copenhagen with Borgergade, Landmærket, Adelgade, Læderstræde and Prinsensgade. It was in that area most Jews who immigrated from Eastern Europe settled in the early twentieth century. (Copenhagen City Archives)

My grandfather on my mother's side was born in Odessa, Ukraine. They lived in a simple, lower class and not especially Jewish quarter of the city. His parents had moved to Odessa. My great-grandfather came from Pinsk in Belarus and my great-grandmother from Resevilov, probably in Russia.

The family fled from Odessa to Denmark because of the pogroms organized by the Cossacks and priests, who came with their crosses. It happened most often when the weather was good. They often had to shut the windows. Many were killed, even Russians, when it was the Cossacks who attacked. At some point the family felt that the situation had become untenable and that it was essential to escape. That was in 1906 when my grandfather was nine years old. Why and how they ended up in Copenhagen, I do not know. But they, like my grandparents on my father's side, settled in the Prinsengade area. I have no knowledge of how active their Jewish affiliation was. The only thing I know is that my great-grandfather became one of the founders of the Jewish Craftsman Association.

"Viking-Jews" or "Russian Jews", religious or atheists, with Jewish consciousness or totally assimilated, whether you were a lawyer in Copenhagen, or a judge in Assens, if you had ancestors who had lived in Denmark for generations or whether you were a relative newcomer tailor from Odessa or shoemaker from Bobruisk, it didn't make any difference when the Germans began their action against the Danish Jews in October 1943. "Viking-Jews" or "Russian Jews", they were all in the same boat.

Notes

1   Sam Besekow (1911-2001) was a famous Jewish theater director.
2   A shtetl is small town with a large Jewish populations, which existed in central and eastern Europe before the Holocaust.
2   The Social Democrat newspaper.
3   The Social Democrat newspaper.
4   Just outside Copenhagen municipality.
5   Food prepared according to Jewish dietary rules.
6   A piece of parchment with specific Hebrew verses from the Five Books of Moses. The parchment is in a capsule which is affixed to the doorpost.
7   Chanukah is the Jewish holiday commemorating the rededication of the Temple in Jerusalem at the time of the Maccabean revolt against the Seleucid Empire. Each night throughout the eight-day holiday an additional candle is lit.

3

The Prelude to the Action against the Danish Jews

The Cooperation Policy during the Occupation

Early in the morning of 9 April 1940 Germany attacked Denmark with land, sea and air forces. The resistance was sporadic and a few hours afterwards the Danish government gave the order to bring the fighting to an end. Germany gave the Danish government an ultimatum: either surrender or the Danish defense would be destroyed.

Handbills were dropped by air with the message:

> It is not the German government's intention to get an offensive posture in the battle against England. The sole purpose is preventing Scandinavia from becoming a battlefield for Britain's expansionist war.
>
> For this reason, heavy German military forces have today taken the most important military installations in Denmark and Norway.
>
> The population is asked to continue their daily work and to ensure peace and order!
>
> The German Army and Navy is from now on providing Denmark security against English assaults.

A few hours later Prime Minister Stauning and King Christian X issued proclamations. Prime Minister Stauning wrote:

> German troops last night crossed the Danish border and have made landing in different places. The Danish Government has, under protest, decided to take care of the situation in the country, taking into consideration the occupation that has occurred and ... The country must be marked by calm and order, and loyal conduct must be manifested to anyone who has an authority to exercise.

The choice between surrender or defeat was made. The so-called 'Cooperation policy' was now a fact. The Danish authorities continued to have formal responsibility and the government and Parliament continued to function. This was a significantly different situation from other occupied countries, where German management was established.

The German ambassador to Denmark since 1936, Renthe-Fink, was appointed as plenipotentiary in Denmark and was thus the supreme German political authority in Denmark.

In the autumn of 1942, the so-called "telegram crisis" started, because Hitler felt that the telegram sent by the King in response to his birthday congratulations was insultingly short. This crisis, along with the anti-German mood in Denmark, which had become more marked, led to a sharpened German course towards Denmark. Prime Minister Buhl's government had to resign in November 1942 and was replaced by a government under the leadership of Erik Scavenius, and Renthe-Fink was replaced by Werner Best as plenipotentiary.

Werner Best's name is inextricably linked to the action against the Danish Jews in October 1943, and there are several strongly contradictory views of Best's role in the action. In several ways these views also influenced the various post-war perceptions of Best, expressed in the verdicts of the trials against him after the war in the City Court, the High Court and the Supreme Court.

Werner Best, Karl Rudolf Werner Best, 1903-1989, German lawyer and diplomat.

Best was a member of the German Nazi Party from 1930 and of the SS from 1932. He made a career in the Gestapo until he had a conflict in 1940 with his superior, Reinhard Heydrich. After that he worked in the occupying authority in France.

Following the "telegram crisis" in Denmark in 1942, he was appointed plenipotentiary in Denmark and was instructed to form a German-friendly government. By accepting a government without Nazis, thus continuing the Cooperation policy, he demonstrated, as on other occasions, a willingness to pursue a policy independent of, and sometimes directly against, the instructions from his own country.

He made elections to be held in March 1943 possible and prevented Germany's wish to have the Danish army and navy dissolved. The unrest and strikes in August 1943 caused this policy to collapse, but Best maintained his political responsibility.

He was sentenced to death after the war. That verdict was changed to twelve years in prison. He was released in 1951 and expelled from Denmark and then served as legal adviser to the Stinnes Group.

Werner Best's reputation was, frankly, not very good. The 'Blood-dog from Paris' is one of the names that the illegal press in Denmark used for him. The term was pure propaganda, because at that time nothing was known about his crimes in France, where he was responsible for the deportation of French Jews. He had also played a key role in the police forces responsible for the killing of thousands of Poles.

However, Werner Best demonstrated a completely different attitude when arriving in Denmark in 1942, than would have been expected in light of his actions in Paris. In previous studies, he had found that the Cooperation policy in Denmark had resulted in Germany not having to use as many resources in Denmark, compared to other countries they occupied. In addition, under the Cooperation policy the important Danish export of agricultural products to Germany functioned impeccably.

Let us have a look at the general situation in Denmark in August, September and the beginning of October 1943, before this story returns to my family and my arrest on 4 October 1943.

August and September 1943

The Cooperation policy meant that everyday life for most people in Denmark continued more or less normally during the first few years. In the course of 1943 however, the situation became critical.

In 1943, the government had been in office for the entire four-year parliamentary term and according to the Constitution, general elections should be held. Due to the occupation, the issue of an election was problematic. In Berlin, the view was held that elections could create unrest, and that the Danish Nazis risked losing face.

Prime Minister Scavenius, however, succeeded in getting Werner Best to convince Berlin that it was appropriate to hold the election.

1943 was also, in many ways, the year when it became increasingly clear that Germany's military success was at a turning point and that Nazi Germany was hard pressed.

In January 1943 the final Soviet attack began against German troops surrounding Stalingrad. The last German forces were defeated in Stalingrad in February.

In July, there was a tremendous armored battle at Kursk, 450 km southwest of Moscow. The German offensive, aimed at weakening the possibility of a Soviet offensive by surrounding the Soviet army, was stopped.

In July and August, Allied forces conquered German and Italian forces in Sicily. This opened up the Mediterranean seaway and Mussolini's power was severely weakened. He was brought down and arrested in July.

There is probably no clear connection between developments in the war in Europe and the situation in Denmark, where acts of sabotage and demonstrations were on the increase. It cannot be ruled out that the recent military setbacks of the Germans may have contributed towards the population's increasing fatigue with the German occupation.

In addition to an increase in sabotage, including the significant sabotage of Forum[1] in Copenhagen in broad daylight, there was also quite violent unrest in several places in August. Strikes and civil unrest spread to a number of provincial cities.

On 19 August a German officer was knocked down in Odense. He had been sandwiched between the protesters at the railway station and other protesters in King's Garden. He could not get back to the railway station where he came from, so he retreated to the King's Garden, where there were hundreds of excited protesters. He pulled out his gun and fired a few shots in the air and then into the crowd. He was grossly abused and lost not only his revolver but also one of his boots which were then "abducted" by the crowd in triumph. The police tried to establish order in the city but without much luck. In Asylgade the crowd overturned one of the police cars.

Best's policy of having relatively problem-free cooperation with the Danish authorities was under pressure, and the events in Odense meant that he was now seriously on the defensive. On 27 August Best demanded on behalf of the German government, that Odense pay a bill of 1 million kroner within 5 days, and that the government should take the necessary measures to find and hand over the people guilty of abusing the German officer. If that did not happen, ten residents of Odense, selected by the German authorities, would be arrested until the extradition of the culprits had taken place.

Danish demonstrations, German reprisals, and acts of sabotage went into a downward spiral. The basis for the hitherto model of the Cooperation policy was gradually vanishing.

General Hermann von Hanneken had been, since 12 October 1942, commander of the German military forces in Denmark. According to the historian Hans Kirchhoff, Hanneken's main military objective was to bring

The German plenipotentiary, Dr. Werner Best, with the Prime Minister and Minister of Foreign Affairs Erik Scavenius, 1943. (The Royal Library/Christian Henriksen)

the defense against a potential invasion up to the same level as in France. This was hampered by the rather limited German resources in Denmark. He tried to stifle anti-German demonstrations and actively fight sabotage.

He was not, in the same way as Best, focused on getting the Cooperation policy to function under the now heightened circumstances, and Best, undoubtedly, felt that he risked losing his position as the absolute superior German political authority in Denmark.

Hermann von Hanneken, 1890-1981, German general, Commander of the German troops in Denmark, October 1942-January 1945.

Von Hanneken established a tougher course against the resistance movement, which brought him into conflict with the German plenipotentiary Werner Best.

After extensive strikes and turmoil in July and August 1943, under pressure from Berlin, Werner Best demanded that the Danish government, among other things, establish a ban on meetings, introduce a curfew, and establish the death penalty for sabotage. When the government rejected the demands, von Hanneken introduced military emergency status on 29 August 1943 and dissolved the Danish military.

Von Hanneken was acquainted with but not involved in the action against the Danish Jews in October 1943. It was conducted by German police under the direction of Rudolf Mildner. Thus the evacuation of the Danish Jews could happen without interference from the German army and navy.

In January 1945, von Hanneken was deprived of his command and sentenced to eight years in prison by a German court for corruption. He was pardoned and demoted to Major, after which he was sent to the frontier service.

He was arrested by the US and then handed over to Denmark, where, in 1948, he was sentenced to eight years in prison at the City Court for his responsibility in the German counter-terror and deportation of the Danish police. In 1949 he was acquitted by the High Court and expelled from Denmark.

In a report to Berlin about the situation in Denmark, von Hanneken gave a somewhat gloomier picture of the situation than the impression Berlin got from Best's reports. When Hitler was informed by other channels of the event with the German officer in Odense, Best was ordered to meet with Hitler on 24 August. It turned out Hitler did not meet with him. Instead, Best received Hitler's rage from the German Foreign Minister von Ribbentrop.

The following day, 28 August 1943, the Danish Government was informed that an immediate state of emergency was to be declared for the whole country.

The note contained, among other things, orders for a ban on assembly, the banning of strikes, a curfew, a prohibition of intimidation of Danish citizens because of their or their relatives' cooperation with German authorities, censorship of the press and the establishment of swift court procedures concerning acts contrary to the issued orders.

The crucial order was the death penalty for sabotage and the involvement in sabotage, as well as for the possession of firearms and explosives.

The German government expected acceptance from the Danish Government of the measures by the same afternoon at 4 p.m.

At 3:30 p.m. the same day, Nils Svenningen, the Permanent Secretary of the Ministry of Foreign Affairs, sent a note attached to the Prime Minister's card to Werner Best with a clear conclusion: "The implementation of the measures required by the German authorities will destroy the Government's ability to keep the population at peace and the Government therefore regrets that it does not find it proper to contribute to the implementation of these measures."

The commander of Denmark's coast guard, Commander Paul Ibsen, sent an order to all Danish ships on the same day that they should try and get to a Swedish port, or alternatively to sink their vessels in order to prevent them from being taken over by the Germans. Thirteen vessels managed to reach Sweden and twenty-nine were sunk at Holmen, in Copenhagen. The majority, however, were taken over by the German navy.

On 29 August 1943, the Danish Government resigned. A state of emergency was declared, and Hanneken was given executive powers in Denmark.

The army was disarmed and about 500 people were arrested. Most of them were quickly released but around 140 were detained in Horserødlejren,[2] including the Danish Chief Rabbi M. Friediger.

During the following days, the Permanent Secretaries of the ministries agreed with the politicians to continue their work, thus replacing the government's previous cooperation with the occupying power. The Permanent Secretary of the Ministry of Foreign Affairs, Nils Svenningsen, became first among equals, and was the one who had close and practically daily contact with Werner Best.

Nils Svenningsen, (1894-1985) Danish diplomat. At the beginning of his career in the Ministry of Foreign Affairs, Svenningsen served in the Berlin diplomatic mission from1924-30.

In 1932-37 he was in charge of the trade negotiations with Germany as head of the Economic Department in the Ministry.

As head of the Political/Legal Department from 1940, and as Permanent Secretary from 1941, he was in a prominent position carrying out the Cooperation policy with Germany, and was Foreign Minister Scavenius's closest collaborator.

After 29 August 1943, he conducted all important negotiations with the occupying power and as the head of the group of permanent secretaries, he was the main driver behind the efforts to preserve a Danish administration until the liberation.

As a result of post-war criticism of the cooperation policy, he was sent to Stockholm as head of mission from 1945-50. In 1951-61 he was again named Permanent Secretary, now in close cooperation with Foreign and Prime Minister H.C. Hansen. Svenningsen was also ambassador to London from 1961-64.

Best was well aware that his position as the top German authority in Denmark was uncertain. However, he received von Ribbentrop's support to try and resolve the political crisis, which eventually took the form of a new government. At that point, Best's position was not as weak in relation to von Hanneken as might be imagined.

Before getting deeper into the circumstances that led to the decision to initiate action against the Danish Jews, one must reconsider various disturbing events during that September that should have made the Danish Jews, or at least their leaders, very concerned.

Passivity? Or were the Warning Lights Very Dim?

29 August 1943 was a turning point of the occupation and also became a turning point for the Danish Jews. The reassuring words from the Minister

for Ecclesiastical Affairs Fibiger to Chief Rabbi M. Friediger on 8 December 1941, that "as long as a Danish government has some authority in this country, the Jews have no reason for anxiety", had lost its authority.

Max Friediger, literally Moses Samuel Friediger, (1884-1947), Chief Rabbi of Denmark. Born in Budapest, died in Copenhagen, buried at the Jewish cemetery in Copenhagen.

Friediger was educated at the Hildesheimer seminar in Berlin, which belonged to the Orthodox Jewish movement. He became Dr. Phil. in 1908 and Rabbi in 1909.

He held positions in Pohrlitz in Mähren and in Oderberg, Schlesien, before being appointed Chief Rabbi for the Jewish Community in Denmark in 1920, a position he held until his death.

On 29 August 1943, he and his son Arthur were arrested by the Germans, among many other Danes. When the persecution of the Danish Jews started in October 1943, they were deported to Theresienstadt, from where they were rescued by the White Buses in April 1945. A total of 470 Jews were deported from Denmark to Theresienstadt.

Denmark's priests had come out earlier with sympathetic declarations when 149 clergymen in the Greater Copenhagen area stated, in November 1941, in a Ritzau telegram,[3] their deep compassion with "our Jewish compatriots because of the suffering their fellow believers are experiencing elsewhere, which fills every Christian with dismay."

Around 5 o'clock on the morning on 29 August, Chief Rabbi Friediger was taken from his home. Both he and his son were arrested. On the same day, approximately 140 other important Danish citizens were also detained in Horserød camp. Friediger was told that morning that they were only being brought in for interrogation, but they were detained in Horserød camp, and from there were sent to Theresienstadt on the morning of 2 October, together with other Jews who had been arrested during the night when the Germans launched the so-called Jewish action.

Throughout the occupation, until the fateful days of late September 1943, the leadership of the Jewish community had almost unlimited confidence in the Danish authorities. This view was understandable, as a measure of their confidence resided in their status as the old Danish Jewish generation (so-called "Viking Jews"), who were deeply integrated into Danish society.

The issue of how the official community acted, or rather their inaction during this fateful period, had a strong, emotional impact when considered after the war. Was their passivity a result of the unlimited trust in the Danish authorities? Was it the result of careful reflection that one should not act in a way that could give rise to anti-Semitism, creating doubt about the authorities' assurances that the Jews were not a separate group but an integral part of the Danish population?

It is difficult to imagine this passivity in the light of a few very concrete attacks on the community in August and September of 1943.

The lawyer Arthur Henriques, Secretary of the Jewish Community, was in his summer house on the morning of Tuesday 31 August 1943. His office was located at Nybrogade 10 in Copenhagen, where he kept the Ministry's official records.

Three men broke into his office at 10:30 that morning. They were told by the bookkeeper that Henriques was on vacation. Undeterred and threatening with guns, the men forced the law firm's staff to hand over approximately fifteen records for the period 1810-1935. The operation was led by Paul Hennig, who worked for the Gestapo. The bookkeeper found that the telephone line on her desk had been cut.

The Copenhagen police were informed of the robbery but after negotiations with the Ministry of Foreign Affairs, they took over the investigation. Whether the police were involved again at a later stage is unclear.

After the war Hennig denied having participated in the operation. His explanation was that the operation was undertaken by a colleague at the Gestapo. An operation like that was considered by the Gestapo to be a private operation and was, as such, forbidden. As Hennig's colleague was about to be promoted, he was afraid of the consequences of violating the ban on such operations, so Hennig offered to take the blame, as he felt he had nothing to fear. In a post-war identification, however, the bookkeeper expressed with certainty that Hennig was one of the three who broke in.

When Nils Svenningsen confronted Werner Best over the event at Henrique's office, he denied any knowledge about it. He calmed Svenningen down, saying that the Jewish question was "überhaupt nicht angeschnitten worden" (has not been raised at all).

About two weeks later, on 17 September, another serious warning occurred which did not set off any alarm bells, or at least not nearly enough. The Gestapo took the community's librarian, Josef Fischer, at the morning service in the Synagogue, to the community's office in Ny Kongensgade. The operation was led by Fritz Renner, a criminal assistant in the Gestapo, and possibly Paul Hennig's superior in Dagmarhus.[4] Josef Fischer was forced to show Renner everything in the library. The Gestapo took census lists of Jews in Copenhagen from 1911, 1916 and 1921. They took twelve to fifteen printed Jewish genealogical tables, approximately ten church records about Jewish communities in the provinces, and an old tax registration with names, without addresses.

Contrary to the "visit" at Arthur Henriques' office, this operation was carried out with considerable visibility as the Gestapo arrived in a large car. Again, Werner Best succeeded in reassuring Nils Svenningsen.

Precisely because that operation was conducted in such a visible way, it was used by Best in the post-war trial as one of many examples that he did not want the Jewish action to be successful. The operation was, he claimed, a clear warning to the community that something was going on.

In his biography of Nils Svenningsen, Viggo Sjøqvist, historian and former head of the archives in the Ministry of Foreign Affairs, suggested that Svenningsen may have been easily overruled and reassured by Best, because at that time he was busy with other essential concerns, such as organizing some kind of leadership for the country after the government had resigned on 29 August.

Although the alarm bells did not lead the community's leadership to seriously react, the President of the community, C.B. Henriques and Vice President Karl Lachmann, went to see Nils Svenningsen in the Ministry of Foreign Affairs on 25 September. They wanted to confront him with the rumors that something was going on. They were reassured by Svenningsen, who stated that he was not aware of any current danger.

The word 'passivity' is used cautiously in this chapter. Consideration must be paid to the position the community found itself in. It was influenced by the fact that trying to escape, which was considered illegal, could well have provoked exactly the thing that they were trying to avoid: a German action against the Jews.

The Telegram of Fate? Best's Telegram of 8 September 1943

The question in this section heading indicates there was some uncertainty about whether the action against the Danish Jews was already determined in Berlin headquarters in August, or whether it was Werner Best's telegram from 8 September that started the process off.

Hans Kirchhoff writes in his biography of Duckwitz (2013) that "there is a consensus today among historians that the initiative for the action against the Danish Jewish came from Copenhagen, and that the process leading to the decision was started by the plenipotentiary with telegram No. 1032 of 8 September."

"The inevitability of an action against the Danish Jews, the need to demonstrate drive and to show Hitler, von Ribbentrop and especially Himmler 'SS spirit', and consideration of his position in managing the occupation, led Best to send the most famous and most analyzed of the thousands of telegrams he sent to Berlin", writes Niels Birger Danielsen in his Werner Best biography.

Gestapo (Geheime Staatspolizei) was the secret police organization established in Prussia by H. Göring after Hitler's takeover of power in 1933. When Himmler became Chief Police Officer in 1936, the Gestapo joined the Security Police under R. Heydrich, and then worked closely with the SS.

SS is an abbreviation for Schutztaffel, the protection corps. They were an elite Nazi corps, founded in 1925 under the SA as bodyguards for Hitler. They had black uniforms and were led by Himmler. They functioned after Hitler took over, in line with the SA, as police reinforcements. They were separated from the SA in 1934 and became stronger as time progressed.

SA is an abbreviation for Sturmabteilung. The SA was founded by Hitler and the NSDAP in 1920. The SA troops were supposed to maintain order at Nazi meetings and create turmoil at other party meetings. The SA also conducted terrorist attacks against the Nazi's opponents and the brown-uniformed SA became a feared presence on German streets. After the Nazis came to power in 1933, much of the SA's terror was directed against the Jews.

NSDAP is National Sozialist Deutsche Arbeiter Partei (National Socialist Labor Party)

RSHA is the Reichssicherheitshauptamt (Reich Main Security Office).

In his telegram to the Foreign Minister von Ribbentrop, Best wrote: "In the context of a consistent implementation of the new course in Denmark, in my opinion, a solution to the Jewish question and the question of the

Freemasonry in Denmark must now be considered. The necessary precautions for that have to be taken under the current state of emergency, as they at a later stage might lead to reactions in this country ...".

Joachim von Ribbentrop, (1893-1946), German politician.

Von Ribbentrop became member of the NSDAP in 1932 and he quickly became Hitler's foreign policy adviser and faithful supporter. He was Ambassador to London 1936-38 and Foreign Minister from February 1938 until Germany's collapse in 1945. During the war the Foreign Ministry lost much of its influence.

His greatest success was the German-Soviet Non-Agression Pact of 1939. He also attempted to spread the genocide of the Jews to countries that were allied with Germany.

Von Ribbentrop was as one of the top-level Germans put on trial at the Nuremberg. He was convicted of war crimes and crimes against humanity, and hanged.

In the telegram Best tried, to some extent, to focus on all the problems in "solving the Jewish question", if not done during the state of emergency. The King and the Parliament would stop participating in governing the country, there would be the risk of general strikes, etc. Even if the list of potential problems was about the timing of an action against the Jews, it also seemed like a manifesto, that any action carried out, even under the state of emergency, could give rise to the reactions mentioned.

Best also reminded Berlin of his previous request to have more police available, which he considered a necessity if he planned to arrest approximately 6,000 Jews.

With some caution, one might conclude that Werner Best did not seem to be overwhelmingly excited about initiating the action.

Why then send the telegram? His motives have been subject of many historians' analyses. This work cannot sort out the inconsistency. One can note, however, that there can be multiple reasons for decision-making of great consequence.

Undoubtedly, because of his experiences during the problematic visit to Berlin on 24 August, Best felt strong pressure, combined with his desire to defeat von Hanneken in their struggle for power. On the other hand, he must have been fully aware that an action against the Danish Jews would further complicate the hitherto mostly cooperative relationship with the Danish authorities, thus making his work and personal life more complicated.

Best's seemingly good strategic compass may also have envisaged a situation in which Germany would not emerge from the war victorious. During this possible aftermath it could prove useful not to have been too anxious to initiate an action against Denmark's Jews.

The subsequent events seem to indicate Werner Best's lack of enthusiasm for a successful implementation of the action against the Danish Jews.

Some historians are of the opinion that it was not a lack of enthusiasm by Best, but a cunning and strategically thought out plan to get the Jews out of the country without German intervention.

This view, in particular, was espoused by the Polish historian Tatiana Berenstein. Her conclusions evolve from her background concentrating on Duckwitz's career and activities before October 1943. She also holds the view that a number of the dates in Duckwitz's diary are incorrect.

Georg Ferdinand Duckwitz was a maritime expert at the German Legation in Copenhagen. It was Duckwitz who in September 1943 informed the leaders of the Danish Social Democrats about the forthcoming action against the Jews. The image shows Duckwitz lighting the eternal flame in Yad Vashem's Hall of Remembrance in April 1971. (Yad Vashem)

In short, Berenstein's conclusion is that the escape of the Danish Jews was the result of a strategic decision, based on Best's view that not enough resources were available to implement the action. By leaking the information about the forthcoming action, he got the Danish Jews to disappear by themselves, so that he could declare Denmark "Judenrein".

The historian Bent Blüdnikow also questions Duckwitz's role and mentions (in an article in a historical periodical) that it seems surprising that Duckwitz never wrote a word in his diary about the horror in the East. He probably knew about it from a number of sources, while at the same time there is concern for the Danish Jews from his diary. "Could it be that this concern for the Danish Jews was deliberately entered in the diary to give himself plausible deniability after the war?" asks Bent Blüdnikow.

The maritime expert at the German Legation in Denmark had a central role in the events.

G.F. Duckwitz, Georg Ferdinand Duckwitz (1904-1973). German businessman and diplomat.

Duckwitz worked as a businessman in Denmark in 1928-33, and in November 1939 became affiliated to the German Legation in Copenhagen as a maritime expert. He gained considerable influence there, as he had the confidence of the German plenipotentiary Werner Best who, among other things, helped him when he was suspected of slipping loyalty to the party.

In an understanding with Best, Duckwitz leaked the planned action against the Jews, in September 1943, to the leaders of the Social Democratic party and the later Prime Ministers Hans Hedtoft and H.C. Hansen, thereby contributing to the failure of the action.

During the general strike in Copenhagen in the summer of 1944, he brokered the negotiations between Best and Danish politicians, and during the last days of the occupation in April-May 1945, Duckwitz made an active effort to promote negotiations with the Allies about the surrender.

After the war he made a career in Western German diplomacy, including as Ambassador to Denmark 1955-58. Duckwitz ended his career in 1967 as State Secretary at the Ministry of Foreign Affairs in Bonn.

On 11 September, a few days after sending the telegram to Berlin with the recommendation that a Jewish action should be launched, Best briefed Duckwitz about the telegram. Best seemed to be confident that the authorities in Berlin would choose not to approve the action. Two days later Duckwitz, with Best's approval, flew to Berlin to discourage launching the action.

Duckwitz had a thorough knowledge of Denmark and Danish sensibilities through his work there as a businessman. Later, as a member of the German Legation, he had good contacts with leading members of the Danish Social Democratic Party, not least with the future Prime Minister Hans Hedtoft.

The historian Hans Kirchhoff, who has studied Duckwitz's history extensively, writes that Duckwitz and Best had a long conversation on 16 September. Duckwitz wrote in his diary that Best was inflexible but probably in his inner thoughts agreed with him about the consequences of an action, which he warned him about.

Duckwitz's journey to Berlin did not help much, because already on 17 September Werner Best received a telegram with a formal announcement from the German Deputy Secretary Andor Hencke, that the action against the Jews in Denmark must be implemented. Andor Hencke, on behalf of von Ribbentrop, requested that Best carefully prepare proposals for "implementing transport of the Jews, which in principle has been decided and, in particular, to indicate how many police forces (Best) needed for this ...". It is also added that "This matter must be kept in strict confidentiality."

The head of security, SS-Standartenführer Rudolf Mildner, who had just arrived in Denmark, most likely with Best's approval, flew back to Berlin in order to get the Jewish action stopped. Mildner, who had a record as a war criminal, may have been opposed because he had hoped to create some cooperation with the Danish police in combatting sabotage, something that would be completely impossible if a Jewish action was taken. Von Hanneken also opposed the campaign.

The inquiries to Berlin did not help. Notwithstanding the fact that the attempts to stop the campaign failed, the actual events show that a lot was done to hinder its success.

On 23 September 1943, Foreign Minister von Ribbentrop, after a meeting with Hitler, wrote a memo to the Führer, in which he referred to "The Führer's instruction that the transport of the Jews from Denmark must be carried out in accordance with the plans ..." and further, to Werner Best's statement that "... the implementation of the action against the Jews will lead to a significant sharpening of the situation in Denmark. ...". Von Ribbentrop ends by asking for "instructions as to whether the Führer wishes the action to be implemented now and, if so, whether it would be right to implement it while there is still a state of emergency."

A further confirmation of the decision to initiate an action against the Jews in Denmark was stated in an internal memorandum of 25 September. The German Ministry of Foreign Affairs, directing the responsible office manager for Jewish questions, stated that 'Mr. RAM [The Minister for Foreign Affairs] has, in accordance with the Führer's resolution, ordered the removal of Jews from Denmark. However, at the same time, Mr. RAM also requests that the action be conducted, as far as possible, in such a way that too much excitement in the Danish population is avoided."

Dr. Rudolf Mildner arrived in Denmark in 1943 from Kattowitz, where he had the position of head of Gestapo and was chairman of the political committee of the Auschwitz camp and a member of the SS court.

He had already left Denmark by January 1944.

During the Nuremberg trials he was the prosecutor's witness in the case against Ernst Kaltenbrunner, SS-Obergruppenführer and the commander of the Endlösung (the Final Solution to the Jewish problem).

Mildner insisted that he had tried to prevent persecution of the Danish Jews, but that he had been ignored by Himmler. He escaped in 1949 and disappeared. Adolf Eichmann claimed to have met Mildner in Argentina in 1958. However, that was never verified. He was not convicted of any crimes.

Kirchhoff also has a description of Duckwitz's visits and contacts in Stockholm, which were allegedly intended to get as many Jews as possible to Sweden.

On 28 September telegram no 1328 arrived from Berlin with the order that the transport of the Jews should take place. At 2:45 p.m. Best confirmed, in telegram no. 1144, that it would happen, probably on 1 to 2 October, depending on whether "the ship ordered from Hamburg arrives in Copenhagen. The action will be carried out on a single night ...".

At the same time, Duckwitz was told by Best when the action against the Jews would start. Duckwitz forwarded this information on the same day to

Vilhelm Buhl, Hans Hedtoft and Alsing Andersen in the Workers' Assembly Building in Rømersgade 22 in Copenhagen. Hans Hedtoft then went to C.B. Henriques, President of the Jewish Community, to pass along the information to him. Despite the increased warning signs, Henriques still believed strongly that such a thing could not happen in a lawful society like Denmark. His answer to the message was, "You lie".

C.B. Henriques and his Vice-President Karl Lachmann visited Nils Svenningsen in the Ministry of Foreign Affairs the following morning, and his reaction was almost the same as Henriques' the day before. At 3p.m. that same day, Henriques met with the other members of the Board of the Jewish Community and informed them. Three of the other seven board members had already escaped.

In addition, Svenningsen visited Best on 29 September at 5.30 p.m., where Best spoke in such a way that it was now clear to Svenningsen that an action was about to take place.

It should be noted that the attempts to change, mitigate, or stop implementation of telegram no 1032 were not few. The real motives for that are only speculative. It is no wonder that after the war the main players gave different explanations that put them in the best possible light.

Kirchhoff has a very important section on this in his Duckwitz biography. "It has been discussed who should take credit for having warned the Danes, Best or Duckwitz? Best always claimed that it was he who ordered Duckwitz to inform his Danish contacts. Duckwitz's statements were more varied, from completely neglecting Best's involvement and thus taking all the credit for himself, to an explanation that is close to Best's account."

As a small postscript to this story, the issue of Duckwitz's role was also discussed in the Jewish Youth Association while I was on the board. The discussion was whether to appoint Duckwitz with the title "Ben Adam", an important Jewish honorary title. That did not happen, due to the combination of uncertainty about Duckwitz's role, and that honoring a German, without conclusive certainty of his potential merits, would cause unrest in the Jewish community in Denmark.

Historians' interpretation of Duckwitz's role is not clear, and therefore the doubt in the Jewish Youth Association was not completely unfounded.

Despite the uncertainty about Duckwitz's role, he had a brilliant career in the German Foreign Ministry after the war. In Israel he was honored by being awarded with the honorary title "Righteous Among the Nations", a title that since 1963 has been awarded by Yad Vashem (Israel's Holocaust Museum) to people who under great personal risk helped Jews during the war.

Notes

1   A big sports and exhibition hall in Copenhagen.
2   Horserødlejren is today a prison in North Sealand. It served as an internment camp during the war. In this book the notion Horserød camp is used.
3   Ritzau is a Danish news agency.
4   The German Headquarters in Copenhagen.

4

Betrayed and Detained

We Went Underground

The leadership of the Danish Jewish community was now sure that an action against them was imminent. Rabbi Marcus Melchior had been informed by an acquaintance of former defense minister Alsing Andersen.

Thursday 30 September 1943 was Rosh Hashanah, the beginning of the Jewish new year. The holiday began the evening before, on 29 September.

After the morning service on Wednesday 29 September, where because of the special morning service prior to Rosh Hashanah there were about 100 congregation members present, Rabbi Marcus Melchior informed them what was about to happen. He asked everyone to take the necessary precautions, and to spread the word to friends and acquaintances alike. In addition, the Rosh Hashanah services were canceled.

Neither my parents nor my grandparents attended the service in the synagogue that morning. I don't know when and how the message reached them.

My parents had met in the Prinsensgade district, where many of Copenhagen's Jews lived. They were married in 1939, and although the marriage ceremony took place in the Jewish community center, not the synagogue, my father still wore evening dress with a top hat and white gloves. My parents lived a simple petit-bourgeois family life, where most of their time was spent earning a living to pay the rent for our small one and a half bedroom apartment on Bredahlsvej 17 in Valby (Copenhagen). My father's profession was cutting leather into the shape of shoes, which was the first step in the process of making new shoes. He was of the opinion that this process was a more advanced part of shoemaking than is normally thought of when one says *shoemaker*. That distinction does not have any meaning to people today, but it relates to something he told about his arrival in the Sachsenhausen concentration camp, which I will return to in a later chapter. My mother was a clerk, who worked in an office.

My parents' wedding photo from 1939. (Private photo)

My grandfather on my father's side was also a shoemaker, which served him well in Theresienstadt. My grandmother was a housewife and was illiterate. They also lived in very modest circumstances in a one and a half bedroom apartment with my uncle, who was 23. He is also part of this story.

My grandfather on my mother's side was a tailor and my grandmother worked in a factory which made cardboard boxes. Her lungs were probably destroyed by the combination of too many small cigars and from the fumes from glue in the factory.

The rumors about imminent action against the Danish Jews had been in the air for several days. Most of the Jews, however, did not consider it too seriously. After having lived a relatively normal life during three and a half years of occupation, it was hard to believe that the situation had suddenly completely changed. All indications show that my family was not particularly alarmed. As will be apparent in our fairly long stay in the Horserød camp, there were several signs that the situation was still not really taken seriously.

When asked how my parents reacted after what happened in August 1943, my mother said that although they had heard rumors that the situation did not look good for the Jews of Eastern Europe, they did not think that anything could happen to us. After the introduction of martial law, however, she said that "all was obviously different. We remained in our home in the month that followed, until we heard the rumors, and we were told that we should go into hiding and try to get out of the country. When we started thinking about getting away, many Jews were considering leaving their children in Denmark. But I thought, unfortunately, that he [i.e. me] had to come with us, because I felt certain that we would get to Sweden. I did not consider at all that we might end up in Germany."

Whether children should go with their parents or whether they should try to place them elsewhere was a tremendously stressful problem. It was a situation that was characterized by complete uncertainty about the future. Furthermore, they were in a situation where many practical problems were pressing and had to be solved very quickly. There were not many opportunities to discuss it thoroughly with close relations and trusted friends.

As noted, there were close contacts between Duckwitz and the Swedish authorities prior to action against the Jews. Even after the raid on 1 October, the Swedish government continued trying to help Danish Jews, and the Swedes suggested that Jewish children from Denmark could be sent to Sweden. Neither of these efforts were successful.

Up to 150 Jewish children were left in Denmark, and it is only in recent years that there has been a focus on the severe mental stress that their parents, foster parents and the children suffered in the years after the war.

But I "unfortunately" stayed with my parents, quoting my mother.

"We first heard rumors that we should go into hiding in early October or perhaps it was at the end of September", she explained. My parents were probably aware that the situation was serious when they learned that my grandfather and aunt had been arrested by the Germans on 1 October. When I write "probably" it's because in one of my mother's letters from Horserød camp, it seems she expected that my grandfather and aunt would come home shortly after their arrest, and therefore did not consider the situation critical.

Since the situation had become serious, one had to think carefully about who your real friends were. There were those that you could safely rely on, even if they knew that by hiding us they exposed themselves to great risk. Did they have the courage to hide us without really knowing for how long, how great the risk was and what the consequences would be if it was discovered?

My mother continued to recount that "in the first place, we had to move from our home. The first night we spent with some friends, but after that they did not dare to hide us any longer."

During the night of 3 October my mother stayed with a colleague from the printing company, Bording, where she worked at the time. She has no recollection of where my father and I were that night, but it was probably at my aunt Lea and uncle Børge's home.

Our friends took out a loan with our silverware as a guarantee so that we could get money to pay for the crossing to Sweden. They forgot to renew the loan agreement, and after the war we got 600 kroner (the value of approx. € 1,814 in 2016), which were the proceeds from the sale.

My grandparents went into hiding at the apartment of the caretaker in the apartment block where they lived. My grandfather's boss lent them 1,000 kroner three times (€ 9,000).

Mr Bording offered my mother assistance, possibly financial, but she did not really understand what it was all about. One of her colleagues, Børge Bøg-Jeppesen, had on a few occasions addressed my mother in a bit "too friendly" a manner. At least she had felt it to be embarrassing. When she went to her workplace to inform Mr. Bording that she would not be coming in any more, several of her colleagues told her it was important that she spoke to Bøg-Jeppesen. What he had to tell her was very important, they said, and she should not leave until she had spoken with him. She ignored that because of the various comments he had made to her.

After the war she often thought about whether he had been connected to the Danish resistance movement, and whether it could have changed her/our lives if she had spoken with him. She kept those thoughts to herself for 55 years, without mentioning them to anybody. She only told me the story and her thoughts about it in 1998. Later I tried to find out if there was something to it. I searched the name online and intended to call everyone with that surname, hoping to find somebody who had any connection to the man. I was lucky. One of the first people I came into contact with turned out to be his nephew. He told me that Børge was his uncle, and that he had died a few years before. He also told me that his uncle could be a bit of a womanizer, and that he probably had contacts with the resistance, because there were weapons in the back of his wardrobe.

A few years ago the Danish Resistance Museum established a database of names of members of the resistance movement. This meant that I eventually confirmed this, as Bøg-Jeppesen's name was in the database. His association with the resistance movement was Region VI (Copenhagen), O.2: Detachment Christiansborg, Amalienborg Detachment, Company Abrahamson.

I will not attempt here, nor in later chapter about Ravensbrück, to cast more light on my mother's suspicions about what happened in her workplace. The possibilities are most likely that a) we either would have managed to escape safely to Sweden or that b) our attempt to get to Sweden would result in our arrest and deportation to a camp. However, as I have now verified that Børge Bøg-Jeppesen was in the resistance, it's interesting to note that apparently his colleagues at Bording were either aware of or suspected that he was in some way connected to the resistance.

I was always told that we had trouble finding a way to escape to Sweden, soon after the action against the Jews started, because we did not have enough money to pay for the crossing. How much was needed to pay for the escape? Was the 600 kroner and the 3,000 kroner sufficient for the six of us: my parents and I, my grandparents and my uncle?

It was well known that in most cases it was necessary to pay for being taken across the Sound to Sweden. Many years after the war, it was somehow deemed inappropriate to pose the question about whether it was reasonable to pay the fishermen, sometimes large amounts, who ferried Denmark's Jews to Sweden. It is understandable that it seemed inappropriate to damage the heroic status bestowed on the fishermen who offered their assistance, but with the passage of time, several historians have re-examined this delicate issue.

In 1995 Rasmus Kreth and Michael Mogensen wrote a book, *Flugten til Sverige* (*The Escape to Sweden*) in which they examined some of the amounts people had to pay to get across the Sound. They also examined the risks of sailing Jews to Sweden. They argue that it quickly became apparent that the risks for the fishermen were limited. They investigated some of the amounts paid and concluded that at the end of September and in early October, when large numbers of Jews were looking to escape, "ticket prices" in some cases increased to astronomical amounts. One example is 4,000 kroner (€ 12,100 in 2016 prices) per person.

If that was the per person price, the amount of money that we apparently had at our disposal would not have gotten us very far.

In September, when the crossing to Sweden was still at its beginning, the price was about 850 kroner per person (€ 2,500), but as the demand increased explosively around the 1 October, prices increased as well. Immediately after the culmination on 8 and 9 October, the average payment was between 1,300 and 1,500 kroner (€ 3,900-€ 4,500). By mid October the amount fell to about 1,000 (€ 3,000) and later 500 kroner (€ 1,500).

Journalist and author Thomas Hjortsø published the book *Den Dyre Flugt* (*The Expensive Escape*, 2010) in which he tries to follow the money behind the Jews' escape. He also tries to peel away some of the halo surrounding the fishermen, and mentions that the price could easily have been about € 4,500 per person in today's money.

In *Rambam 22*/2013, a magazine about Jewish culture and research, Thomas Hjortsø wrote a story which also questioned the general glorification of the fishermen. Although the fishermen were given heroic status, he asks whether there could be a "false gratitude". He states that the thanks for having survived the German action against the Jews in 1943 should be directed to those who deserve it. As the events took place 70 years ago, it may be in order to consider whether there are those who do not deserve a "thank you".

Here, as with many other situations, there were some rotten apples. But I do not understand the argument that suggests that the risk of sailing Jews across the Sound was not that great. The situation was totally chaotic and one neither had Facebook nor Twitter to share one's experience of the crossing. There was no certainty that there was accurate information conveyed among the people involved. The risk was great. Although the transport of Jews did not have serious consequences for most of the fishermen who were caught by the Germans, one could not be sure the Germans would continue this surprisingly lax attitude.

How would it help a fisherman to know that 95 per cent of the crossings went without many problems, meaning there was only a 5 per cent risk of being caught? Being caught meant the boat was confiscated, the fisherman went to jail, or worse. What if the fisherman's crossing was among the 5 per cent?

Considering that in October 1943 a total of 7,742 people fled to Sweden, and that between the 4 and 16 October 6,670 refugees had arrived to southern Sweden, of which 90-95 per cent were Jews, then the opportunity we had to get to Sweden was in the early phase of the escape. The impression

I got from my parents, that we only got the opportunity to get to Sweden relatively late, was due to lack of money. This seems not to be the case.

Even though it is certain that my parents did not have much money, it was probably not that bad for my grandparents. This story is not particularly flattering.

My grandmother rented a shop in Thorsgade (Copenhagen) with someone my family knew via some kind of business relationship. The person, who I will call H, and my grandmother, worked together buying all kinds of linen that H, who had good contacts with the Germans, then sold to them. Quite a lot of money was involved, which leads me to believe that my grandmother probably had sufficient funds to pay for our escape.

This book is about real people of flesh and blood, and it has therefore been important to me that all are mentioned by their proper names. With H, about whom I have solid information, I have made an exception. The reason for that will become apparent later.

H actually appears in relation to my mother's family some years earlier, in 1940, when my grandfather was employed in his tailor shop on Toftegaards Allé 24 in Valby (Copenhagen). H had taken the tailor shop over from a Jew, whose name I also know. My grandfather took over the shop in 1941. It was given the name Valby Skræderi.

In the "family history" it was said that H felt that in some business arrangement he had been cheated by a person (a Jew?), which had made him very vindictive. The story was that he directed his vengeance against Jews in general. Whether it had anything to do with the two business relationships with my family, I have no idea.

It was now 4 October – Assembly Point: Syrefabrikken[1]

One day H told my grandmother that he had a contact who could bring us to Sweden. On Monday 4 October, my parents and I met my grandparents in their apartment on Ægirsgade 36, in Copenhagen, along with my uncle Bernhard, who lived with his parents.

In her lecture in 2003, my mother said virtually the same thing as in the Shoah recording from 1996, and in other interviews, that "my in-laws had a friend, a so-called friend, who promised to provide a passage to Sweden for us."

Notice that she says "a friend, a so-called friend". This is important in understanding what followed.

In light of the call by Rabbi Melchior not to stay at home, and my mother's description that we had not slept at home, it seems a little daring that we were all to meet with my grandparents in their flat in Ægirsgade, but we did.

Now that the situation was real and crucial decisions had to be made, doubts came back to my mother about what they should do with me. She said that "The question was whether we should take him with us or hand him over to somebody. But I did not really feel that I could give him to somebody else, resulting in bringing him with us. We should join my in-laws and my brother in law."

H said he would get a taxi to pick us up. The car then took us to the spot in Amager² from where we would be able to get to Sweden.

The weather on that October-night was not bad. The temperature was 10°C, there wasn't much rain, and the wind was fresh. All in all, it would be a crossing under at least reasonably good weather conditions. But it turned out to be a very different evening than we had expected.

My mother explains it in this way in her lecture to the Hvidovre Club in 2003:

> On 4 October we left the flat by car. There was a curfew so we had to get to Kastrup (Amager, not far from the Copenhagen airport) in time, and from there we would get on a boat. It started getting dark as we reached one of the side roads close to the meeting place. The so-called friend went out and said that he would be back soon. He just wanted to get in contact with the person who would sail us over the Sound.
>
> We waited for a while in the car, but our 'friend' came back accompanied by a German who pointed a submachine gun into the car and ordered us to get out.
>
> We were taken to the road alongside the sea. We could hear noise, bustle, shouts and screams. A big action was going on. At one point two women carrying a package of bread came walking towards us on the opposite side of the road. The German went over to them and asked them what they were doing, as it was almost curfew time.
>
> While they explained themselves, my brother in law, who had recently finished service in the King's Royal Guard and therefore was extremely fit said, 'I am leaving.' In an instant he disappeared behind a hedge and hid himself in some gardens. When the German came back he asked 'Where is the tall guy?' 'We don't know', we said, 'we don't know him'. 'That will cost you, if we don't find him', the German said.
>
> At one point we were split up. My husband and father-in-law came in one direction, in one of those big cars with a tarpaulin over it, and

we got into a taxi, in which there was already a married couple and a little 13 year old girl who had been separated from her family.

It seems quite clear from that description that H had betrayed us.

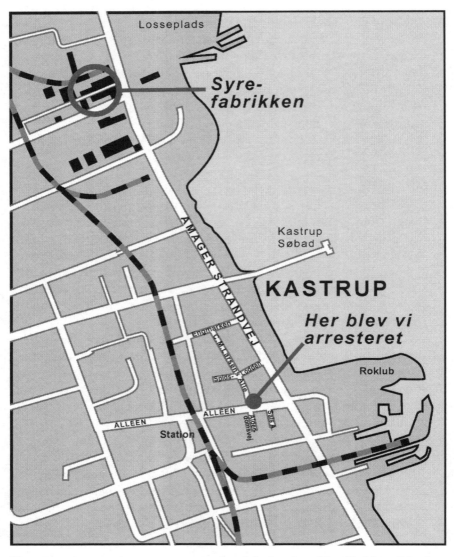

The area on Amager where we were arrested, and the location of Syrefabrikken. (Map from 1945)

The bridge at Syrefabrikken, 1943. It was from there that we were going to be sailed to Sweden on 4 October 1943. (Tårnby Stads and Lokalarkiv B4328)

Helper or Informer?

Despite my parents' clear perception that H had betrayed us, they never investigated the matter further after the war. They didn't even mention him during the trial, which, among other things, resulted from an article in *EkstraBladet*.[3] The silence was complete.

In short, we should have met at Syrefabrikken on Amager, from where we would have sailed to Sweden. However, the transport from the factory had been betrayed to the Germans, and all the Jews who were at the meeting place were arrested. The informers were identified and tried after the war. That happened initially in the District Court, and when the verdict was appealed, the procedure went to the High Court.

My father and my grandfather testified after the war to the police and in court. They both explained that at about 6.30 p.m. we drove down Amager Strandvej on our way to Syrefabrikken, from where the transport to Sweden would leave. When we were close to the factory our car turned onto a side street. At that moment a civilian stepped out into the road and said, in German, that he was German security police. The man was armed and guarded us on the sidewalk.

Shortly after a German car arrived and my grandmother, my mother and I were taken to Dagmarhus, while my father and grandfather were taken into Syrefabrikken.

In his testimony in the District Court on 15 January 1947 my father recollected the incident at Amager Strandvej in October 1943. He was not inside the factory but outside on the road when the action started. He and several others were arrested by the Gestapo. The Gestapo man stopped several German cars in order to the take the arrested away. There was a woman in the first car that stopped who was shouting "He shot me in the stomach." The person next to her said that they were going to a hospital.

It is worth noting that both the explanation to the police in 1945 and the evidence presented in District Court in 1947, do not have anything directly related with our arrest. We were arrested before we arrived at Syrefabrikken, therefore it's not certain that my father's and grandfather's explanations were precise in their detailing of what happened outside the factory.

My memory of my parents' recollections, which was also articulated in the Shoah interview and at the Hvidovre Club, was that H asked the taxi to stop, whereupon he got out of the car and came back a short while later with a Gestapo man who pointed a submachine gun into the car, ordered us out and arrested us. In one interview, however, my mother expresses some doubt about H's actions. She said that it could well have been a coincidence that H simply met a Gestapo man.

That explanation is not consistent with my father's remark in the police report where he said that "as we were about to get out of the car, a civilian German, who was armed, came along."

My uncle Bernhard, who was also in the taxi, was sure that he could remember where we were arrested, when I talked to him about it in July 2013.

On the morning of 4 July 2013 I picked him up at his home. He had just turned 93 but seemed of completely sound mind. We drove to Amager to find the place where we were arrested. We were driving around in the area where Syrefabrikken was at that time, and where the old port of Kastrup is located. When we got to Alléen, which is a side road to Amager Strandvej, and the corner of C. M. Larsen's Allé, my uncle was in no doubt. "It was here", he said.

In 1943, he recounted, we were driving on Amager Strandvej, turned onto Alléen, and then again just around the corner to C. M. Larsen Allé, where the taxi stopped.

It was a normal taxi and H was in the car. The car must have been quite big, as we must have been 6 adults, myself and the driver.

As we stood there on the spot on 4 July 2013, my uncle started talking about the situation on 4 October 1943, and explained that there was a German on the spot who immediately arrested us.

When he recounted the events again half an hour later, we were still walking up and down Alléen and Amager Strandvej, still talking about the events of that night 70 years ago. He was now absolutely sure about it. "H got out of the car to see if the passage leading to Syrefabrikken was OK, and then came back with a German."

He said several times, in the course of our conversation, that H was a bastard who wanted to get rid of the Jews because he had been deceived by them, and that they were his competitors.

He went on to say that the German took us from the corner of C. M. Larsen's Allé over to the opposite sidewalk of Alléen, and that we then walked down Amager Strandvej.

My uncle and father were in agreement about what happened, which my mother also touched upon in the interviews. As we walked with the Gestapo man on Amager Strandvej, Bernhard told H that if he, Bernhard, locked the arms of the German, H could take his submachine gun. H refused to do it.

My mother was carrying me in her arms, and Bernhard told my father that he ought to carry me, so they could better run away if the opportunity arose. The opportunity only came for Bernhard himself.

H was also detained and taken to Dagmarhus and Horserød camp and then released the following day.

Saturday, 9 October, a few days after we were arrested, H submitted his explanation to the Copenhagen police, because he had been arrested and detained by the Germans, not the Danes.

He explained that he had some acquaintances (my grandparents) who were Jewish, and that my grandmother was employed in his business. My grandmother had asked him the previous week if he would assist her and her family finding a particular road in Kastrup, as they did not know the area very well.

H continued that no mention was made that the family would be traveling. They agreed that he should come to my grandparent's home on 4 October at 6 p.m. When he arrived, according to his explanation, it was obvious we would be traveling somewhere, as we had prepared hand luggage. He said that he was told we needed to go to a place called Alléen in Kastrup.

A car came to pick us up, we drove to Alléen, and got out. Then we walked to Amager Strandvej, where we were suddenly stopped by a civilian German policeman who asked for our Ausweis (identity document). We did not have any, and were arrested. That was H's account.

As with many of the other Jews who were arrested in Syrefabrikken H says that the family and himself were taken to Dragør and then to Horserød camp, where he stayed for about 3 hours. Then, he says, he was taken to Dagmarhus and to Vestre Fængsel[4] and that he was interrogated in both places.

In conclusion, H admitted that he had helped us find the way to Alléen in Kastrup, but that he had nothing to do with any further planning, and also that he had no connection with groups which helped Jews to escape.

The events and explanations clearly give rise to many questions.

My father's testimony, given shortly after the war in connection with the trial against the informers, is probably more precise than the allegations that he, my mother and my uncle made several years later. But the testimony was given in a different context than its relevancy in assessing what exactly happened that evening on Alléen. It seems unlikely that H would have deliberately tried to get hold of a Gestapo man on Amager Strandvej. It would have been far simpler for him to have drawn the Gestapo's attention to the fact that we were all gathered in my grandparents' apartment in Ægirsgade.

H may well have been just as frightened by the situation as everyone else and, because of that, refused to help trying to disarm the German.

And finally, if my parents had been so sure about the role of H, why didn't they try to clear this up after the war? It could have been attempted with a lawsuit, despite their propensity to keep a low profile.

My understanding now, after much thought since the war about what really happened, is that "death should, so to speak, have a reason." H became a useful *scapegoat* in the family history.

The serious accusations against H, which proved not to be well-founded, led to the conclusion to keep his name to myself, using only his initial in this book.

It may be useful to look into what usually happened to people who helped Jews with their illegal escape.

The Germans normally handed arrested helpers over to the Danish authorities, as these kind of illegal actions were under Danish jurisdiction. The cases were judged by Danish courts, and after a paragraph with only mild sentences. Despite the fact that the Germans knew that those arrested had helped Jews, they also accepted, for a long time, that the police consistently released them immediately after interrogation. At some point the Germans made a fuss about this, but the Gestapo did not interfere. Helpers who had been arrested, were handed over to the Danish police in the first three weeks after the action against the Jews.

For example, some fishermen were arrested on 4 October. They were taken to Horserød camp and handed over to the Danish police on 9 October. They were released the same day and did not appear in court until more than six months later. They received a very mild punishment and the sentence was not even served.

What happened to Bernhard, after he had managed to run away when we were arrested?

A short while later he tapped on the front door of a house to get help. The man who opened the door was not prepared to help, but a grown up son who had heard what was going on came out of the back door and offered to help Bernhard. They walked together towards the center of Copenhagen. "As far as I remember we only talked about football on our walk into town", he says. When they arrived at Sundby[5] they split up, and Bernhard stayed for a few nights at a former colleague's place.

Bernhard went to see H a couple of days later, but he would not let him in and slammed the door. Neither my uncle nor my parents wanted to get in touch with H after the war.

Bernhard then went home to the flat in Ægirsgade. My grandparents' neighbor had the key. When he arrived he saw that the neighbors were emptying the flat. The carpets were rolled up, and the chandelier had been taken down. Comically, the neighbor was walking around with my grandmother's hat on her head. Bernhard stopped what was going on and had the household items stored in the basement of some acquaintances.

He was then "hospitalized" at the Municipal Hospital's Psychiatric Department. After about a week a nurse appeared and told him that he should take the tram to Hellerup,[6] where there would be a boat which would bring him to Sweden. He went there without knowing much more, and was approached by a couple of young men who asked him if he was going to Sweden. When he replied in the affirmative, they told him to turn right at the next corner and then just walk straight on. That story sounds a bit fantastic, but he insists it happened that way. He got across the Sound to Sweden.

Upon his return from Sweden after the war, he went to Amager and knocked on the same door where, one and a half years before, he had been rejected help, just to tell the man that he did not have to feel guilty about his refusal helping him in October 1943.

What I have recounted of Bernhard's story is virtually all I could ever get out of him. His steady response to further questions was always "It was a terrible time. My youth was ruined. I will not talk about it any more."

As for the 5 of us who were still out on Amager Strandvej, we were soon approached by a car containing a Danish Hipoman (member of the Hipocorps, a brutal police force of Danish volunteers), and a German soldier arrived. My grandmother, mother and I were taken into the car and driven away. Also in the car was a married couple, Poul Kempinsky and his wife, who was not Jewish, and a 13 year-old girl named Annie Smaalann. The car took us to Kastrup Airport and then further to Dagmarhus, which in 1943 was the German headquarters, together with Shell House. The Gestapo also had a branch there.

Another car arrived. In the back seat was a woman who moaned "He shot me in the stomach." My father and grandfather were taken into that car. I only found out about what happened to her and why she was driven around in that car, from an article in *EkstraBladet* from 19 November 1945. That article opened the door for some additional information about what had happened in Syrefabrikken.

Infernal Noise, Shouts and Screams – The Gestapo Raid on Syrefabrikken

"Infernal noise, shouting and screaming" my mother said, when she told the story.

The departure point for the crossing to Sweden was Syrefabrikken. That was where we were heading to. But the crossing had been betrayed. By whom? What had happened?

The Copenhagen police was already aware in September 1945, who they should get a hold of. At any rate at least one person, who according to the police report "during the persecution of the Danish Jews might have killed a woman, most likely Mrs. Rena Pfiffer Madsen." In some places the police refer to her as Regina, but here I use her real name.

During the interrogations in connection with the trial, details about the raid on Syrefabrikken were disclosed about two informers who were involved in the case. The raid was among the actions against the Danish Jews where the Germans made the most arrests at the one time, probably second only to the discovery of the Jews hidden in the church attic in Gilleleje. While the Gilleleje incident has been examined a number of times in histories of those times, the arrests at Syrefabrikken are only mentioned sparingly.

The police wrote a summary of the case based on a number of interviews. That summary was sent to the newspapers in Copenhagen. The intention was to get in contact with Jews who were arrested in connection with the raid on Syrefabrikken, in order to gather as many witnesses as possible. This was successful, and several of those who were arrested testified during the trial.

The police inquiry led, among other things, to the following article in *EkstraBladet*. The headline on Monday 19 November 1945 was:

Sold 21 Jews to the Gestapo for 600 kr.

The informer who made possible the Germans' surprise attack on the planned Jewish escape on Amager Strandvej arrested

The front page of *EkstraBladet* from 29 November 1945. The article says among other things "including a Jewish Woman with her two-year old child. In Ravensbrück the Jews were placed in underground bunkers and for 6 months they did not see daylight, so that they were blind on 25 April, when they were transferred to Theresienstadt."

In Akts. Dansk Svovlsyre- & Superfosfatfabrik, located on the corner of Amager Strandvej and Syrefabriksvej, on 4 October 1943, the German police arrested 25 Jews who were waiting to travel illegally to Sweden. During the raid a Danish citizen, who at the moment is imprisoned by the Allied Military Authorities, shot and wounded the opera singer Mrs Regina Phiffer Madsen, who after several hours was taken to Nyelandsvej's camp hospital, where she died a few days later. The informer in this affair is now in police custody.

During the raid 25 Jews were arrested, and after a short stay in Horserød camp they were sent to German concentration camps. Most of them were sent to Theresienstadt, where one of them, a tailor, Mr. Choleva, died shortly afterwards from illness. A 6 month old Jewish girl also was sent to Theresienstadt and the others to Ravensbrück, including a Jewish woman with her two-year old child. In Ravensbrück the Jews were placed in underground bunkers and did not see daylight for 6 months, so that they were blind when they were transferred to Theresienstadt on 25 April. During their stay in the German concentration camps, they suffered from serious diseases. It can thus be noted that the above mentioned two children are now suffering from tuberculosis.

Both informers have confessed

The informers were unskilled worker Ernst Pedersen, 3, Ungarnsgade, and waiter Heinrich Chr. Vanseløv, 108, Holmbladsgade. The last one was arrested in July, charged with subversive activities and trading illegal cigarettes. At the time there was no knowledge or suspicion that he had also been guilty of treason. He was given a sentence of 6 months for other offenses. He was sent to prison in Rudkøbing Arrest, presumably in the belief that he was now well under control.

But through a thorough investigation by Police Commisioner Andst and his staff, they identified these informers, who have now both confessed during interrogation, in Dept. F of police headquarters, to their infamous crimes.

Went to Dagmarhus

Both explained that they met a friend one day who was helpful in getting Jews sent to Sweden. That friend, during the conversation, urged them to refer Jews whom they knew to him, and he could probably manage to get them out of the country. Kaj Pedersen and Wanseløv pumped their friend for more information, and found out where the Jews were to meet and depart from.

After they received this information, they went to Dagmarhus on 4 October, where they contacted the German criminal police and gave them the information. Before coming, they had drawn a sketch of the harbor and Syrefabrikken in Kastrup, where Jews would gather and remain until a boat for the crossing was found. This sketch was handed over to the Germans.

50 kr. per Jew

The two criminals were promised that if they facilitated the arrest of Jews they could expect 50 kr. for each Jew, fit for work, who was arrested.

A few days after the German's action was completed, the two bandits went to Dagmarhus where they were given 600 kr. to share.

The Germans said that 12 Jews fit for work had been arrested and the 600 kr. was the payment for the information. It appeared that the Germans had cheated the informers, as more than 12 Jews fit for work had been arrested.

The case remains under police investigation and the police believe that Pedersen and Wanseløv committed several similar crimes, not yet revealed.

The article specifically mentions my mother and me by writing "... including a Jewish woman with her two-year-old child. In Ravensbrück the Jews were placed in underground bunkers and for 6 months did not see daylight, so that they were blind when they were transferred to Theresienstadt on 25 April. During their stay in the German concentration camps, they suffered from serious diseases." The description is not entirely accurate, but mostly it is.

On 14 November 1945 a few days before the article from 19 November in *EkstraBladet*, my grandparents gave testimony to the Copenhagen police, and on 17 November it was my father's turn to testify. It's strange that my mother was not asked to give evidence, or at least she didn't do that. One reason might be that she (and I) did not arrive at Syrefabrikken after we were arrested. Neither did my grandmother, but she testified nevertheless.

The police reports were presented to the Copenhagen City Court in January 1947. The trial of Ernst Kaj Pedersen and Heinrich Christian Vanseløv began with an indictment that they had informed the Gestapo in Dagmarhus about an illegal transport of Jews that was about to depart from Dragør. That resulted in the German police raiding Syrefabrikken in Kastrup and arresting 22 Jews who were then deported to Theresienstadt and other concentration camps.

Where had Kaj Ernst Pedersen and Heinrich Christian Vanseløv received their information about the planned departure? That question was not answered during the trial.

Vanseløv said that Kaj Ernst Pedersen told him that he had been told that on the very night a transport of Jews would leave. Kaj Ernst Pedersen said, for his part, that Vanseløv had overheard a conversation between himself and a person who was helpful with getting Jews out of the country. The explanations varied about the events: of who had spoken with whom and who heard what from whom.

The manager of the factory explained his role in the sequence of events during the persecution of Jews in October 1943. Through his connections with the resistance he was able to facilitate fellow Jewish citizens' illegal departure from the country. He had made the factory available for that purpose.

On 2 October he got the message that at nightfall on 4 October, he would receive 27 Jews who were going to Sweden. It had been arranged with two fishermen, who had boats for this purpose, were to be ready in the harbor that was close by the factory.

By nightfall on 4 October Jews gradually came to his home, which was immediately adjacent to the factory. Once they were all assembled – 27 should have come he says, but there were only 22 – they were taken over to the factory, where they were hidden in one of the buildings. He then went back to his own house in order to change his clothes. When he returned shortly after, the Gestapo had arrived, occupied the factory and had arrested all of the Jews.

The "missing" five were probably my grandparents, my parents and my uncle. I, as an almost two year-old, had probably not been counted in the calculation.

The Danish citizen Hans Michael Diehl, who worked for the Germans in Dagmarhus, participated in the raid on Syrefabrikken. The resistance was aware of what he did in Dagmarhus already in March 1943. In the illegal paper *Frit Danmark* (*A Free Denmark*), which was "Published by a group of Danes", in issue number 11, he is among "the names of some of the informers we know, and we are therefore in a position to give specific warnings against them."

Diehl explained that the German security police in Dagmarhus had received information that there was a transport of Jews who were going to leave from Syrefabrikken, and he had been ordered to join the raid. Usually it was the Gestapo who took care of the arrests, but Criminal Secretary Nass indicated that although the German security police usually only had the task of dealing with ordinary criminal offenses, all of the security police participated in persecution of the Jews.

Late in the afternoon, Nass, Diehl and three other Germans went off in two cars to pick up Ernst Kaj Pedersen and Vanseløv at Langebro. They then went to Kastrup in order to scout the site and also to scout out whether from Syrefabrikken there was a path leading down to a bridge which led to the harbor.

Kaj Ernst Pedersen and Vanseløv were later allowed to get off at Amagerbrogade, and the Germans, along with Diehl, continued to Copenhagen airport. There they parked their cars under the supervision of

The Danish citizen Hans Michael Diehl worked for the Germans in Dagmarhus. He participated in the action on Syrefabrikken where he shot opera singer Rena Pfiffer Madsen. (Frøslevlejrens Museum)

the two drivers. They then proceeded along Amager Strandvej. Before doing so, they split up into two teams that were to follow one another at a safe distance so as not to attract too much attention.

When they reached Syrefabrikken, they rushed in and, according to statements, there was a lot of shooting in the air. Inside Syrefabrikken Nass and his assistants called for back-up and the arriving Gestapo took over.

What exactly happened during the later part of the raid, which ended with a murder, is unclear. The understanding of the exact sequence of events is far from unanimous. A key factor in the inconsistent explanations is that the Jews, including Rena Madsen, who had a handbag in her hand, were ordered to put up their hands.

In 1987 Rena's husband, opera singer Jens Egon Christian Madsen, told that she was Jewish and born in Poland and that she originally was called Rena Pfiffer and had performed at the Viennese opera. She came to Copenhagen to give a concert and they fell in love and got married.

It was obvious that Rena would also try to get over to Sweden in October 1943. Her husband said his wife had been contacted by flutist Poul Birkelund, who was one of their good friends. He told her to go to Kastrup Syrefabrik, where there was a ship ready to take refugees to Sweden. When Egon Madsen came home that day, she had already left.

Apparently she was not quick enough putting her hands up, and Diehl lashed out at her with his pistol. Whether he deliberately hit her, or whether it was an accidental shot, is not clear. He claimed that he did not understand when and how a shot was fired.

She was bleeding and complained of severe pain in the abdomen and asked to be taken immediately to a hospital. The Germans got a car and Rena was thrown into it. The explanations about what was done with her are also inconsistent. Instead of going directly to the hospital, Diehl took her to Dagmarhus, where he got her an ambulance that, after half an hour, drove her to the camp hospital at Nyelandsvej.

Before that, they drove her around on the roads of Kastrup, although she repeatedly asked to be taken to a hospital because she was in severe pain. The Germans responded by saying that it was their business, and they continued driving around looking for other Jews, who had reportedly escaped. They may also have been looking for my uncle Bernhard.

Another person, who had also been taken into the car, like my father and grandfather, asked the German to go to Sundby Hospital with Rena, but the German replied that he should keep his mouth shut. They were then taken into Syrefabrikken, and the car with Rena Madsen continued.

That evening her husband received a call from the police. They told him that his wife had been injured and brought into the camp hospital at Nyelandsvej, where he could visit her. He contacted Dagmarhus to get permission for the visit.

RENA PFIFFER - AMELIA (MASKENBALL)

The opera singer Rena Pfiffer Madsen was shot by Hans Michael Diehl in the German action against the Jews who were assembled in Syrefabrikken. (Theater Museum Vienna)

It turned out that the bullet had damaged her liver and gallbladder. She died four days later, on 8 October.

Before she died, she managed to whisper to her husband what had happened, and how she had been hurt. She said that a German patrol suddenly came into the hall, where the Jews were waiting for the crossing. The Germans' Danish henchman, who was standing with a gun in his hand, had ordered their hands up. Rena had kept her handbag in one hand, and suddenly the traitor hit her in the stomach with the gun and yelled that she should let go of the bag. Rena thought at first that it was the hit that hurt, but it turned out that, accidentally or not, the idiot had actually fired the gun into her stomach.

Egon Madsen later said that it was reported that the transport had been betrayed by a girl in a baker's shop in Amager. That is probably not true, but at this point there is also no certainty.

The manager of Syrefabrikken was taken by the Gestapo to Dagmarhus, where he was asked if he knew two men called Karl Erik Abel and Villy Nielsen. He denied this and was subsequently taken to Western Prison. He was released after three days at the request of the Industry Association on the grounds that the factory could not do without its employees.

After the war the manager told the police that he knew that the two had been involved in helping Jews go to Sweden, and that the transport they were involved with departed from the port outside of the factory.

One of them, Karl Erik Abel, was executed by the Germans on 2 May 1944.

The second one, Villy Nielsen, confirmed after the war that the two had helped the Danish Jews leave the country illegally. It began immediately after the start of the action against the Jews. On that day, 4 October, they had a shipment which was scheduled to depart from a nursery on Syrefabriksvej. During his testimony he referred to a few conversations about specific individuals and he grumbled over how the information about their pending transport had reached the wrong people.

It was from the nursery that 13 year-old Annie Smaalann should have been taken to Sweden. She was also arrested on Amager Strandvej. She was in an apartment in Amager with her mother, sister, grandparents and two uncles, one of them who with his wife and children. There was also a young couple they didn't know who had asked if there was room for them on the boat. Annie did not know anything about whose apartment it was, just that it was there where they had to meet before going down to the harbor in Copenhagen. She did not remember exactly how long they were in the apartment, but thought it was half a day.

The uncle, who was not accompanied by his wife, took the lead, and said that they should not all go down to the port together, but rather in a few groups. He said that the young couple and Annie's sister should go with the first taxi. The sister began to cry, and would not leave her mother. So it was Annie who came with the young couple in the first taxi.

When they were near Syrefabrikken the taxi was stopped and a man in civilian clothing with a gun shone a flashlight on them. Annie was taken into a car parked nearby and where there were already other Jews.

Out in Amager the process ended with some of those arrested, mainly the men, being taken directly to Horserød camp. The women were taken to interrogation in Dagmarhus and later during the night were transferred to Western Prison.

It is not known why the two groups were treated differently.

My mother said that "At one point we were separated. My husband and my father-in-law were taken in one direction, in one of those big cars with the tarpaulin, and we got into a taxi, which already had a married couple and a little 13 year-old girl, who had been separated from her family." It was Annie Smaalann.

What happened with all the people after the arrest?

A total of twelve of those who were arrested at Syrefabrikken were sent to Theresienstadt on transports from Horserød camp on 13 October 1943, and returned from the camp with the White Buses in April 1945.

They were my grandfather Sjaje Katznelson, my grandmother Gisse Katznelson, Alex Eisenberg, Wolfgang Karl Isenstein, Rosa Margrethe Isenstein, Rigmor Adler, Ber Nachmann Kasinsky, Doba Kasinsky, Daniele Kasinsky, Frieda Hertzberg, Edith Cholewa and Sulamith Cholewa.

Interrogation in Dagmarhus and a Night in Western Prison

Later in the evening we arrived at Dagmarhus. My mother said:

> We were interrogated in Dagmarhus. I heard that Poul Kempinsky was questioned. He told the Germans something and was then released.
>
> Ib needed to go to the toilet and I was allowed to follow him. When I came back, another lady was interrogated. She apparently behaved somewhat aggressively, and I heard the German shouting "I demand the truth and only the truth." He pounded his fist on the table and said, "Look at him, who was just here. He told the truth and was allowed to leave."
>
> Then it was my turn to be interrogated. I was simply paralyzed by fear. Perhaps I could have lied about everything by saying that I was not Jewish. He did not believe that I was Jewish. I had blonde hair [my mother had red hair], and he probably imagined that as a Jew one would look different. Then he asked for my papers, but I did not have any because I had forgotten my bag in the car. I was totally confused.

So I must admit, he put the words in my mouth when he said: "You are not a Jew". And, stupid as I am, I did not dare lying, so I said: "Yes I am". And he asked if my husband was a Jew. "Yes he is", I replied and then there was not much to do. He said "schade" (It's a shame).

The one who was typing asked what he should do. "Write", he said. That was a note that we should be taken to Western Prison. When everyone had been interrogated, we were all taken to the prison. We stayed there, I think, one night and a day. It was not a long time.'

In Western Prison my mother was not interrogated again.

When Annie Smaalann was interrogated in Dagmarhus, they were only interested in getting the location of her mother out of her. She could not tell them that for obvious reasons, and the value of not knowing anything about the apartment on Amager proved to be helpful.

I was ordered to wash the floors in the prison. I was definitely not in the mood for that, but I had to do it, said my mother, adding "We spent the night in jail and sat there most of the day. I cannot remember if we got anything to eat. If we did, I certainly had no appetite. At one point we were told that we had to leave."

We were taken to Horserød camp where we were united with my father and grandfather. My grandmother was with us in Dagmarhus, but in the many interviews with my mother, she didn't mention anything about her.

Horserød Camp

My mother continued:

Then we arrived at Horserød camp on October 5, in one of those big cars covered with a tarpaulin. It was a large military truck. We drove along Jagtvejen. People were walking along the sidewalk. It was the most beautiful autumn weather and the sun was shining. We sat there and could not shout to anybody. We sat behind a tarpaulin. I tried to put a hand out so somebody would notice us, but it was hopeless. We were maybe ten people in the car. We didn't know where we were going. We had no idea.

She also told about the strange, unreal feeling of seeing people who were free, while we were sitting there, arrested. She also remembered that the German driver had to ask for directions several times to find the way to the Horserød camp. "When we arrived, we were sent into some wooden huts."

Horserød camp was established in 1917 for the purpose of housing prisoners of war from Russia. In 1920 it ended up serving as a camp for interned prisoners of war, and it was then transformed into a colony for infirm children, until Germany occupied Denmark in 1940.

At the beginning of the occupation German immigrants were interned in the camp.

In 1941 the Danish communists were detained in the camp, and from September 1943 Jews were interned there as well. Those who were taken hostage on 29 August, were also there.

It was, strictly speaking, a kind of concentration camp, but in contrast to the German concentration camps, it was not governed by the SS.

After the liberation, the camp was used for the internment of traitors.

By the time we arrived at Horserød camp, quite a few Jews had already been detained there, and more arrived in the following days.

We all ate in a large hut and lived in a smaller one. My mother had the feeling that Horserød camp was divided into two camps, one for the "prominent", who were taken hostage on 29 August, and one for us.

Ralph Oppenhejm, in his book *Det Skulle Så Være. Dagbog fra Theresienstadt* provided descriptions of things as they were before 13 October.

The setup, going to eat, was almost the worst. First the men had to get something to eat. When they were sitting at the table the Germans rang a bell, and then the women had to line up. Even if it was raining they had to remain in line until the men were ordered to leave the hut. We sat at seven long tables, and a few from each table had to go to the door leading out to the large kitchen, to fetch food.

My mother's description of the meals are more prosaic. Until 29 August 1943 the camp was under Danish rule, and it continued partially like that after that date. So it is not strange that she says that there was Danish service, and that there was a Danish policeman and a Red Cross nurse, about whom she said that "there were so many rumors, such as that she was an informer. Rumors about who you could trust, and who could not be trusted. About who was full-Jew and who was half-Jew [a German notion; a half-Jew was a person with one Jewish parent and a non Jewish parent]. That's what it all depended on at that time, about who could leave and who could stay."

One's "Jewish fraction" was essential. The Danish Nazi, Paul Hennig, came to Horserød camp along with the German criminal assistant Renner and interrogated us separately. Hennig's primary interest was to determine whether some were half-Jews, or so-called Aryans. Those who fell under the last category were released.

That these words were something the prisoners talked about is clear from my mother's remark that "the first words Ib could say were full-Jew and half-Jew. They were all the words he heard. They were the first thing he learned to say. The days passed with rumors about what would happen, when we would go home, and so on."

Paul Hennig, 1902-86, was a fanatical Danish anti-Semite. He had been a member of the Waffen-SS in 1942 and was a member of the anti-Semitic party, the Danish Anti-Jewish League.

He worked for the Gestapo in Dagmarhus in a small unit that had the task of collecting and processing information about Danish Jews. He also led the action against the Jewish community's archive, and he was the one who interrogated the detainees, both in Horserød camp and on the ship *Wartheland* at Langelinie quay, in order to separate full Jews who should be deported, from half Jews who should be released.

Toward the end of the war many Danish Nazis, including Paul Hennig. went to Frøslevlejren (a camp in southern Jutland), presumably to be in a kind of sheltered place for fear of being liquidated by the Resistance.

He managed to disappear after the liberation on 5 May 1945 but was arrested in southern Jutland in December 1945. In 1947 he was sentenced to death by the District Court for the preparation and implementation of the action against the Jews. The High Court changed the verdict to life imprisonment in 1949, confirmed by the Supreme Court. He was released in 1956 and died in 1986.

Paul Hennig, born in 1902 in Copenhagen, was genealogist. In the period from May 1942 to June 1944 he was an official in the Waffen SS. Around the middle of September 1943 he was under the command of the Sicherheitspolizei in Dagmarhus, and later the Sicherheitspolizei in Shell House.

His education was apparently used when there was doubt as to whether the captured Jews were full-Jews or married to a non-Jew. He explained in court after the war that his daily work was to investigate the internees' descent with possible release in mind, and he almost took pride in how many Jews he "succeeded" in getting released. In other testimony a German says that Hennig, in cases where there was doubt, would hand in recommendations which were followed. Nobody verified Hennig's studies.

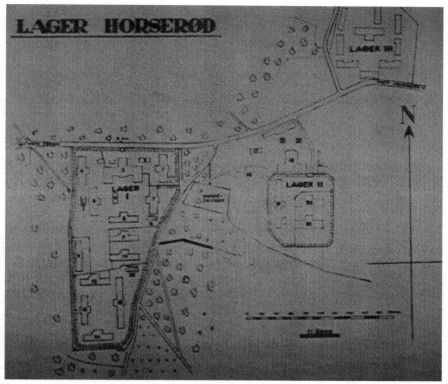

Map of Horserød camp. The map is German and allegedly made just after 29 August 1943. The "Jew camp" at this time is the fenced "Lager II". The internment camp is located in a beautiful area in North Zealand. It was set up in 1917 to house prisoners of war from Russia. After the occupation of Denmark the camp functioned as a kind of German concentration camp, but was not placed under the SS. (Horserødlejren's Museum)

Hearing the stories of some of whom were interrogated by Hennig, one does not get the impression that his efforts were directed at getting Jews released.

Sven Hoffgaard was a half-Jew and his wife full-Jew. They were arrested during the action against the Jews in the church attic in Gilleleje. To Sven, Hennig said that if he could decide, then all Danish Jews would be sent to Germany, so that they were no longer seen in Denmark. After the war, predictably, Hennig challenged whether he said that. He said that if he really meant that, he could easily have done so by simply distorting the papers.

Corrie and Sven Meyer and their two boys were on their way to a boat and were allegedly encountered, by chance, by a German guard. Corrie was Dutch and a full-Jew. Sven and the boys were baptized. To Sven, Hennig said that if it was up to him alone to decide, Sven and his family should have been sent off long ago. According to Hennig, Sven was just the type who did not belong in Denmark. By marrying a Jew, he had placed himself outside of Danish society.

My mother also remembered Paul Hennig, who repeatedly questioned her. When she explained that she had been baptized, he said that it was of no importance. In an interrogation in connection with the trials against him, Hennig said that "he may well remember that he had seen her somewhere. If she had been in Horserød camp, he had most likely questioned her, and in that case, he may also well have said that it did not matter that she was baptized."

He explained that it required all four of a person's grandparents to have been baptized in order for that relationship to have any impact on an individual. Because my mother herself was a half-Jew, married to a full Jew, she must, according to the German rules, be interned.

German Provisions on Full and Half Jews and other "Fraction Jews"

These terms were defined in the Nuremberg laws of 1935.

According to German terminology a person was a Jew, regardless of religious affiliation or even understanding, if the individual had at least three grandparents who were affiliated with a Jewish congregation.

A person who had one or two Jewish grandparents, was also considered to be a Jew, if the person satisfied one of the following conditions

a) a member of a Jewish congregation at the time the Nuremberg laws were adopted;
b) married to a Jew;
c) was married to a Jew, or was in a marriage concluded after the prohibition of mixed marriages;
d) was from an adulterous affair with a Jew, born out of wedlock after 31 July 1936.

A person who did not belong to any of these categories, but had two Jewish grandparents was classified as Jewish Mischling of first degree, while a person with only one Jewish grandparent was Mischling of second degree.

It couldn't be said that the Nazis were not interested in details!

Some days before 13 October, Hennig came to Horserød camp with a movie camera. The Jewish detainees were lined up in two rows, men and women separately. He filmed them, first in two rows and then some of the Jews individually. The latter were selected as "distinct Jewish types". During the trial after the war he claimed there was no special purpose in filming the Jews. The camera was private, his wife's, and it was purchased to film their child after his birth.

This explanation is different from what some of the detainees told the court. To them Hennig said that the film would be used as propaganda to show the Danes what Danish Jews looked like, and that they were interned.

A few years ago the film was unexpectedly found in a police archive. The film can be seen on videnskab.dk's website http://videnskab.dk/kultur-samfund/dansk-scoop-i-holocaust-forskning.

In the version of the film that can be viewed on the internet, the close-up shots of some people are pixelated in order to hide their identity, as the images can be offensive to those concerned and to their descendants. There is a panning shot over people lined up in front of a barrack building. About 29 seconds into the film one can see my father, who is stooping slightly with his right foot forward. He has dark hair.

On the morning of 13 October some SS officers arrived in Horserød camp. An order was given that all half-Jews, even if they were married to a full-Jew, should gather in a separate group. The full-Jews were to be deported to Germany the same day. This was about 175 people. Those who were separated would stay. They were taken to a barrack building for the sick until the others had left.

The picture is from the film that the Danish anti-Semite Paul Hennig filmed on the 12 October 1943 in Horserød camp, in order to show the Danes how Danish Jews looked and to show that they were now interned. My father is seen in the middle of the picture, stooping slightly.

My grandparents were in the group deported to Germany on that day. My mother said that my grandmother tried to commit suicide at the railway station in Elsinore by eating some pills. It probably wasn't very dramatic because there are no descriptions of a delay in the onward transport of the 175.

My parents and I, Corrie and Sven Meyer and their two boys and the Hoffgaard family all had the same "characteristics" of the Germans' Jewish classification, but apparently it was not obvious that we should also be deported, although it turned out differently.

The Agreement that Prevented the Danish Jews from being Sent by Transport

To better understand Paul Hennig's efforts to separate full-Jews from half-Jews, and in general the Jews being split up into two groups in Horserød camp, we have to return to some events in October. Svenningsen finally succeeded getting in contact with Best around 1 October, when Best tried to avoid a confrontation with the official representative of Denmark.

As early as the night of the action, Best promised, as Hans Kirchhoff cited in *The Holocaust in Denmark*, that the deportation would not be repeated, and promised that half-Jews and Jews married to Aryans would not be persecuted. However this should be seen against the background that in the order given for 1 October, every full-Jew and half-Jew were to be deported.

At the meeting with Best on 4 October, Svenningsen expressed how seriously the treatment of the Jews was considered. The threat by Svenningsen was that cooperation with the permanent secretaries in the ministries could only continue as long as there were no new "extreme actions".

Many of the subsequent actions were aimed at preventing us, who had remained in Horserød camp, from being deported to Germany, and to get those back who, according to the Danish Government's understanding, were deported in error.

The pressure to clarify the conditions of people deported in error – the children, the old and so on – continued.

On 25 October the Danish ambassador in Berlin, Otto Carl Mohr, handed over a memorandum to the German Foreign Ministry. It dealt with Best's commitment of early October, as well as some other issues the Danes had repeatedly expressed, such as the release of children under 18 years, getting a list of the deportees, and permission to visit them in Theresienstadt.

The views of the German authorities were mixed as to how far they would go in accommodating the Danish views. Hans Kirchhoff described it this way: "By then the key German players had positioned themselves. The political leadership, i.e. von Ribbentrop, along with the head of the legal department, supported his representative in Denmark [Best]. The ministry's 'expert' on Jews, together with Von Thadden and Wagner, held a position in between, relative to the radical Eichmann. What was left now was for the head of the Gestapo, Heinrich Müller, to decide and he proved to be less stubborn than his Jew expert."

Von Thadden did not receive this request very positively, and expressed that Best might have been misunderstood. However, there were some openings in von Thadden's reaction.

Best was asked to come to Berlin on the 29 October. He had several meetings, including a visit with the Gestapo head Müller. A few days later Müller ordered Eichmann to Copenhagen with the task of clarifying the details with Best. Hans Kirchhoff writes that the overall deal, in practice, was settled.

After the meeting with Eichmann, on 3 November, Best sent telegram no. 1353 to the Foreign Ministry in Berlin, which in many ways would be crucial for those who had been deported, and those who were going to be.

It is difficult to completely grasp why Eichmann accepted Best's proposals, in light of the fact that he was upset over the failure of the action in Denmark. I will not go deeper into a number of factors that may have played a role, but will mention that the meeting with Best was quite brief and took place between other business Eichmann had that day. In the telegram Eichmann stated that he told the Reich Security Main Office [Reichssicherheitshauptamt] that he would make the following proposals:

1) Jews over 60 years will no longer be arrested and deported.
2) Half-Jews and Jews in mixed marriages who are arrested and deported, must be released and brought back to Denmark.
3) All of the deported Danish Jews are to remain in Theresienstadt and in the foreseeable future receive a visit by representatives of the Danish administration and the Danish Red Cross.

I request information about whether the Reich Security Main Office will proceed with Eichmann's proposal.

How much or how little did that help us? One can immediately see that Mohr's request for the release of children under 18 was not included in Best's telegram, whereas the point about the over 60 year-olds was included.

Neither my grandparents nor my parents could be "rescued" by the 60-year rule, which, incidentally, applied only for the future.

The point about half-Jews and Jews in mixed marriages was a little more difficult to understand in relation to us. It is clear that my grandparents (on my father's side) did not fall into that category, and they had no chance of being released.

But what about my grandfather on my mother's side? My grandmother was born and baptized Christian. She converted to Judaism on 18 June 1920 and married my grandfather on 2 July 1920. Paul Hennig is obfuscating with his explanations about this issue.

What about my mother, and thus indirectly my father? My mother was born in 1917, almost three years before my grandmother converted in 1920. The ministerial registration does not reveal when my mother converted, but most likely it was together with my grandmother in 1920. Was she thus a half-Jew? Paul Hennig explained after the war that it was necessary for a person's four grandparents to have all been baptized if that relationship was to have any impact on the person. As my mother was a half-Jew, and she was married to a full-Jew, she would, according to the German rules, be interned.

Whatever the interpretation of the above mentioned points, the provision in point 3 proved to be of greatest importance. The Danish Jews were to remain in Theresienstadt, and would be visited there by the Red Cross.

Most researchers have interpreted point 3 as an absolute assurance that the Danish Jews were protected from being sent to the extermination camps. The historian Arthur Arnheim, in an article in the magazine *Rambam*, addressed a somewhat different interpretation. He noted that point 3 contained two commitments, and the two are not divided into two different points. His opinion was that they should be interpreted in context, which could indicate that the Danish Jews were only protected until the Red Cross visit was over. One cannot rule out that interpretation, but the essential thing is that the Danes, no matter what was the original intent of the formulation, were not sent away in transports, and many of us received better treatment in Theresienstadt.

There have been different interpretations among the detainees about the visit from the Red Cross. My mother's opinion, in contrast to a statement that is emphasized in a later chapter about the visit, was that "the visit gave us a kind of safety, and we were aware that someone outside the camp knew where we were and were keeping an eye on us."

Perhaps a Brain Tumor: Attempts to get my Grandmother Released

There was no doubt that both my paternal grandparents were 100 per cent Jewish, and therefore clearly belonged in the group that should have been taken to Germany. And yet.

The head of the Psychiatric Department at the municipal hospital, Dr. Reiter, wrote a medical report "on request" about my grandmother on 11 October 1943, just before the deportation of the group to Germany. It is unclear who had made this request. Perhaps it was my uncle who managed to escape when we were arrested on Amager Strandvej. He was being hidden at the Psychiatric Department of the municipal hospital until it could be arranged to get him to Sweden.

In the medical report Dr. Reiter stated that my grandmother, for a number of years, had suffered from a serious digestive disorder. In 1937 she suffered a serious head injury, and that she had constant headaches, dizziness, double vision, spinal fluid changes and much more. He mentioned that it was likely that she had developed a brain tumor and that hospitalization for an eventual operation might be necessary.

Contact with the Germans about the case led nowhere, and on 22 October the Foreign Ministry made a notation in the file that Kriminalrat Bunke had said that my grandmother had been taken to Germany.

Erich Bunke was head of the Gestapo department for combatting sabotage, and issues concerning Jews. In the chaotic days when Denmark was liberated, he managed to escape to Germany and disappeared.

The Foreign Ministry did not give up that easily, although the notations made in the file on 16 November clearly indicate that the case was considered hopeless, and that it should be shelved. A few days later, however, on 18 November, the deputy head of department, Frants Hvass, stated, with the consent of the head of department, that yet another effort should be made and that the medical report should be sent to the Danish Legation in Berlin, asking whether they thought that an appeal to the German authorities could lead to my grandmother being admitted to a hospital in Denmark.

Time was passing, more than six months, and it was not until 11 May 1944 that the Danish Legation in Berlin informed the Foreign Ministry that the German Foreign Ministry had reported that my grandmother was under medical observation by Jewish specialists in Theresienstadt, which had excellent sanitary conditions. The named official in the German Foreign Ministry added that the Danish representatives at the upcoming Red Cross visit would probably have the opportunity to familiarize themselves with the sanitary facilities in Theresienstadt.

We Remain in Horserød Camp

Probably the same day as the large group in Horserød camp was deported to Germany, the so-called Jewish barracks were emptied, and there was no longer any separation between men and women.

The group that remained in Horserød camp, which later in November were deported, included my parents and myself, Corrie and Sven Meyer with their two children, Peter and Olaf, who were 1 and 2 years older than me. There was also Sven and Karen Hoffgaard with two adolescent daughters, Kate and Lillian. Remaining at Horserød was 13 year-old Annie Smaalann who was arrested together with us near Syrefabrikken, Salomon Feldmann and his wife as well as Michael Singerowitz, Carl Suskowitz, London, Löb and Heller. The latter two were agricultural trainees.

The Danish authorities, which were otherwise highly restrictive in allowing Jews from Germany to come to Denmark in the 1930s, let some young Jewish men and women come to Denmark in order to learn agriculture for eventual emigration to Palestine. They were typically 14-18 years old. Their stay was funded by Jewish resources and they were not paid for their work by the Danish farmers. Löb and Heller belonged to that group.

My mother said about 13 October that "we knew they were going to Germany. We could not imagine otherwise. The Germans organized a collection of money in the camp so that somebody would go to Elsinore and buy soap, food and other things, so that they had something for the 'trip.'

We all had money in order to pay the fishermen for sailing us to Sweden. So the money we had was handed over. Items were bought, but we did not see any of it, and neither did those who were leaving. These things were obviously for the benefit of the Germans."

Ralph Oppenhejm also mentioned what happened, but he wrote that those who left from Horserød actually did get what was purchased.

> In the afternoon we were told that we had been allowed to send a couple of men to Elsinore to buy supplies. They bought preserves, butter, eggs, clothing and toiletries in large quantities. Many shops declined payment. Everything was now taken into the waiting train, along with the packed lunches we got from the camp. Then we were given orders to get into the train, in the old third-class compartments … Then the train left.

Jytte Bornstein writes in her story, *My Journey Back*, that her mother, among other things, helped buy things in Elsinore, and it appears from her story that most of the food simply disappeared.

Annie Smaalann, who remained with us in Horserød camp until we were deported, was only 13 and completely on her own. Whether she remembers correctly or not is unclear. Years after the war she said that nobody paid special attention to her. "Maybe I isolated myself and people had enough with their own problems", she says. It sounds outrageous and perhaps not completely accurate, but it may well be that she felt it that way. My mother said that "everyone did what they could to comfort her, and she seemed to be doing fine, because we did not notice anything special."

My mother's letters to my grandmother from Horserød camp, along with one letter to my aunt, were saved and are now in the Jewish Museum's archive in Copenhagen.

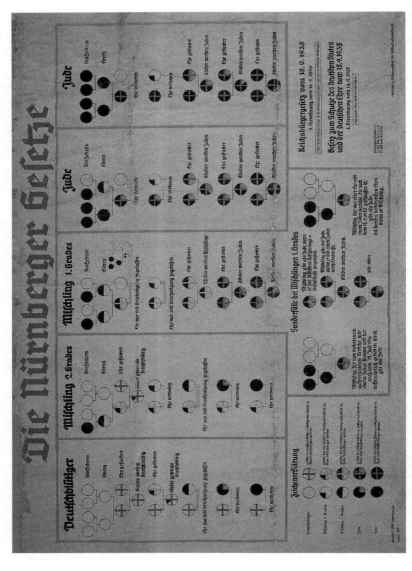

Schematic overview of the German Nuremberg Laws of 1935. The laws define who, according to the Nazis, were 100 per cent Jews, half - Jews and other "fraction Jews". There was so much talk about it that in Horserod camp, my mother noted, that 100 per cent Jew and half-Jew were some of the first words I learned to speak.

The Danish anti-Semite Paul Hennig. He became member of the Waffen SS in 1942 and a member of the anti-Semitic party, the Danish Anti-Jewish League. His task in Horserød camp was, among others things, to decide how the prisoners fitted into the provisions of the Nuremberg laws and, consequently, who should be deported. (National Archives)

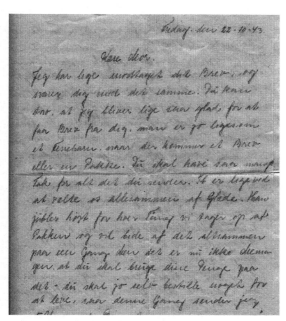

My mother's letter from Horserød camp to my grandmother, 22 October 1943.

In many ways some of the letters are remarkable, because they illustrate life in the camp as fairly uncomplicated and peaceful. What thoughts my mother might really have had about what was waiting for us, she kept well hidden. It may be due to the fear that letters were censored. Or was it simply that the seriousness of the situation was not yet clear to her?

In the lecture she gave at the Hvidovre Club, it also comes out clearly that her concerns were not very serious. She said: "So all in all, we calmed down again. We were, after all, in Denmark, and we thought that at some point they would set us free again. Why were we there? And there were rumors every day."

Letter from 14 October 1943:

Dear Mother.

Many thanks for all the good things you sent us. Ib is so happy with malt extract, that you can't believe it. I just cannot understand that you have not written a letter with the package – hopefully nothing is wrong? Let me know how everything is with you. Here we are well. We get good food and Ib is happy and satisfied. He is playing outside all day, and it is something which does him well. Have you talked to Bording? I would appreciate having news from them.
Answer me as fast as you can. I would love to hear from you all.

Many kisses and greetings
From Max, Ib and Karen.

Remember the address: The Internment camp in Horserød. No 1

P.S. I think we can only receive letters when they are in a package, but do not spend so much money for it. Just remember, if you send something, then put a letter in the package.

The following letter from 18 October suggests that my mother, who knew that my maternal grandfather and aunt had been arrested by the Germans, was not aware that they had been deported to Germany on the same day they were arrested on 1 October.

Letter from 18 October 1943:

Dear Mother.

Now I send you yet again a little greeting. Some letters might have crossed each other, but I have now received your letter, and you may now write to me without a package. You write that you have sent toiletries, but I have not received them. On the other hand I have a comb, a wash cloth, soap, and a good cleanser, because I am breaking out in spots on the face due to the sharp air. A little powder and a puff would not be bad, but it could be saved if I could just get my bag. Could you talk with H [the same H as mentioned in the chapter "Helper or Informer?"], he should know where it is. I forgot it in the car and he could try to get it back. There is also what remains of my salary for the month, 75 kroner. Can I get some more biscuits and a few sweets? I got a letter from Gerda. It was good that you were together. Happy Birthday, hopefully it will be different next year.

I have seen my birth certificate and the letter from the lawyer Per Holm, but I do not understand why Annie and Dad have not come home.

Let me soon hear from you again.

I am happy that Ida and Børge stay with you.

Ib often asks about you, and he wants his "Cille" with Grandmother. Otherwise he is happy and healthy and is completely spoiled. He sleeps two hours in the middle of the day, every day, and there's a nice sand pit, where he plays with the other children. He has begun to talk so well and I would wish you could hear him on his second birthday.

Take care all of you and write from time to time

Many kisses and greetings
From Ib, Max and Karen.

That same day, 18 October, my grandmother went to the Foreign Ministry. She informed the ministry that my grandfather and aunt were arrested by the German police on 1 October at 10.15 p.m., and that she had filed my grandfather's naturalization certificate on 4 October at Dagmarhus, as well as her own certificate of baptism and her parents' certificates of baptism and their marriage certificate. At Dagmarhus they told her that my grandfather had already been taken to Germany by ship on 2 October, and that they didn't have any information about my aunt's fate. She also informed them that her lawyer, Per Salomon, had filed a written application for their release on 9 October.

My grandfather received Danish citizenship in 1927. The Foreign Ministry's file also indicated that he was not a member of the Jewish Community and that he was not orthodox.

My grandmother also told the Foreign Ministry that my mother, who was born out of wedlock, along with me and my father, who was 100 per cent Jewish, had been arrested in Kastrup by the German police and were deported to Horserød camp, along with my grandparents.

The foreign Ministry noted in the file that as my parent's marriage was not dissolved, and that they are only separated, that the official recommended that the ministry should try not only to get my mother and myself released, but also my father.

In a draft drawn up by the Foreign Ministry, in German, to the German authorities, there are two comments. One is that the Ministry of Foreign Affairs did not hide the fact that although my mother was born of an Aryan mother, her father was 100 per cent Jewish and she was "legitimized" in connection with her parents' marriage. The second comment is that the ministry was inclined to ask for the release of my father as well. The form was dated 6 November.

Now back to my mother's letters. The letters from 22 and 27 October were also very much about everyday issues, and my mother's main concern seemed to be my grandmother's economic situation. However, small worrisome comments about the future started to appear in the letters. "How do you think it's going to be [a week ahead]" and "We hope that better times will come for all of us. After all we are all here with a good conscience. We have not done anything wrong."

Letter from the 22nd of October 1943:

Dear Mother

I just received your letter, and respond to you immediately. I am so happy to get letters from you. One feels just like a child on holiday when there is a letter or a parcel. I am so grateful and send you many thanks for everything you send. Ib is about toppling us all with joy. He rejoices aloud about everything we take out of the package and will bite it all at once. But you should not spend your money on it - you yourself have to work hard in order to get something to live from, so this time I send you 5 kroner with the letter.

I am very glad that my bag has been found.

Well, there is no special news. Everything is calm and quiet out here. Better nothing new than bad news, as the saying goes, yet we all hope that before long there will be a change (preferably for the better), but gradually we learn to be patient, and we must not complain. You ask if you could visit us. I do not think it is worth the trouble to spend money getting up here because you will probably only get a brief glimpse of us, and we are not allowed to speak to each other anyway. It is good that you have visited Mr Nedergaard, so that people at Bording are aware of the situation.

Father has a birthday today, but unfortunately you cannot celebrate it with him. In a week's time it is Ib's birthday. How do you think the situation will be then?

Dear Mother. Lea writes that you have been looking for a birthday present for him. If you can, I would love to have a pair of dark blue leggings for him. I have seen in the newspaper that they have some wool and thread that can be buttoned on the side of the leg. They cost 7.50 kroner at Simon Olesen. He has toys out here, so you should not spend much money on him, as he does not have any understanding of it anyway.

Yes Mother, then I will stop for now with many loving greetings and kisses from the three of us out here.
Karen.

Letter from 22 October 1943 to my mother's sister and brother-in-law:

Dear Ida and Børge.

Thank you for the letter, it is wonderful when there is something to read, and I read them so many times that I end up knowing them by heart. Congratulations on your birthday. You will get a nice thing from me when I come home, if it does not last too long, otherwise you better get money to buy it yourself. Do not send your own powder to me. If I get my bag I can manage with what is in it. You should definitely not give me your birthday present. It is bad for mother that she has lost so much weight. I wish that she didn't have to work. I bought a nice warm coat at CG for Ib, so do not think about that. What are you doing on Sundays? It is the worst day out here. Now I have to finish the letter - for Ib has been on the potty for half an hour and now he is cross - he says that I have to come with toilet paper because he has finished. Believe me, he speaks quite well now.

Kisses from Ib and loving greetings from Max and Karen.

Letter from 27 October 1943:

Dearest Mother

I just received the package with everything you sent. You have no idea how it all makes happiness. Believe me, the small suit of clothes was admired by everyone here, and it suits him so well. Thank you very much. I am just sorry that you spend all your money on it, but here are 10 kroner to help you. Have you received the 5 kroner I sent the last time? Director Hans Bording said to me that if it was difficult for you, you should turn to him personally, and you should take advantage of that offer.
Dear Mother, next time I hear from you, please send an empty suitcase, because as you write, it is good that we are well, but it is not certain that we can stay here. We don't know anything yet, but I take it as it comes, and then it is good to have a suitcase for our clothing. We may well hope that better times come for all of us, for we are all here with a good conscience. We have not done any harm.
Now at the end the warmest greetings and kisses and the hope to see you soon my loving Mother, I miss you so terribly.
A thousand kisses from Max, Ib and Karen.

On 30 October I turned two years old. Indications show that the birthday was not very different from what it would have been if we had not been interned in Horserød camp. There was no shortage of birthday presents. My mother said that one of the prison guards, Larsen, was very nice and kind, and that he was sorry for the situation on our behalf. It was he who bought the rocking horse I got as a birthday present. Another sign that conditions in Horserød were much better after 13 October was that a couple of Danish officers managed to get permission for gymnastics.

Letter from 30 October 1943:

Dear everyone

I just want to tell you how Ib's birthday went. The time is 1:30 pm and he's sleeping at the moment, but it is also really necessary. He is completely out of his mind. He received presents from 8 o'clock in the morning. Max bought him a nice rocking horse, which he did not want to ride on. He will only carry it under his arm. He got wooden building blocks, sand molds, buckets, chocolate, a horse and carriage, a picture book and more is to come. At 3 o'clock we are going to have afternoon coffee and I bought two layer cakes which we are all going to share.

I finish for now, I am going to do gymnastics.

Loving greetings from Karen.

Now two and a half weeks went by without a letter, and as stated in the letter from the 17 November, there were now tighter restrictions on how many letters are allowed to be written.

Letter from the 17th of November 1943

Dear Mother

I will send you a few words again, although I haven't yet had an answer to my last letter to you. I reckon that this letter will cross yours - because I am awaiting a response from you every day as I have not heard anything from you since the 6th.

There are other rules out here now for the receipt of letters and packages. We are allowed to receive one package a month, and I think it will be best at the end of the month. On the other hand we are allowed to receive and send letters twice a month, on the 15th and the 30th and respond the 16th and 1st.

Yesterday I got a letter from Gerda, in which she writes that she has been with you and Mrs Kahn, but I understand from the letter that she was disappointed that she had to leave early. How are you all of you? Here everything is as usual. We received a letter from Mrs Jensen. At Ægirsgade, from where she was writing, everything is fine. Nothing will change until she sees my in-laws again.

Mr And Mrs Ebbesen have been so kind to us. They send so many nice packages out here, and we just received a package from an acquaintance of Asger Jensen. There was a jar of real honey, biscuits and apples. They are people that we hardly know, so I must say it is considerate. We have not even received a postcard from Asger and Inge.

On Saturday, it is my birthday, and I will certainly think much of you. Do you remember my birthday last year? It was not a very good one either. God knows when all our hardship will be finished. One might think about what we have been through as the 'seven lean years'. But as long as we are here we should not complain, but it is unavoidable not to feel a little homesick.

I am sure you will be surprised when you see Ib again. He has grown a lot, and he says everything, even naughty words which he has learned from some small boys out here. When I put clothes on him in the morning, and it does not matter which clothes I put on him, he says "I have got it from Aunt and Børge". He believes that anything he gets is from them.

Well, now it is almost 12 o'clock and we are going to eat. We get a hot meal at this time of the day, so I will end my letter now – and you will then not hear from us until about the 1st of next month.

Many loving greetings to you all from Max, Karen and Ib.

It was now about five weeks since we had arrived at Horserød camp. There was hardly any doubt that we had been kept back because there was uncertainty as to which category, under the Nuremberg laws, we belonged.

Although it must have been for "racial" reasons that we remained in Horserød camp after the others were deported, the story in our family was that it was because of my maternal grandmother's attempts to get us released that we remained. It was due to the fact that my mother was a half-Jew, and that she had a small child, and that this fact "delayed" our deportation to Germany.

I never talked to my grandmother about what she actually did when we were arrested, but there is evidence of her efforts to get us released in the police interrogations of December 1945 and January 1946. They are of her and Paul Hennig who remembered, apparently quite clearly, my grandmother's visit to Dagmarhus. The reports did not seem to confirm the story that it was her inquiries in Dagmarhus as the reason for our family not immediately being deported.

When my grandmother heard that Jews married to Aryan women should not be detained, she went to Dagmarhus, on the morning of 3 October. She pointed out that she was Aryan and baptized. She initially approached Dagmarhus to see if my grandfather and aunt could be released. At that point they were already on their way through Germany. My parents did not know anything about what happened when they were arrested. My mother was only told the story of when they were arrested when she and I arrived to Theresienstadt in late April 1944.

As 3 October was a Sunday, my grandmother was asked to come back the next day. She was told that she should speak to Fritz Renner, but she realized later that it was Hennig she needed to talk to. Renner was, among other things, an accomplice in the shooting of a refugee's helper on 9 October in Tårbæk.

She explained to Hennig that she was Aryan. He said that she had to get a certificate proving this and submit it together with an application written in German. He said she probably had to get a lawyer to do it for her. The application should state that she suspected that her husband and her daughter were arrested by mistake.

From the lawyer, Per Holm, she got the application, and they both went to Dagmarhus and handed it over to Hennig.

In the meantime, my parents and I had been arrested and detained in Horserød camp, and so my grandmother's inquiries in Dagmarhus also included us.

My grandmother then also got hold of my mother's certificate of baptism and handed that over to Hennig, who said that he would consider that issue as well.

During the first conversation with Hennig, my grandmother said that he said that "Are these Jews completely stupid? It was shouted on loudspeakers on the ship that those who were married to Aryans should report themselves, and that her husband could have just done that."

At the same time Fritz Renner came by chance into the office, and when my grandmother complained that the application had not been forwarded, Renner took the application and gave it to a uniformed German named Nagel, and instructed him, as far as Hennig understood, to ensure that the application was sent.

In January 1944 Renner announced to my grandmother that the application had been refused, and that she should not expect to see my grandfather and my aunt any more.

Hennig, who was present, threw one of the Jewish official ministerial protocols on the desk and said "that she had been hanging around too closely to Moses" and "that he knew about all her relationships, so there was no hope." The same day (or another day) Hennig said, "How the hell could you think of marrying a Jew?"

One day when she spoke with Hennig about my father, he said "he was the most filthy, disgusting Jew pig whom they had ever seen up there."

After this final refusal from Dagmarhus, my grandmother approached Dagmarhus once again and asked why her daughter could not be released like the Schultz sisters[7], who were also only half-Jews. To this Hennig apparently answered "that when you have the devil as your great-grandmother, one could achieve much in this little country, but if you were a poor tailor's wife, nothing would be done for you. After all the government had left, and the king was sitting reading *Socialdemokraten*[8]."

My mother completed the story about our time in Horserød camp and said "then time passed in Horserød, always with both rumors and hope. Some came into the camp, and some were released."

The 23 November – Deportation to Germany

On the 23 November we were told to pack all of our things. We were moving on.

My parents always believed there was most likely a link between a bomb attack at Café Mokka on Strøget in Copenhagen and the Germans' loss of patience and decision to deport the remaining Jews. That's the same conclusion made in Corrie and Sven Meyer's book *Theresienstadt:The Staged Deception*. They believe our fate was sealed when a number of German officers and soldiers were killed in the sabotage. A number of other researchers also came to the same conclusion.

The attack took place on 27 October at Café Mokka on Strøget in Copenhagen. It happened about a month before we were deported to Germany. The café was frequented by Germans and Danes who worked with the Germans. Today the incident would be called a terrorist act. This was not a typical attack from the Danish Resistance. The explosion took place during regular hours with the aim of killing and wounding those present.

The explosion was on the front pages of the all the Danish newspapers.

The headline on the front page of the newspaper *Politiken* on 29 October was "Terrible effect of a delayed action bomb in the crowded room". The devastation was indescribable. There were about 250 people in the café when the bomb exploded, shortly after 10 o'clock in the evening. Four people – two German soldiers, a German policeman and a Danish woman – were killed, and 40 were wounded.

As punishment for the attack, a state of emergency was imposed with a 8 p.m. to 5 a.m. curfew in the entire Copenhagen area starting 29 October, which lasted all the way until 10 February 1944. As a result of the curfew tram and S train operations were also stopped, and restaurants and entertainment were closed at 7 p.m.

The time span between the explosion at Café Mokka on 27 October and our deportation to Germany on 23 November, almost a month afterwards, is so long that it seems unlikely that the attack was the reason for our deportation. But the explosion probably created an unfavorable climate for any attempt to ease up on the part of the Germans.

Hans Kirchhoff, in *Holocaust in Denmark,* writes that Svenningsen, on 27 October, pushed Best towards getting us released from Horserød camp. "It was probably entirely cases that did not fall within the action against the Jews, that these people had been exempted from the deportation that took place recently", Svenningsen declared in Dagmarhus. "Why were these people not released? Their relatives were troubled and continuously addressed their concerns to the Danish authorities." Best promised to look into the matter. Whether he did so or not, we were deported anyway.

The departure from the Horserød camp was by car, and we were taken to Elsinore.

"When we arrived at Elsinore, we were counted and called out in the usual way with the purpose of confusing people by yelling and screaming. The leader of the operation was a Dane named Juhl. He counted us again when we boarded the train. It was an ordinary train. It was no cattle car", my mother said.

Hans Wilhelm Adolf Juhl, also called Gestapo-Juhl, was not Danish as my mother thought, but a German SS officer. He was head of the local Gestapo in the Elsinore area.

He was born in Schleswig-Holstein and spoke and understood Danish quite well. He was a member of the Nazi party even before 1933 and came to Denmark shortly after the occupation.

He was one of the most zealous Nazis and was, among other things, responsible for the raid on the church attic in Gilleleje on the night between 6 and 7 October.

It is estimated that he was responsible for the deportation of more than half of the Danish Jews who were deported to Theresienstadt.

He was not convicted for his crimes after the war.

More people came on the train as it drove south through Zealand. We were 19 Jews coming from Horserød camp. In Copenhagen, an additional 31 prisoners, mostly from Odense, came on board. Among them was 18 year-old Poul Nielsen, whose crime had been to distribute illegal papers. Poul Nielsen, who passed away in October 2018, recently wrote a book about his stay in Sachsenhausen *Only a Number. 18 months in KZ Sachsenhausen*, published on Auschwitz Day on 27 January 2016. The prisoners from Odense were not Jews, but Poul Nielsen had a clear recollection that there were six Jews on the train to Sachsenhausen. However, he had no specific recollection of my father.

Map with a marking of a number of concentration camps, including the three camps we were prisoners in: Ravensbrück, Sachsenhausen and Theresienstadt.

My mother told about the train journey:

> We traveled south through Denmark and came to Germany. The train stopped for quite a while. I forgot to tell about three young men when we were on our way south through Zealand. They were in Denmark as agricultural trainees [except London], and they had come to Denmark from Germany and Czechoslovakia. They knew what was going on in Germany, and knew the seriousness of the situation much better than we did. They said that they did not care about how, but they wanted to jump out of the train.

The three young men were the previously mentioned London, Löb and Heller.

> I think it was my husband who persuaded the three. One of them was Czech. He was trembling with fear. I have never seen a man who was so nervous. He knew much more about what was going on than those of us from Denmark. We did not really know how terrible it all was. And when we reached Roskilde, my husband said 'there is a mental

hospital in Roskilde, try and get off the train and find the hospital. They will hide you for sure and help you in getting to Sweden.

Annie Smaalann remembers that there were whisperings before the three jumped off the train. She found out, after the war, that they had discussed whether they should try to take her with them when they jumped. They ended up deciding not to because they found the risk too great if they were caught.

There was probably a lot of talk on the train about it for a long time, as the train was driving rather slowly. When it stopped, three to four German soldiers who were on board went out and patrolled.

The trip from Elsinore to Roskilde took quite a while, so I will not rule out that my father was involved in the discussions, although he might not have had quite as decisive an influence on what happened as my mother recalled. He does not appear in the report that Gerhard Löb wrote.

After the war Löb said that he hid in several places in Denmark, with friends and acquaintances, after the warning he received on 30 September, and that he'd also made contact with the Resistance. He was arrested in the first half of November on the way to Stubbekøbing, where he was scheduled to sail to Sweden on a fishing boat. He was then detained in Horserød camp.

On the train from Elsinore, he said he had a friendly conversation with Corrie and Sven Meyer. Sven said that a cousin of his wife had succeeded in jumping off a train in a similar situation. Löb, Heller and London then talked about that, and they agreed that the next time the train stopped, they would jump out from each compartment at the moment the Germans jumped on the train and closed the doors.

The three were aware that their flight could create problems for us, but Löb said that Sven said that it was perfectly in order, and that they would close the windows after they had jumped out. When the train stopped, and set in motion again, a bit before Roskilde train station, all three of them jumped out.

They had agreed that each of them should take care of themselves if the Germans discovered and came after them. Later in the evening Löb was taken into protection by the Danish police in Roskilde, and they also managed to find and protect one of the others who, according to my mother's statement, was terribly nervous. Just before they were about to go to Sweden, the third one also joined them.

In 1942 Löb's parents were deported to a concentration camp in Riga. From there they were ordered into a forest and shot. On the question of whether we also considered escaping, my mother said:

No, we had a small, two year-old child. Jumping out of the window onto a train track! There were Germans at each end of the carriage. We could not imagine that it would have been possible. They were healthy and fit young men. They could do it. We would never have been able to do it.

The train arrived at Gedser, and we were transported by ship to Warnemünde. On our departure from Horserød camp each of us got 5 kg of food. The three escapees left their packages with my father. In the meantime the group of prisoners from Odense had joined the train, so the packages benefitted them as well. In Germany we also boarded an ordinary train.

One of the Danish women from the resistance movement, Klara Sørensen, who was also on our transport to Germany, said that the Jews were in a separate compartment, and that she could hear the chatter as well as crying children. My mother continued:

We then arrived in Germany. We stayed for very long at the first stop. We got a bit to eat. It looked like rye-bread-and-beer porridge. It did not taste particularly good. And most of us, as we had already received good food in Horserød camp, and we had also our packages from the Red Cross, were relatively ok. So we threw out what we did not like. Then the German soldiers said to us "Wait and see, you will get something much worse afterwards".

When the train was near Berlin, it was stopped. It was not possible to continue. Allegedly there had been a bombardment of the rail network.

It has not been possible for me to verify whether that explanation is correct, or whether it was planned that we, at least temporarily, should be taken to the camps where we later ended up. The closest I determined is that there was heavy bombing of Berlin in November and December, including on 23 November, when there was an air raid alarm between 7.26 p.m. and 9.19 p.m. Berlin was completely covered by clouds that night, and with the technical equipment at that time, it must have been quite difficult to determine exactly where the bombs were supposed to be dropped. This does not prove that "our" network was bombed, even if there were air raid alarms more or less at that time.

The train stopped, and the women and children were ordered out of the train. The train went a little further, and then the men were ordered out as well, among them my father. They were taken to Sachsenhausen concentration camp.

Klara Sørensen also recounted the dramatic event when the Jewish families were separated from each other, and she also explained that we were ordered onto a truck to take us the rest of the way to Ravensbrück. My mother continued:

> In the middle of the night we were stopped. There was a small group of women on the train. They were communists, and then there was us, the small group of Jews. We were told to get off the train. Only the women and children, not the men. I had the boy and the suitcase my mother had sent me in Horserød camp with some clothes for us. I could not carry the boy, the clothes and the bags as well as the food. Naive as I was, I thought, oh well, we'll probably get something where we are going, so I left the Red Cross package, unfortunately.

It was now 24 November and we had arrived at Ravensbrück. Among the Jews there were my mother and me, Corrie Meyer with her children Peter, and Olaf, Klara Feldmann, Karen Hoffgaard and her daughters Kate and Lillian, and 13-year old Annie Smaalann.

What kind of camp was it?

Notes

1   The name of the company is "Aktieselskabet Dansk Svovlsyre & Superphosphat-Fabrik". It was called Syrefabrikken (could be translated Acid or Chemical Factory). The term Syrefabrikken will be used in this book.
2.   Amager is an island in Copenhagen.
3   *EkstraBladet* is a Danish daily newspaper.
4   Vestre Fængsel (Western Prison) is the main prison in Copenhagen.
5   Sundby is an area on Amager.
6   Hellerup is a suburb to Copenhagen.
7   More about the Schultz sisters in the section "My Father's Ten Days in Berlin".
8   A Danish daily Social Democratic newspaper.

5

Ravensbrück – "Welcome to Hell"

"Welcome to Hell". That was what a young Danish girl said when Ellen W. Nielsen arrived at Ravensbrück in December 1944. That is quoted from an article in a local magazine about Ellen W. Nielsen. Ellen helped people to escape and participated in illegal work with, among other things, weapons transport.

Ravensbrück was one of four concentration camps established in Germany before the war. It did not differ much from other camps: forced labor, medical experiments, individual killings and mass extermination, murder of sick prisoners, beatings, gas chambers, crematoria and forced marches. But Ravensbrück was unique in the sense that it was the only major camp for women.

In 1940, there were 4,000 in the camp, and 84 died. By the end of 1941 there were 12,000 prisoners. In 1942 they began killing the prisoners by firing squad, and they began to take groups of women in transports. In 1942 the first medical experiments started, the first Soviet prisoners of war arrived, and the first large groups of children came to the camp. In April 1943, the SS started a crematorium with two ovens. Before that, the corpses were burned in Fürstenberg.

In 1944 the SS enlarged the factories and increased exploitation of labor from the camp. They built a gas chamber near the crematorium and extended it with a third oven. It is assumed that the commander received notification that the death rate was too low, and that the camp did not have the capacity to receive deportations from the Polish camps that were being evacuated, unless drastic steps were taken to increase the death toll at Ravensbrück. The number of prisoners rose from 17,300 in January to around 35,000 in late July. By transporting some of the women to Majdanek for extermination, this figure was brought down to 34,500 in August, but later that month 14,000 Polish women arrived from Auschwitz. In September women from Warsaw were placed in a hastily erected tent city. Due to transports and the gas chambers, the number of prisoners was reduced to 43,000 in late December.

In 1945 there were still medical experiments going on. Dr. Clauberg sterilized Roma women and their young daughters in January. The guards poisoned dozens of prisoners in February. From January to April the SS assassinated 7,000 women and children in the small gas chamber.

In the last days of March 1945, the evacuation of the camp started, but during the first three weeks of April 6,000 women were gassed. The evacuation was a tragic event. Red Cross delegates met with the commander Fritz Suhren to try to prevent an evacuation and eradication of the 17,000 prisoners who were still in the camp, but their request failed. On 26 and 27 April, the SS evacuated 11,500 of the remaining prisoners, and there were only 3,000 very sick women left when the Soviet army liberated the camp on 30 April. The Soviet army realized that most of the prisoners died along the roads and in the forests.

The evacuees were pointlessly sent off on a march to one of the remaining pockets still under German control.

Although it was a women's camp, the camp's commanders were two men. But Ravensbrück had the largest number of female SS guards, between 550 and 600. The worst one was an assistant, Dorothea Binz. A former prisoner described how she would walk up and down the rows searching for the most vulnerable and frightened women and almost beat them to death.

There were many children in Ravensbrück. They came in transports with their mothers or were brought to the camp alone. Gemma Gluck writes that there were 500 clean-shaven 'skeletal children' in the camp while she was there.

Crematoria ovens were running 24 hours a day. As there were still problems with the capacity the furnace temperature was increased, so that one of the ovens ended up exploding. Ravensbrück's archives show that 32,000 women were killed in the gas chambers, and in no other concentration camp in Germany was the proportion of murdered prisoners as high as in Ravensbrück.

"We, the small group of Jews from Denmark, were placed in the prison, and not out in the camp itself, so we did not experience the 'camp life' directly", says my mother. After the war several of the Danish women who were interned in Ravensbrück wrote accounts of their experiences in the camp. Extracts from reports by Ellen W. Nielsen, Ragna Fischer and Astrid Blumensaadt describe the conditions in the camp.

The clothes they were given on arrival were canvas trousers and chemise, a petticoat, a prison-dress and sweater and woollen stockings, which were held up by a string. Moreover, they were given camp boots with wooden soles. The clothes were replaced three times in the year and a half they stayed in Ravensbrück, and they were only allowed to wash their underwear once a week in cold water with artificial soap.

The women in the barrack buildings were woken up around 4 a.m. and had to be at a roll-call half an hour later. In this short time they had to wash themselves, if they were among those who were lucky enough to get some of the scarce water, make their "beds" and drink half a cup of artificial coffee, which was the only breakfast they got. As there was little space, they had to take their meals sitting or standing in the bunk beds. They shared their spoons and mugs with those who had nothing.

"Beds" is too nice a word for the bunks they slept in. They were wooden frames with straw sacks. In the wide blocks they had a "sleeping-bag" of cotton fabric and pillow case and two blankets, and it made a terrible noise to make the beds. The beds had to be made according to military tradition with sharp edges, and the straw sleeping bags were to be shaken so it reached a specific height.

The madness of evil meant that all beds had to look perfectly even, even though the mattresses were dirty and infested with vermin. If not, the prisoners were severely punished. Often there were raids where stored food was searched. The search was attended by female SS with whips in their hands. Each barrack building was subject to a head of the barrack room. Often it was the camp's criminal prisoners who had that rank. Ellen's head of the barracks room, Lisa, had strangled her husband with her bare hands.

The first roll-call of the day (of many) lasted one to two hours. Out in the darkness and the cold the camp's women stood in rows of five in order to be counted. It was indescribably cold and the prisoners were forbidden to move. No stamping of feet, no nose blowing.

There were also roll-calls as punishment, often on Sundays, where they had to stand even longer. The reason for the first roll-call was punishment, Ellen witnessed, such as when one prisoner was missing. She was nowhere to be found. It turned out she was lying in the barrack room dead. There were two to three roll-calls a day, most of them lasting 2 to 3 hours, and once there was one that lasted about 8 hours.

After the roll-call the various working groups marched out. Ellen's work in the main camp consisted initially in spreading garbage and digging sand. Sometimes she was, like the others, beaten with leather straps by the SS women. It was not always the supervisor who did the beating. It could also be a passerby who suddenly started beating the prisoners. Gradually Ellen learned several tricks that the prisoners employed to fool the guards. They might hide, work more slowly when they were not under strict surveillance, or obtain a little cabbage, onion or a potato.

The working day lasted 10 to 11 hours interrupted by a half-hour lunch break. Initially the prisoners got three potatoes for dinner, but later, only a mug of soup. Afterwards there was another roll-call before the work would start again. Late in the day the exhausted prisoners would stand for a roll-call again before they could return to the barrack rooms and get their ration of soup. Then the high pitched sound of the siren sounded, announcing night's rest in the camp.

They never got an uninterrupted night's sleep because most of them were ill. Ragna Fischer says:

> But hunger was not the worst, the worst was our stomachs. One could not avoid getting dysentery and stool ran before we managed to get out. We did not dare to keep our pants on at night so as not to make them a mess, and if we took them off, we were freezing terribly. If we managed to get out and sit down somebody came and beat us.
>
> The food consisted of a black liquid in the morning that had a slight resemblance to coffee. At noon cabbage soup or rutabaga soup was served with a small cup of potatoes. In the evening either a disgusting soup filled with great flour dumplings or grits soup. The bread was divided into four parts for those who had not worked, and three to those who had worked.

The camp commander, during the period that my mother and I were in Ravensbrück, was SS-Sturmbannführer Fritz Suhren, who was the commander of the camp from August 1942 until it was liberated in 1945. Shortly before the Allied forces liberated Ravensbrück, Suhren took one of the inmates, whom he thought was Winston Churchill's niece, to a US base in the hope that her presence would save him. Suhren's attempt failed. He was convicted and hanged in 1950.

My Mother and my Five Months in Ravensbrück

My mother's report on our arrival at Ravensbrück is here intertwined with some of Corrie Meyer's stories.

> We got into a big nasty, cold room. There was a German female prison guard. She kept shouting "close the door" for there was a terrible draught, and it was cold outside. There we sat and waited on a bench all night and did not know what was going to happen. At one point I saw a number of naked people from behind, and I thought – they were completely bald – can this be women, no it must be men. It turned out they were women who had just arrived. They were shaved completely bald. They were going into some shower thing. We were

very afraid of things like that. We had heard from Jews from Eastern Europe about poison gas connected with shower, but it did not happen.

Annie Smaalann, who at the time began to get more attached to Karen Hoffgaard, who had a daughter her age, remembers:

> It was the only time during the war that I was beaten. We had been told that we had to stand up every time a Gestapo woman passed by. I did not stand up at one point and then I got a blow. Moreover, it seemed like they did not really know what to do with us. Maybe that was why we did not come out in the camp.

My mother continues to say that

> When we had been sitting there all night, we were taken out to the camp itself. It was a horrible sight I will never forget. Not only the sight, also the smell and the noise. All these poor people who were not proper people anymore. They were in their prisoner clothing, some of them with bare feet, some had clogs. A few stood over a waste bin, trembling. They probably had typhoid or something like that. They were standing trying to pick some food out of these waste bins. It was as if it was a different world. We did not realize properly that it was real. We were taken through this hell, frankly speaking, into a tiny room where we were packed together.
>
> And again waiting and waiting time without knowing what would happen. Then a few prisoners came with a few large zinc tubs, with something warm. It was a kind of soup, a rutabaga soup. It was warm, even if it did not taste very good. They were very interested in hearing from us about how the war was going. Will it end soon, what will happen?
>
> We could tell them that there was no specific prospect that it would end soon. We asked them in turn how it was here. They did not answer very positively. All they advised us was that everything we had in our suitcases, we should put on. No matter how, just put it on, otherwise it will be stolen.
>
> We began to dress in what we had of clothing. My boy had one set of knitted sweaters on after another. At the end he could barely keep his arms along his body. He was looking as a small wool lump.

Map of the Ravensbrück camp as it was in 1943. No. 26 on the map is the prison, no. 28 is the crematorium and no. 11 is the barrack building for sick prisoners (Revier).

My parents and my son and daughter in front of the crematorium in Ravensbrück in April 1995. We were imprisoned in the building seen behind the crematorium on the left in the picture. We were first imprisoned in the top cell, to the right of the picture, and later in one of the cells at the base of the prison. (Private photo)

The day came to an end. Then someone came and picked us up. We were taken into a prison in the concentration camp. At the end of the prison and up some stairs were a number of cells.

It was there we would stay. The doors were allowed to remain open so that we could get around to each other, even though we were in the cells.

Corrie Meyer also describes our situation. The next few paragraphs are views and partial quotes from her stories in her book with Sven Meyer *Theresienstadt: det iscenesatte bedrag.*

"To begin with", she says, "we were grateful that at least we had somewhere to lay down, a proper WC and a washbasin with running water. But soon it lost novelty and the cell was so small that we could barely move without stepping over each other's legs."

The floor was covered by two straw mattresses, and then there was just room for a toilet, a washbasin, a folding table and a small stool, which was nailed to the floor. But the next day the situation became worse. Corrie was

"Our" cell corridor in the prison. There were 78 cells on two floors. The prison was built in 1939. (Memorial Museum Ravensbrück and Brandenburg Memorials Foundation)

so nervous that she could not help but sob. For my mother it was almost impossible to bear it. And then we children quarreled non stop over the toys I had. When Olaf did not cry and scream and Peter was quiet, I was screaming. The second night was even worse than the first. Everyone got on each others' nerves, and Corrie and my mother were constantly quarreling over nothing.

The next day the supervisor woman came and picked us up. We were allowed to bathe. My mother says: "How happy we were, not only for the lovely warm shower and the feeling of being clean, but also because it interrupted the day's monotony. And then the woman explained that we would be moved to another department where the children would have better playground."

And so we ended up in the so-called "prominent department". Our predecessor, we heard, had been a Polish countess, and a niece of General de Gaulle had also been in the department. Why should we get that honor?' In Corrie's opinion, we could thank Peter, Olaf and me for it. "If we had not had the kids with us, I don't think that we would get out of the small cells", Corrie says.

The first floor had a series of three cells at the one side and a large room with one cell at the other. In the middle there was a large staircase leading to the basement, where there were 6 cells. One cell was the WC and laundry room, the other five were ordinary cells which were not used while all of us were there.

Was our placement in the prominent department because of the special treatment the Danish Jews got as a result of the cooperation policy? Or was the reason more banal: that our arrival was apparently somewhat unexpected for the camp management? They had placed the non-Jews from Odense, who came with us that night, into the camp itself. That they actually continued to keep us in the prison, seemed to indicate that it had had something to do with specific agreements for the Danish Jews.

We now heard from one of the prisoners who brought us food that the concentration camp was called Ravensbrück and that it was one of the most infamous camps for women in Germany.

At the beginning we were choosy and threw the black pudding and everything we did not like into the toilet, because we did not dare to let anything go out again. But later on that changed completely. We really got so used to the black pudding that we ended up liking it.

At 6 o'clock in the morning we got "coffee" and our bread ration for the day. At 12 o'clock we got our lunch meal and at half past six the evening meal.

The lunch meal consisted of potatoes with either white, red or green cabbage or turnips or rutabaga. It was always the same for days in a row, so that often, when we had cabbage, even a week after, you could find cabbage remnants between beets or rutabaga.That's how well all the pots were cleaned!

The dinner was usually a kind of flour soup with dumplings that prisoners called wallpaper paste. We hated it, and often went right into the toilet. On rare occasions we got 'nudlen', which was a cause for celebration.

We were allowed to be in the big living room, and at the beginning we were, but later on it was so cold that we could not stand it, and we kept constantly together in a cell to keep warm.

My mother continues: "Then it was Christmas, and my boy started to get ill."

The prison meal at Christmas was even worse than usual. We had agreed that we would at least try to make something out of the evening of a Danish Christmas Eve. Each of us gave something. My mother had a little bit of raspberry marmalade, only a small mouthful for each, and she also gave a piece of crisp bread with honey.

We did not go outside. We could only get fresh air by standing in front of the open living room windows facing a small depressing garden. In this

Photo of barrack buildings in Ravensbrück taken from the tower of the Kommandantur (Headquarter). The front barrack building to the left where we were hospitalized with serious diseases, was the barracks for the sick prisoners (*Revier*). It was built in 1939. (Memorial Museum Ravensbrück and Brandenburg Memorials Foundation)

way we illegally made contact with some fellow prisoners, who were "aired" there, with two SS "Totenkopfregiment" officers who had been arrested for black market trading. They told us that we should be happy not to be in the camp, because out there were the most horrifying and appalling conditions. There were also transports leaving from the camp, to where, nobody knew. One of them told us that she had been told that she was to be sent to the concentration camp Dachau. The other one had a stomach decease and looked like a living corpse.

Once we managed to look out of the window onto a narrow courtyard as some Germans passed by. They pointed to the chimney of the crematorium and held their noses.

One Sunday there was roll-call. All prisoners, the sick as well as the healthy, had to go to the square. We in the prison had nothing to do with this, but we tried to see some of it by standing on the high end of the bed and staring through the cell window that was ajar. What we saw was deeply shocking. Thousands of women and young girls had to stand up and stand for hours in the gray rain. We saw them all go by, young and old. Last came the sick, supported and dragged along by others, and if they could no longer stand, they sat or lay on the ground, but they had to participate at the roll call.

What was said or rather roared, we could not hear, as there was a building that blocked the view. We only saw women pass by, and then the rows at the end with the sick who stood, sat or lay outside in rain for hours.

She continues to talk about me:

> He was shivering with fever. I did not know what to do. But those who came with the food or bread were not the Germans, they were bible researchers [Jehovah's Witnesses]. I asked one of them to get hold of a doctor. It took a while, but then a female German prison guard came. She took him away from me. I remember I was standing on the landing when they walked away with him, down the prison corridor. I thought, God knows where they will take him, and I wondered what would happen. I was not allowed to go with them. Time passed and I did not hear or see anything about what had happened to him, until about 10 January.

> Then we, the Jews from Denmark, were again told to pack our things. It was at night. We packed and came down another prison corridor and were standing there in a row. Then they took me out of the row. I thought that there must be a reason why I was being held back. The only reason must be, that he was still alive, and perhaps I would somehow get him back.

> I said goodbye to the others. One of the others said to me "I am happy that you're staying here, it is closer to Denmark". But honestly, I did not feel happy. I did not know, and neither did the others where they would end up. That was the question, but we had no choice.

It was 10 January 1944. Corrie Meyer and her two sons Peter and Olaf, Karen Hoffgaard and her two daughters Kate and Lillian, Klara Feldmann Annie Smaalann were told to pack. After two days of waiting, they left Ravensbrück and arrived at Theresienstadt on 13 January.

> They left, and I came back to the empty cell and sat there all alone. I thought, Only God knows what would happen now. As time passed I expected all sorts of things. But when that day had passed, I was taken down into one of the cells in the basement level with a small window high up, and with a kind of wire mesh in the glass.

A picture of me from 1943 that my mother had brought with her to Ravensbrück. Of the cardboard at the back of the photo she made playing cards so she could play solitaire. (Private photo)

It was a solitary cell, and there was a hatch. Bread was put through this hatch, otherwise I was not in contact with anyone. After a while I lost sense of time. How long had passed, I could not really tell anymore. I was despairing. First of all, I kept thinking about how stupid I had been not to lie in Dagmarhus. Had I done so I might have been let off. Honesty lasts longest, as the expression says. I kept thinking that I might have done something differently. Lied. Both at that time and in all years after the war I blamed myself that I did not lie when I was interrogated at Dagmarhus.

But now I was in the mess and I had to try to keep myself up, one way or another, not to lose my mind. During the nights I tried to repeat to myself things I had read and tried to let time pass without having too many black thoughts. I also tried to exercise a bit.

Why I had taken a photo of my boy with me, I do not know. After all he was with me. There was cardboard on the back of the photo. Then I thought about dividing the cardboard into 52 pieces. I managed to get a pair of scissors and something to write with. I made 52 playing cards out of it and could play solitaire, but they quickly became faded and worn out, and I also soon got tired of it.

The time completely alone in the cell felt very, very long. One night I heard them coming down the corridor. Stomping boots. A door was opened. The cell doors always rattled. I heard an adult man crying,

A sickroom in the *Revier*. This photo is - like the photos of the barracks and Cell corridor - from an album from 1940-41, which would prove that everything looked orderly and efficient. As it appears from my mother's description, there were croweded bunks with sick prisoners in the rooms when we were hospitalized in the *Revier* (Memorial Museum Ravensbrück and Brandenburg Memorials Foundation)

completely in despair, but then it stopped. Whether they covered his mouth, I do not know. I could hear them drag him off, probably for interrogation.

Another night I heard somebody, it may have been a Russian prisoner, who started singing "Black Eyes Have You, Sonja, Sonja". I think that is the name of the song. She had a very, very beautiful voice. There was absolute silence in the prison.

Another time all the lights went out. I became desperate and panicked and shouted "Licht, licht". It was a bit comical that somebody rushed to me and asked "Was wollen Sie, Tee? (what do you want, tea?)".

I asked the prisoner, who came with the bread, if she could get me some knitting needles. She promised to forward the request. And she actually came back with a pair of knitting needles. Then I unravelled my boy's clothes. I unravelled his knitted sweaters and I knitted them again.

Time passed, I did not have any clue about it. Then they came back with him. The boy. I felt great joy with the reunion. He had become a little weakling. He was thin, malnourished, he had big marks, blotches and sores all over the body from malnutrition. Not because I think they had done him any harm, but he was malnourished and could only speak German. He spoke a bit of Danish when we left Denmark, but now he could speak only German.

I tried the best I could, to speak in German. Then we gradually turned into Danish. I tried to entertain him a bit, playing some singing games with him.

Shortly afterwards they came and took him away again. The purpose was to treat him. But he did not know why they took him away and I remember that he cried out when they took him away. I could have asked if I could join, but I didn't, and I would probably not have been allowed anyway.

They came back with him again after treating him. His back had been washed so that one could see the small light down on his back which caused the nurse Schwester Emmy to say: „Wir haben ja einem Mann bei uns" (We have a man with us).

My mother continues her story.

Then I suddenly began to get ill myself. I got a high fever and had a big abscess in my throat. I could not breath. High up near the ceiling there was a window with steel wire in it, so it was not very transparent, but it could be opened a bit. I tried to climb up to get some air. I was nearly suffocating because of the abscess. I could not take care of the boy as I was lying down, almost unconscious.

Every time the Jehovah's Witness, or whatever she was, came with the bread, I told her that I was ill and needed a doctor. She said she would try to get one, but at the same time she was happy that I gave her my bread. I simply could not eat it because of the abscess, and the boy couldn't either. It was like pure sawdust. But she was happy for the bread.

It took a very long time before a doctor came. It's not because I mistrust her for not forwarding the message, but it benefitted her every day that I did not take the bread. Finally, a German doctor arrived. When he saw me he said I needed to be taken away, but I was allowed to take the boy with me. We crossed a large courtyard which was wet from the rain. There were a lot of barracks around. At that time it was very quiet.

We came to the *Revier*, the German word for the infirmary, which was the medical ward in Ravensbrück.

The *Revier* was divided into several rooms. In each room there were 6 bunks, 2 in each bunk. Fortunately, or unfortunately, I have to say, I had my boy with me, so I was allowed to lie with him. There were all kinds of diseases: tuberculosis, diphtheria, typhus, everything. Seriously ill people were hanging over the edge of the bunks to see who was coming.

My boy had been there. He had been there when he was taken away. They knew him and had obviously taken care of him. They asked each other "Where is the mother?" They did not know that I was in the prison. Now we were together.

When I wrote a feature article in Politiken[1] about our time in Ravensbrück (*Two-year-old was sent to Ravensbrück*), I was called by an unknown woman, Emma Florentine Kristensen, who told me that she had seen me in Ravensbrück in 1943 and that she remembered me. Both she, who was then19, and some other young Danish girls, became very concerned by the news that a Danish child had come to the camp. She told me that she saw me through the window in the *Revier*. In the years after the war, she often thought of me when she saw a 2 year-old child, assuming I was dead. She was greatly surprised when she suddenly saw a photo of me as "an elderly gray-haired man".

We agreed that I would visit her, but unfortunately it did not happen right away, most likely because I did not want to be too realistically confronted with the past and then the note with her name and telephone number was lost. I only found it in 2012 in connection with a relocation, and by then Emma had unfortunately passed away.

On the internet there was information about an upcoming book about Emma called *Emma's War*. The information was that Emma kept her experiences to herself for more than 60 years, until 2006, when she mentioned it to her hairdresser. That was the start of a long and warm friendship between the two women, and over the next few years Emma's story came to life in conversations, on recordings and in writing. It is called a profound personal account of surviving a madness and cruelty that exceeds the imagination, but also the moving relationships with fellow prisoners, as well as glimpses of compassion by the German prison guards, who had

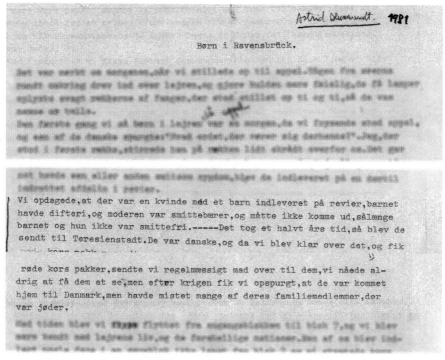

One of the women from Odense, who came to Ravensbrück with us, Astrid Blumensaadt, gave the Royal Library notes about her stay in Ravensbrück. In one of the notes "Children in Ravensbrück" she said that they sent food to my mother and me in the *Revier*, but they never saw us. (The Royal Library)

become part of the Nazi barbarity. I don't know if Emma mentioned me in her reports.

The women who came from Odense were taken straight into the camp to work. They got their Red Cross packages immediately after their arrival, and it was a huge help.

They had heard that there was a sick Dane in the *Revier*, so they put something together from each of their Red Cross packages. A few pieces of sugar, a slice of sausage, a bouillon cube. There was a bit of everything in those packages. One of them brought it to us.

One of the Danish prisoners, Astrid Blumensaadt, gave the Royal Library some notes about her stay in Ravensbrück. In one of the notes *Children in Ravensbrück*, she writes:

> We realized that there was a woman with a child in the *Revier*. The child had diphtheria, and the mother was infected and was not allowed to get out until the child and her were non-infectious. It lasted about half a year and then they were sent to Theresienstadt. They were Danish and when we realized that and got Red Cross packages, we regularly sent food to them. We never managed to see them, but after the war we were told that they had returned to Denmark.

Astrid Blumensaadt concluded by writing that we had lost many of our family members, who were Jews. That is not correct, unless she was referring to a couple of our very distant Norwegian relatives who perished in Auschwitz.

My mother continues:

> I was happy because there was a slice of sausage, which I wanted my boy to eat. And believe me, he would not eat that slice of sausage. He only wanted the white dots inside the sausage. I tried to explain to him that if he ate the whole slice he would also get the white dots. But there was nothing to do. He did not want it.

> We were by and large treated well by the prisoners, who took care of us. A German officer came to us occasionally. At one point he quickly put a bag of sweets under the "blanket" for me. Schwester Emmy, another prisoner, was also very kind to me. She tried to get some mashed potato in me by making a small drawing with a fork to make it look a bit appetizing.

But undeniably, our situation was not good. She continues:

> I was very, very ill. Unfortunately, I infected him so he got ill again.
> There we were, down-at-heel. Nobody could help us or take care of
> us. It was other prisoners who took care of us. Then there was another
> prisoner who was Russian. She was obviously more realistic than I
> was. She said to me "Leave him. Give up and try to save yourself. You
> are young, you can come home, you can have another child. You
> cannot do anything for him. Let him go".

It was a less brutal way of expressing that she should let me die. And my
mother continues:

> It was hard advice to get. Of course, I could not comply with it. But
> there was not anything I could do.
>
> Some of the prisoners were doctors. One day they came and took
> him away. They could see that it was impossible to have us together. I
> could not do anything for him. They could just as well take him. At
> that point I was so ill that I did not care at all and was relieved that
> now I only had myself to care about.
>
> All the people around me were also ill. I remember that the toilets
> were far down the corridor and it was long, dark and and cold.
> Everybody was ill and had dysentery or simply diarrhea. Before
> managing to reach the toilets they would have "accidents". It was a
> terrible mess. We lived in these conditions every day.
>
> One night I was told to get out of bed and leave. Where to, I did
> not know. I was again taken across the courtyard. I had the
> opportunity to see what was happening on the square one morning.
> It happened every morning at a time about 4 to 5 a.m. All the prisoners
> were out there in the yard in rows. There were thousands.
>
> They had to be counted. It was cold and it was dark. They were
> counted and if the number was not correct then they were counted
> again. They were cold and some fainted both of hunger and of cold.
> But fortunately I was spared that because I was in the prison, or in the
> *Revier*.
>
> The night I was told to pack I was returned to the prison. My nose
> was bleeding constantly. And who was in the prison corridor on a
> bench? It was my boy. We were once again re-united, and there was
> again cause to rejoice. It was hard to keep back my tears but I did not
> want to show him how sad I was.

Our visit to Ravensbrück in April 1995 was undeniably somewhat unreal. The sun was shining, the trees were leafing out, and everything was nice and proper. Our cell, which we saw again, was newly painted, and the toilet and washbasin in the cell looked new. It gave a totally bizarre and inaccurate impression of what had been our reality.

I have tried to see if I could get some additional information about our experience in Ravensbrück. The lists of those who were detained in the camp were only fragmentary and in April 1945, the SS destroyed virtually all the data, so inmates testimony is all that's left.

On 24 April 1944, while we were still in Ravensbrück, the ministry of Foreign Affairs tried to get us released. A note was handed to Dr. Mildner on 13 December 1943, and the next day Mildner announced that our case had been carefully investigated, but that unfortunately there was not much prospect of a favorable outcome. He promised, however, that a new review of each case might be made.

My grandmother went to the Ministry of Foreign Affairs again on 27 January 1944. She said that she – after the five incorrectly deported[2] had returned from Theresienstadt - had been to Dagmarhus again and talked with (probably) Paul Hennig about getting us released. Considering Hennig's behavior previously, it is remarkable that my grandmother said that Hennig said it would be important that my mother had been married before the German Nuremberg Law came into force. I wonder if he meant it or if my grandmother remembered wrongly that the Nuremberg laws had already come into force in 1935, several years before my parents got married.

He advised her not to simply put a 10-øre stamp on a letter to the Ministry of Foreign Affairs, but to demand to speak to the relevant head of division in person and demand that the case was presented to Dr. Best, "because she could not expect that the ministry would make the same effort for an ordinary wife of a tailor, as was made for the wife of Commander Schultz".[3]

The Ministry of Foreign Affairs wrote that they told my grandmother that they were making the greatest efforts for all incorrectly deported people without distinction amongst them; they had repeatedly presented the case to the German authorities and that my grandmother, who they described as a sensible woman, had understood it.

At the same time that we were almost dying in the *Revier*, the Ministry of Foreign Affairs was continuing the process of trying to get us released. On 4 February 1944, the lawyer Per Holm applied for divorce on behalf of my mother. It must be a misrepresentation of facts that it was on my mother's behalf. In the *Revier* we did not have any contact with the outside world, but this is all irrelevant.

It might suggest that it was Per Holm's idea to move that way. Apparently, based on my grandmother's conversations in Dagmarhus, she had gotten the idea that a divorce could be of importance, and that my mother and I could probably come home if there was a divorce, whereas a judicial separation would not be enough.

The Ministry of Foreign Affairs also noted that on 13 December 1943, they didn't mention that my parents had been separated since January 1943. Even if they realized that the prospect of getting only my mother and me back was poor, they still wanted to try and promote the case via the Legation in Berlin, by emphasizing that the separation had been granted almost one year before the deportation.

In the archives of the Ministry of Foreign Affairs there is a little detached copy of a message from Brandt Rehberg, from the beginning of April 1944, that neither my father nor my mother were in Theresienstadt. They noted that they didn't know where my father was and that it was said that my mother and I were in the same camp as the women Hoffgaard and Meyer, and that my mother could not leave because of my illness.

It has not been possible for me to find out how this suddenly appeared, but the note is probably the basis for a letter to the Legation in Berlin from 9 June 1944, which states the same things and also asks if it is possible to provide any information about our whereabouts. By that date all three of us were in Theresienstadt.

Poul Brandt Rehberg was a physiologist, and was involved in the organisation of the escape routes to Sweden in 1943 and later in relief work for the prisoners in Theresienstadt.

He was arrested by Gestapo in early 1945 and was placed on the top floor of Shell House and during the interrogations was tortured. He managed to escape when the Royal Air Force bombed the Shell House on 21 March 1945.

Prior to the letter to the Legation in Berlin on 9 June, the Ministry of Foreign Affairs, on 8 May, requested a response about what happened in the case to get us released.

There has been a lot of discussion about the Danish authorities' lack of effort in the late thirties and during the war, for not having saved Jews who might otherwise face certain death. But when it comes to us, the Ministry of Foreign Affairs really made an effort. In a situation of world war, total chaos in Europe and German occupation, I am impressed by the Ministry of Foreign Affairs' persistence in helping us.

Notes

1   A Danish daily newspaper.
2   The story about the five misdeported and the Schultz' sisters is in the section *My Father's Ten Days in Berlin.*
3   The story about the wife of Commander Schultz is in the section *My Father's Ten Days in Berlin.*

6

Sachsenhausen

In the late summer of 1936, the first prisoners arrived at Sachsen-Mühlen from Moorlaer Esterwegen, to clear the area where the camp was to be. By the end of 1937 51 barracks were completed. There were approximately 40,000 prisoners at any time in the camp and about 100,000 people were killed there.

Sachsenhausen was shaped like an isosceles triangle. There was a two meter high stone block wall around the camp and there were watchtowers and a gatehouse with the inscription *Schutzhaftlager* (detention camp) and a metal gate with the encouraging words *Arbeit macht frei*.

Near the roll-call square was the section where members of the "punished company", the so-called *Schuhläufer*-command, tested German military boots. The prisoners testing the boots had to march daily through sand, wet clay, broken stones, cement, water, pebbles and asphalt. A tour around the roll-call square was about one mile, and the "shoe-runners" had to march round at least 41 times – the same distance as a marathon – without much food and carrying a knapsack that contained 15 kilos of sand.

The SS demanded that during this terrible march the prisoners should be singing. From early morning to late at night songs were heard.

Camp commander Hermann Baranowski roared: "Hier hat niemand zu lachen! Der einzige, der hier lacht, is der Teufel, und der Teufel bin ich." (Here nobody is laughing! The only one who laughs here is the Devil and the Devil is me).

Franz Ballhorn, a former prisoner wrote: "Wir weinen nicht, wir trauern nicht. ... Werden wir je wieder normale Menschen werden?" (We do not cry, we do not curse, we do not mourn. Will we ever again become normal people?).

Sachsenhausen also housed the main administration for all of the concentration camps, and it was the training location for commanders, camp leaders and other KZ staff for all camps. Infamous hangmen such as Ravensbrück's Fritz Suhren and Buchenwald's Karl Otto Koch, whose wife Ilse made lampshades of the murdered prisoner's tattoos, were all trained in Sachsenhausen.

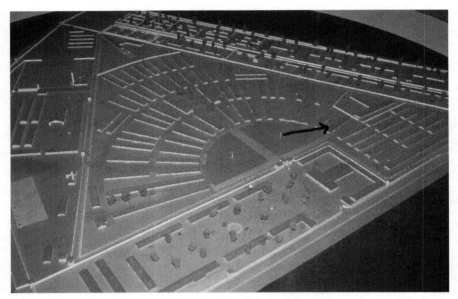

Model of the concentration camp, which is exhibited in Sachsenhausen. The half-circle is the roll-call square where the prisoners would stand for hours and hours every morning and evening. Around the half-circle there were barracks. The bottom right of the model is the Jewish barrack buildings no. 38 and 39. Barrack building 14, where my father came in, was in the first row in the front. It is marked with an arrow.

Sachsenhausen was liberated by the Soviet army on 22 April 1945. Immediately before the liberation, the commander ordered 40,000 ill and hungry prisoners on a march to the north-west. Those who could not go on were either shot or left dying.

The leader of Sachsenhausen while my father was there was Anton Kaindl. He was caught by the Red Army and was sentenced, along with 10 other SS officers, by a Soviet military court. He was sent to the Vorkuta Gulag, a Soviet prison camp in Siberia, where he died in the spring of 1948.

My Father's Six Weeks in Sachsenhausen

We now return to the night of 24 November 1943, where the train from Elsinore via Gedser and Warnemünde was stopped near Berlin because of the alleged bombardment of the track. The women went to Ravensbrück and the men to the concentration camp Sachsenhausen, which is also near Berlin.

The six men from Horserød camp were my father, Sven Meyer, Sven Hoffgaard, Salomon Feldmann, Michael Singerowitz and Carl Suskowitz. In addition, there were about 20 men from Odense who were put on the train in Copenhagen, including the before-mentioned Poul Nielsen. There were already a number of Norwegians in the camp who had been there for a long time.

My father never said much about his imprisonment in Sachsenhausen. On the basis of the relationship between my father and Sven Meyer, this chapter is a mixture of his memories as they are told in the book written by Corrie and Sven Meyer and my father's own account of what happened.

"Max suddenly came wandering in. Despite his illness, he did not want to stay back when we had to leave. I was very happy to see him as he was the only one I really liked." Sven Meyer said that about my father when they were about to leave Sachsenhausen, six weeks later. And my father said, "I slept in the bunk bed with Sven Meyer. We were like two lovers, keeping each other warm."

They arrived at the camp wet and exhausted, after having walked for some time. They were registered and had to hand over all their valuables. Everything was documented in a directory: name, age, nationality and crime. For the Jews, "Jude" was written.

The barracks for Jews had the numbers 38 and 39. After October 1942 all the Jews were deported to Auschwitz and block 38 and 39 were no longer specially designated for Jews. The barracks almost burned down in September 1992. Some young right-wingers from Berlin were accused of starting the fire, but they were acquitted due to lack of evidence. (Erich Hartmann, Magnum)

They were then taken to baths where they undressed, were examined for lice and shaved until bald. All their clothes were put in a large paper bag. Then they were sent to the shower. My father says that he had heard something about gas that came out of the shower instead of water, and he kept somewhat in the background until he realized that there was actually water coming out of the taps.

After bathing they were sprayed for lice, which they did not have, but the Germans were afraid of lice. Lice cause itching and if one scratches with unwashed hands and nails it can cause infections. Then they got a pack of clothes and a pair of large, wooden Dutch shoes. The pack contained a coat, a jacket, a pair of trousers and a hat, all striped and very thin. In addition there were two patches, which were supposed to be socks, a pair of underpants and a shirt.

My father said that "we were taken over to reception Block 14 where the new arrivals had to be in a kind of quarantine for a couple of weeks. There was barbed wire around it. I got the prisoner number 73081. The numbers had to be sewn onto sleeves and pants. Barracks 13 and 14 were connected with a small yard between them. Barrack 13 was for prisoners who were punished."

They were also medically examined to find out whether they were capable of working. As soon as that was done, they were brought to the SS leader of the workforce. My father says that "a tall, good-looking SS man came in and asked them what their profession was. Sven Hoffgaard answered stockbroker, Sven Meyer said salesman, and I said shoemaker, although I cannot really make shoes, because I assumed that I would then get to work inside." As noted previously, when we went underground, he emphasized that his profession was to cut the leather for making shoes, not a proper shoemaker. He regarded his profession as a somewhat finer part of the process of making shoes and when he tells the story of how he answered the SS man he tells it with a big smile.

The senior person in the room was Willy, and if one had not heard the Saxon dialect earlier, one could hear it from him. He immediately informed them that all smoking was forbidden as long as they were in quarantine, and he commanded them to hand over everything. If something was kept aside, it was their own responsibility, and if found out they had to face the consequences, which would not be pleasant. My father and Sven Meyer went in and handed over everything they had, and he said that from time to time they could come and have a little smoke.

When the quarantine was over, they came out into the camp and were moved to another barrack where, in my father's opinion, the food was even more meager than in the other barrack.

When a German came into their barrack room, the first one who saw him was to shout "*Aufstehen*" and everyone would stand up. On one day my father did not shout quickly enough, and the German pulled his head forcefully.

As a rule, they had to get up and go out into the yard at 3 a.m. to wash. They brushed their teeth with their fingers. There was nothing to wipe them with. Once a week they were shaved. It was a pure bloodbath. Bad knives, 20 per cent soap, totally unskilled barbers and quarter-minute lather for a seven day-old beard.

It happened that in the morning, instead of coffee, they got a served a hot flour soup or the like, whatever they called it. The dinner consisted of four or five potatoes and half a liter of cabbage soup.

After breakfast the 40,000 prisoners were placed in the courtyard for roll-call. The Elders of the barracks and of the rooms were responsible for the census.

My dad says that "at 6 to 6.30 a.m., when the prisoners had eaten, some of the prisoners met on the square with backpacks filled with 20 kilograms of sand. They were made to march around and sing. In several places some big waterholes were made. Suddenly they were ordered "get down" and crawl through the waterhole. When it was 11:30 to 12 o'clock, they came in for lunch. Afterwards they had to go back until 5 p.m."

My father also drove stones to the crematories. They were driven on a four wheel trolley, pulled by a leader and eight men. When they had been in the camp for a few weeks, they were allowed to write home. It was, strangely enough, possible to ask for food packs and money.

On the other side of some barbed wire in the camp there were some children. My father was told that the Germans were testing something on them. It was a test of innoculating against contagious diseases.

A few days before Christmas Eve, a Christmas tree was raised where the camp's gallows used to stand. On Christmas Eve itself there wasn't much food, as usual. My dad had ten cigarettes, of which he paid five to another prisoner (an Elder in the room) who supervised the iron door that kept them in. He then got the opportunity to go over to the Norwegian prisoners, who had a lot of food because they got Red Cross packages.

Among the Norwegian prisoners, there were prominent civilians who got particularly lenient treatment. Every month they received a 5 kilogram package from the Norwegian Red Cross.

Later in the evening, he had to pay the last five cigarettes to be let out again.

Both the later Norwegian Prime-Minister Bratteli and the author Øverland were among the prisoners. Speeches were made as well as singing and it was, circumstances being as they were, a good Christmas Eve.

There were some bright spots as well. "Sometimes on Sundays, football was played at the roll-call square. You could go and look at it. That was the only pleasure we had", he says.

I have tried researching the Sachsenhausen archives to see if I could retrieve information about him. I was told that most of the material from the administration of the camp was destroyed by the SS before the evacuation, including almost all the prisoners' personal records and their photographs. The limited material that exists is in Russian archives.

They could, however, confirm both the time of arrival of my father, when he got into the *Revier*, and his prisoner number. He arrived on 27 November and he got into the *Revier* on 27 December 1943.

When there was a roll-call the prisoners in each barrack would stand up. Five in a row, and the rows had to be dead straight.

My father goes on: "One day the senior prisoner of my barracks slammed me very hard on the jaw. 'You're not standing straight', he said. He was a Bible researcher[1], a big powerful man who asked every morning if somebody needed to go to the *Revier*. When he had selected ten, the rest were pushed away."

He then went to the *Revier* with those ten and stayed there until they had been examined. Those who were not hospitalized were brought back.

"The morning I got sick, I felt really bad because of the punch in my jaw and also had a high fever. That day about thirty men signed up. But the barracks Elder did not want to take me to the *Revier*. Then a Norwegian who I knew quite well came by. He said 'What's the matter with you, Max? You have to go to the *Revier*. There are some Norwegian doctors I know'. They took my temperature and said they wanted to keep me."

The *Revier* was also fenced in with barbed wire.

The punch caused inflammation in my father's jaw, for which he would later be operated on in Theresienstadt.

My father was placed in a bunk bed with a German who died during the night. Then he was next to a Frenchman who was so sick that stool ran out of him. He also died.

My father heard that there were Norwegians in the *Revier* and got a Norwegian doctor to get him into their room. His condition was somewhat unstable, but he got enough to eat as they shared food with him. Sven Meyer visited my father and he offered him some of the delicious things he had got from the Norwegians.

The "nurse", who was a German prisoner, was angry with my father because he could not get him food from the Red Cross packages, but my father did not get packages himself. He only had what he got from the Norwegian's packages. The German accused him of raising the thermometer's temperature by rubbing on it, and punished him by sending him outside, almost without clothes, to polish windows.

He says that "one day, probably while I was at the hospital, they asked Sven Meyer about what size shoes he used. He said 43, and then they gave him a pair of military boots with which he was supposed to walk around the square. The boots were not tight, but he had to walk through an area with broken stones while singing all the time. He managed somehow to avoid going back the next day."

Sven Hoffgaard had his own story in Sachsenhausen. He was a stockbroker and was given prisoner number 73099. He was in barracks 19, which was surrounded by barbed wire and completely isolated from the rest of the camp. There were also armed guards. No one was allowed to know what happened in that barrack. When prisoners from this barrack had to go out into the camp, they were always escorted by guards so that no one could communicate with them. Sven Hoffgaard worked in the special counterfeiter command "Operation Bernhard".

My father tells that one day "Sven Hoffgaard was walking through the square with two SS guards, one on each side, but I could not talk with him because he wasn't permitted to talk to anybody."

They were subject to the death penalty for talking about what they were doing. In an issue of a police magazine, Sven Hoffgaard recounts after the war that a couple of SS guards who had apparently said too much were shot, and prisoners who became seriously ill were injected with poison.

The idea of the project was to pump vast amounts of counterfeit notes into the black stock market in neutral countries. They could hurt England's economy by hitting the enemy from within. The Germans also intended to throw significant amounts of counterfeit banknotes over England from airplanes, creating financial chaos.

Sven Hoffgaard stayed in Sachsenhausen until 1 March 1945. Along with the other prisoners in barrack 19, he was sent off because the fronts were moving closer and closer, and Berlin was bombed night after night. They were supposed to have gone to Mauthausen, but as there was not sufficient electrical power there everything was taken to Rdel Zipf, a small camp with three barracks. Everything, including machines, paper, banknotes and prisoners were transported in 14 railway wagons. When the American troops approached the camp, Berlin ordered the destruction of everything: machines, paper and banknotes. However, the burning of the paper and the banknotes was not fast enough, because it was difficult to get the tightly compressed paper to burn, and some boxes were thrown into a lake. The Germans also wanted to bury a portion of the notes for eventual future use. The prisoners were ordered to Mauthausen, where there were gas chambers.

The diary of Sven Hoffgaard. He stayed in Sachsenhausen until the 1 March 1945, after which he was sent to other camps. He was with a group of other prisoners isolated in barrack 19 of the camp. They worked on producing counterfeit banknotes that could damage the economy of England. While he was there he kept a well documented diary. (The Museum of Danish Resistance)

The American troops liberated Mauthausen on 5 May 1945, before the Germans managed to kill their prisoners.

During his stay in Sachsenhausen, Sven Hoffgaard kept a number of diaries, which are now kept in the Museum of Danish Resistance. I tried to find some more personal comments in the diaries, about how he experienced camp life, and possibly if he had mentioned anything about my father. But the diaries are only about purely factual information, like the content of packages he received and when he had his hair cut, etc. The explanation for that may well be both the awareness of what could happen if the notes were discovered by the Nazis, and that these facts were important simply for surviving everyday life.

Michael Singerowitz was mentally ill and things went wrong on one of the first roll-calls. He was extremely confused and one of the SS men almost went berserk, hitting and kicking him. At one point the Germans came and took him. My father asked a Norwegian what would happen to him and was

Tag	Lieferer, Auftrags-Nr.	Bel. Rt.	Zu-	Ab-	Re...	Bel. Nr.	Empfänger Auftrags-Nr.	Bel. Nr.	Zu-	Ab-	Bel.
73051	Wrobel Franz					73076	Jensen Jung A.				
52	Stolzenburg Franz					77	Feldmann Salomon	A. 11.1.44			
53	Watter Erich	A. 6.12.43 laft.				78	Hansen Thines				
54	Goc Kasimir					79	Olsen Lars				
55	Slabkowski Iwan	A. 13.1. ...				80	Jensen Tage				
56	Tobias Jan				✓	81	Katznelson Moses	A. 11.1.44			
57	Muck Stefan					82	Hansen Jörgen				
58	Grzcsik Boleslaw					83	Henriksen Jens				
59	Tomaszewski Antoni					84	Meyer Sven	A. 11.1.44			
60	Ziabka Wladyslaw	1.3.44				85	Nielsen Paul H.				
61	Gwozds Czeslaw	A. 13.1.44 Buch				86	Sörensen Willy L.				
62	Skrzypczyk Jan			*		87	Nielsen Niels				
63	Baran Andrzej					88	Sörensen Edmond V.				
64	Pantschenko Fedor					89	Schjönning Vagn, F.				
65	Jaroszewics Josef					90	Suskovitz Carl	A. 11.1.44			
66	Markowskj Nikolai					91	Nielsen Evin				
67	Zinkewitsch Josef					92	Ziehrer Kaj O.				
68	Pawlowski Alexander					93	Nielsen Paul V.				
69	Goletschenko Georgi					94	Hansen Alfred B.				
70	Uschaatow Wasilj					95	Holbaek Arne				
71	Duhin Boris					96	Müller Alf				
72	Worobiow Michael					97	Singerewitz Michael	A. 6.12.43 laft.			
73	Kamtschenkow Wasyli					98	Unnerup Oluf C.				
74	Starenli Wasily					99	Hoffgaard Sven				
75	Sidnikow Nikolai					100	Rasmussen Jörgen				

Prisoner list from Sachsenhausen indicating that my father left the camp on 11 January 1944.

told "either they give him an injection, or they put him in one of the cars that are driving around which have the exhaust pipes leading into the car's cabin". Singerowitz was sent to the KZ camp Majdanek near Lublin in December 1943, where he died shortly after his arrival.

Around 8 January 1944, Sven Meyer, Salomon Feldmann and Carl Suskowitz were gathered. My father and Sven Hoffgaard were not there, as one would expect. Sven Hoffgaard was isolated in a barrack and my father was in the *Revier* with a high fever. The others were very surprised when my father suddenly joined them. He had obviously heard that they were about to leave and did not want to be left behind.

The four were sent away from Sachsenhausen. They got German transport numbers I/106- I/110. It is important to note that they got German transport numbers. The Sachsenhausen archives indicate that on 11 January 1944 my father was transferred to the Gestapo in Potsdam.

My Father's Ten Days in Berlin

Both my father and Sven Meyer recount that they were taken to Berlin to the Jewish retirement home, 1,500 meters from the Kurfürstendamm on Grosse Hamburger Strasse. The retirement home was established in 1829. In 1942 it was taken over by the Gestapo and used as a gathering place for the thousands of Jews from Berlin who were waiting to be deported. The building had just been bombed when they arrived. The third, fourth and fifth floors were gone. Behind the building was a Jewish burial site. All the gravestones there were overturned and smashed to shards. Of all the former occupants of the retirement home there was only one survivor. The survivor returned in 1945 from Theresienstadt.

While my father and Sven were there they were made to clean up after the bombings.

My father, who still had high fever, was placed in an ordinary house with a number of larger and smaller rooms. He had become very thin, so the woman in the kitchen gave him some extra soup. The house was used as a sort of pick-up place for coming deportations. During the war 55,000 people passed through this pick-up site.

These deportations always had two destinations, Poland or Theresienstadt. When the four men arrived in Berlin, the transport to Theresienstadt which they should have been on had just left. They would therefore have to stay in Berlin for a few weeks until the next transport would leave.

In a note dated 19 January 1944, registered in the German Ministry of Foreign Affairs on 26 January, it was stated that Ellinor Schultz, 44,

Ingeborg Schultz, 42, Panchars Braumann, 22, Julius Grothen, 65 and Inge-Liese Jensen, 7, were *Freigelassene Michlinge* [released Michlinge: that word/cathegory is explained in a box in the chapter *Horserød Camp*]. What is below the note is illegible, followed by *Juden Dänemark*. They returned to Denmark from Theresienstadt because they had been wrongly deported.

Panchar Braumann is Poul Bromann, who in the book *Jødeaktionen i Danmark Oktober-43* wrote that on the way back to Denmark, he had to stay in Berlin in the retirement home in Grosse Hamburger Strasse. He met my father there. Poul got permission to write a note that my father could give to his parents upon his arrival in Theresienstadt and he could then extend greetings to his parents and tell them that Poul was on his way back to Denmark. Poul Bromann was released from Theresienstadt because he was married to a non-Jew.

Another of the five is the wife of Commander Schultz. We met her when Paul Hennig told my grandmother that she should not expect the ministry to make the same effort for an ordinary tailor as it had made for the wife of Commander Schultz.

The woman was the widow of naval commander J.H. Schultz, who was not Jewish. She had been arrested in the evening of 1 October 1943 with her two daughters. The daughters denied being Jews when they were on the ship, but their mother said she was Jewish. When the daughters refused to leave their mother, they were also deported to Theresienstadt. The family had important connections in Danish society. One of them addressed a German Major and pointed out that it must have been a mistake that the wife of the commander had been arrested. Paul Hennig maintained, however, that there was no mistake, as he personally had issued all arrest warrants and had personally drawn up the register.

Nevertheless the daughters returned home in January 1944, while the mother remained in Theresienstadt. The daughters, like the other three adults, had to sign a statement before getting permission to return home, saying that they had volunteered joining their mother and that they would not tell anyone about their stay in Theresienstadt.

From Viggo Sjøqvist's Svenningsen biography, it appears that they could not keep quiet about what they knew of life in the ghetto, and that the information leaked to the Swedish press. After that further repatriations were stopped. Hans Kirchhoff, who thoroughly reviewed the case in his book on the Holocaust in Denmark, states that there are many indications that it was Julius Grothen who had not kept silent about Theresienstadt.

My father's stay in Berlin was only temporary, until the next transport to Theresienstadt arrived. Sven Meyer did not join that transport as he had

My father in 1995 in front of the memorial at the former Jewish retirement home in Berlin, in the area where he was cleaning up after the bombings. (Private Photo)

become ill with scarlet fever and had been hospitalized. He arrived in Theresienstadt only on 19 April 1944.

On 20 January at 2 a.m., my father, Salomon Feldmann and Carl Suskowitz were ordered to pack. They were taken to the central station and put on a train. The train didn't move that night. Suddenly it started. At night it stopped and they were taken off.

The three of them got onto a dirty truck and were taken to Theresienstadt, where they arrived on 21 January 1944. While my mother and I got Danish transport numbers upon our arrival at Theresienstadt, the three men kept their German numbers during their stay there. The same applied to Sven Meyer.

Note

1   Normally a notion for Jehovah's Witnesses in the camps.

7

Theresienstadt

Transport of No. 9 and 10/ XXV/4 to Theresienstadt

In Ravensbrück my mother packed her stuff and was taken back to the prison. "I still did not know what was going to happen and where we were going", she explained. "Early the next morning I came out of the prison again."

We were leaving. A long journey was ahead of us. We were given transport numbers 9/XXV/4 for my mother and 10/XXV/4 for me.

XXV was the number used for Denmark, and number 4 signified the fourth transport from Denmark to Theresienstadt. The first two transports which were numbered XXV/1 and 2 took place on 2 October 1943 respectively from Funen/Jutland and Langelinie (a harbor in Copenhagen). All in all there were 281 Jews. The third transport numbered XXV/3 was the group that came from Elsinore (Horserød camp) on 13 October 1943. The fourth was also from Elsinore on 23 November 1943. Even though my mother and I only arrived in Theresienstadt from Ravensbrück in April 1944, our numbers referred to the group that came from Elsinore on 23 November.

Out of the prison, my mother tells that:

> We got our own clothes. My coat was ripped up and I had sewing thread in the shoes instead of shoelaces. We crossed a large wet courtyard. Two soldiers followed us. One pushed me in the back and said "schnell, schnell" (fast, fast). They wanted us to walk faster. However, it was hopeless. Ib was so ill. We came to a train station and got onto a train. It was an ordinary train, not a cattle wagon. It was one of those trains with compartments. We were seated in a compartment.
>
> There was a man who apparently had to accompany us. He did not introduce himself. He did not wear a uniform. We did not exchange many words, but at one point he did ask me if I had been ill. I obviously answered yes to that question. He asked when I got out of bed. I said that it was yesterday. He did not say anything, but it seemed

to me that he was shaking his head. Whether he was a Gestapo man or something like that, I do not know.

When the train stopped at stations, other passengers entered the train, and I would therefore take Ib on my lap. However, our German "guard" said that I did not have to do so, because a ticket was paid for him.

A passenger said "they smell of hospital." Another passenger gave Ib an orange, and then Ib said "Mutti schneiden" (Mom, please cut it).

At one point our "guard" said that "We are now arriving at Berlin, and we have to change train and it has to be fast."

Fast was not exactly the proper word for me. I could hardly walk and neither could the boy. We got off the train. The man walked briskly ahead of us, probably to lead the way as well as to set the pace, which I definitely could not keep up.

At one point my boy stretched his hands up to me and said "Mom help me". But I could not help him. I could not even lift him 2 cm from

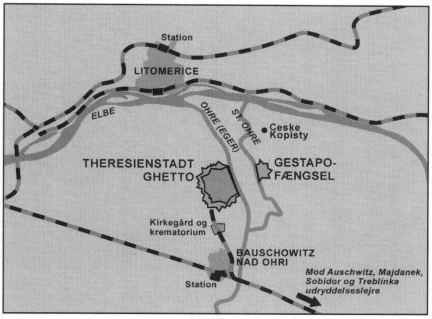

Map of Bauschowitz and Theresienstadt. The small railway station at Bauschowitz is about 3 kilometers from Theresienstadt. It was to that station many of the prisoners arrived before they were taken to Theresienstadt.

the ground. So I had to shake my head. We managed to get on the train in time. Our "guard" also joined us for the next train.

The journey continued. I don't remember for how long and how many hours it lasted. Later during that day we reached the terminus or the station where we got off. It was a small Czech town called Bauschowitz.

We got off, and he followed us into a corner. It was an ordinary city. The houses were neat and the windows looked as though people were living there, but I did not see one human being. It seemed completely empty. The man disappeared without saying a word. He just disappeared. There I was, on this corner with the boy, and had no idea what was going to happen. I must admit that I thought "What are you going to do, how can you get away from here?" It was hopeless. The child was so ill and so was I. There was nothing else to do but to stay and wait for what would happen. I had no idea where I was and I did not have the strength to go very far. I just stood there and waited.

Sign at the railway station in Bauschowitz. The photo was taken on the arrival of Dutch Jews in January 1944. The photo is by Ivan Fric, who was born in Prague in 1922. He was hired by the SS to participate in the filming of the Nazi propaganda film about Theresienstadt. The film crew worked under the strict control of the SS and was forced to sign a contract to the effect that any information about what they saw in Theresienstadt would lead to reprisals against them and their families. (United States Holocaust Memorial Museum)

It was 24 April 1944, a wonderful warm and sunny day. There we were, in Bauschowitz.

Most of the prisoners that came to Theresienstadt at the beginning of the establishment of the camp came via Bauschowitz. They had to walk the last 3 kilometers, from the station in Bauschowitz to Theresienstadt.

In 1942 construction began of railroad tracks that would lead to Theresienstadt at the Hamburger barracks. The tracks were completed in the summer of 1943. The Danish Jews who came to Theresienstadt on 5 October 1943, were taken by the train all the way into the camp.

That was not the way my mother and I traveled the last few kilometers from Bauschowitz to Theresienstadt. My mother said that

> ...a large truck with young people, German soldiers, arrived. They jumped out and signaled that we should get into the flatbed. I do not know what else had been on there. It could have been potatoes. In any case it had been something with soil as there was a layer of mud. The flatbed was high up and it was impossible for me to get up by myself. I was completely helpless and just looked at the soldiers. They continued to signal to me what I had to do. Apparently it was beneath their dignity to touch me.
>
> After a while they realized that there was no other solution. If they wanted to get me up on that truck, they had to help me up. Then one of them grabbed me and threw me up like a sack of potatoes, and then did the same with the boy. There were no side panels, so there was nowhere for us to hold onto. The roads were full of potholes. We drove off, bumping wildly. They were driving crazily fast, I thought. We clung to each other. We jumped further and further towards the edge. I tried to move myself back to the middle of the truck in order to avoid falling over the edge. I managed, using all of my strength.
>
> We arrived at Theresienstadt. I still did not know what Theresienstadt was. It was a small town in Czechoslovakia.

What kind of a place had we arrived at?

Theresienstadt's History

Theresienstadt was founded by Emperor Joseph II in 1780 and named after his mother, Empress Maria Theresa. There were two fortresses on either side of the river Eger (Ohre, in Czech). The city was intended as a military installation, but it became outdated by the end of the nineteenth century, and was abandoned. The smaller of the two fortresses was used for a period of time for dangerous criminals, while the greater fortress fell into decay. A small town with 7,000 inhabitants had grown when, in 1939, the Germans invaded the area. It was a small, under-developed town without modern facilities and with small gray houses, which left a depressing impression.

The Theresienstadt ghetto, which was sometimes also called the *Grosse Festung*, looked, from a bird's eye perspective, like an elongated octagonal star.

Outside the ghetto, on the other side of the river Eger, was the *Kleine Festung* (small fortress) which was the Gestapo's interrogation and intelligence headquarters. In the prison in the *Kleine Festung* prisoners who were considered dangerous to the German empire were detained. Executions also took place there.

In September 1941 Hitler appointed Reinhard Heydrich as protector of Bohemia and Moravia, where Theresienstadt was located.

At the Wannsee Conference in January 1942 Reinhard Heydrich, who was also head of the Reich Security Main Office, explained to the assembled Nazi leaders that Theresienstadt was intended as a privileged camp for Jews. It was his plan that Theresienstadt, among other things, should serve as a camp for the elderly Jews who were deported from Germany and for Jews who had had a prominent career during the First World War, which meant that they had received the Iron Cross of the First Degree. The Christian inhabitants of Theresienstadt were thrown out of their homes to make room for Jews.

An attempt was made on the life of Reinhard Heydrich on 27 May 1942 by a British-trained team of Czech and Slovak soldiers. He died of his injuries a week later. After his death, the development of Theresienstadt continued according to his plans. It was the efficient Adolf Eichmann who now had the overall responsibility for the camp.

Siegfried Seidl, who was appointed SS-Hauptsturmführer in 1942, was mandated to establish Theresienstadt as a ghetto and concentration camp. In July 1943 he was appointed by Adolf Eichmann as commander of the concentration camp Bergen-Belsen. He was succeeded by Anton Burger, who was the head of Theresienstadt until February 1944, when he then was succeeded by Karl Rahm.

After the war, Seidl managed to escape. He was arrested in Austria in 1946 and sentenced to death and was executed on 4 February 1947.

Burger also managed to escape. He lived under a false name in Germany until 1951 when he was arrested and imprisoned in Vienna. A month later he managed to escape again, living on the border between Austria and Germany under eight different assumed names. He died in Essen in 1991 of natural causes. His identity was only revealed in 1994.

Rahm was captured by the Americans in Austria shortly after Theresienstadt was evacuated. He was sentenced to death and executed in Czechoslovakia on 30 April 1947.

In the autumn of 1942, a total of 60,000 Jews were in the camp, which was only intended to have 7,000 inhabitants. One of the few good buildings, a big house in the middle of the camp, was inhabited by SS-men.

As was the case during our visit to Ravensbrück and Sachsenhausen in 1995, it was a beautiful spring day when we visited Theresienstadt. Our impression of the city was completely opposite, just as the visit to the two other concentration camps, compared to the situation in 1944. Two of my children, who accompanied us on the visit to all three camps, said it was shocking and unreal to imagine that there could be up to 50,000 people in that little city, and that it was very difficult to imagine the misery in 1944, as they were seeing flowering trees, green lawns, and not least, the refurbished houses and barracks.

The prisoners' situation was rapidly deteriorating in September 1943, when Eichmann decided to send 5,000 Jews to extermination in Auschwitz. Now it was not only the daily hardships the prisoners suffered, but also the fear of deportation.

Prior to the visit by the Red Cross, which was agreed upon in the discussions between Best and Eichmann at their meeting in Copenhagen in early November 1943, an "embellishment" of Theresienstadt was launched. The new camp commander, SS Sturmbannführer Karl Rahm, was appointed to implement the decision for the "embellishment". No expense was spared. The streets were cleaned and washed. Some houses were demolished and others renovated, washed and painted. Elegant shops were opened with signs "General Store", "Bakery" and even "Cosmetics". Furthermore, goods were brought to the camp to show that the shops were not empty. It was a completely false front. Everything was made only for viewing, to be seen from a distance.

The town square, which had been closed until now, was opened and the area planted. Paths and grass were laid out for promenading. A total of 1,200 bushes were planted. A music pavilion was built with a real stage. A smart café was organized, and the kids got a playground. Not least, the hospital reorganized and everything was renovated.

In the months after the visit of the Red Cross, close to 20,000 Jews were sent directly to Auschwitz to be killed.

On 3 May 1945 Theresienstadt received protection by the International Red Cross. Rahm left Theresienstadt on 5 May, with the last of the SS staff. That day Theresienstadt simply ceased to exist as a ghetto. On 11 May, the city was formally handed over to the Russians. More than 122,000 lives were lost in Theresienstadt.

Theresienstadt's Organization

Theresienstadt was administratively placed under the part of the SS which administered the Prague branch of the Central Office for Jewish Emigration, reflecting Theresienstadt's special status as a transit camp. The leader of Theresienstadt reported directly to the head of this office, Rolf Günther, who in turn reported to Adolf Eichmann in the RSHA.

Theresienstadt had Jewish self management. As early as 4 December 1941 the Germans formed an administrative structure where management of Theresienstadt was carried out by a *Judenälteste* as head of *Ältestenrat*[1].

One should not be misled by the positive term "self-management". The *Judenälteste* and the *Ältestenrat* were actually nothing more than puppets whose task was to execute the orders that came from Theresienstadt's Nazi leadership.

The *Judenälteste* was assisted by two deputy *Judenälteste* and members of the *Ältestenrat*. The number of members of the Council varied somewhat, according to different sources. Most likely there were between 10 and 20 members. The Danish Chief Rabbi M. Friediger was a member of the Council. The Council's main task was organization and administration of the ghetto, with all the issues one can imagine in a camp with about 40,000 prisoners. It was also the Council of Elders that, according to criteria set out by the SS, had the responsibility for picking the thousands who were sent on transports eastward, primarily to Auschwitz-Birkenau.

Every morning the *Ältestenrat* received their orders, when a small delegation from the Council had to report to the SS headquarters. Orders had to be accepted and implemented without any opposition or contradiction.

The Magdeburger barracks was a kind of office building, which was the administration's nerve center. The offices of the *Ältestenrat* were located in that building. The Council members and their families, as well as many of the so-called prominent prisoners, also lived in the barracks. Prominent prisoners were people of high status in society before being deported to Theresienstadt. In 1944 there were 114 prominent prisoners and 85 of their family members.

There were 11 barracks on the outer edge of Theresienstadt, which were used for various purposes. Inside the city, there were blocks of houses with one or two floors. In the center there was a park and a church. Long streets ran through the city from one end to the other. They were called something with "strasse". The transverse streets were called something with "gasse".

On the outer edge of the city, behind the Magdeburg barracks, there was a children's hospital, which was used for some of the patients in isolation.

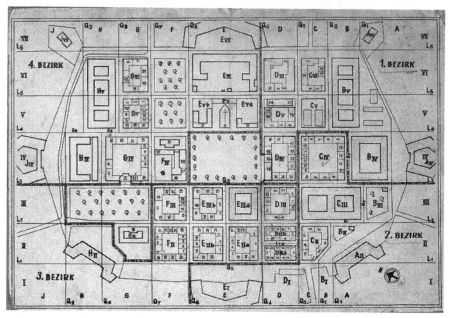

Map of Theresienstadt. In the upper left corner on the map is Dresden barracks, which was used for women and children. If one follows the map clockwise, there is the Kavalier barracks and at the top center of the map the Hohenelber barracks, which was used as a hospital. The Magdeburg barracks is top right. It was used by the Ältestenrat and the prominent prisoners. Then the Hannover barracks on the right side of the map. It was used for men who were fit for work. Then the Hamburger barracks just below the Hannover barracks. It was here that the railroad tracks from Bauschowitz ended. At the bottom right of the map is the Jäger barracks. The Sudeter barracks is at the bottom center. The Genie barracks is slightly above the Sudeter barracks, and the Bauhof barracks is slightly to the left of the Sudeter barracks. Finally the Aussiger barracks is to the left of the map. It was in here that the "Schleuse" was located. (The Danish Jewish Museum/From Ralph Oppenheim's scrapbook)

Just outside the confinement with the 11 barracks there were some barracks surrounded by barbed wire.

It is strange that from Theresienstadt, which wasn't fenced with barbed wire, electric fences or things like that, there were virtually no escape attempts. However, the city was surrounded by walls and ramparts that made surveillance easy. The guard consisted of a small group of Czech gendarmerie, assisted by about 150 Jews in the extremely officious Ghettowache. Only 37 attempted escape, and 12 of them were captured. In Paul Aron Sandfort's autobiographical book *Ben*, he writes that they were told that six young men had tried to escape. They were hanged and left hanging in the gallows for an entire week.

There were three *Judenälteste* in Theresienstadt during the period the city served as a ghetto/concentration camp.

Jakob Edelstein was a Czechoslovakian Zionists. He and his family were deported to Theresienstadt on 4 December 1941 by SS-Sturmbannführer Hans Günther (German major in the Reich Security Main Office). He was "appointed" by Seidl as *Judenälteste*, the first person with that position in Theresienstadt.

In January 1943, Edelstein was removed because he was accused of having tampered with some deportation lists, as the registered number of prisoners in the ghetto was not consistent with the actual number. He remained a deputy in the *Ältestenrat*. On 11 November 1943 he was arrested, and in December was deported to Auschwitz. In June 1944 he was forced to witness the murder of his mother-in-law, his wife and then his 12-year-old son, before he was shot as well.

When Edelstein was removed as *Judenälteste* in January 1943, he was replaced by Paul Eppstein. He was a sociologist who came from Mannheim. He was the one who received the Danish Jews when they arrived in Theresienstadt on 5 October 1943. He also received my mother and me on 25 April 1944. Like Edelstein, Eppstein could not avoid the Nazi's arbitrary sentencing and killing.

In mid 1944, virtually all the big ghettos had been destroyed, and Theresienstadt was the last one which was referred to as a "ghetto". There were rumors among the Germans that an uprising was underway in Theresienstadt. Because of that, 10,000 men who were deemed to be in good enough physical condition to lead an uprising, were sent in transports eastwards. Eppstein was ordered by Scharfürer Rudolf Haindl to deliver about thirty sacks to the Aussiger barracks. Presumably the purpose was that they should be used in connection with the transports.

Eppstein rode a bicycle to fetch the sacks. He was cycling the same way as he had done a number of times. This time however, the Germans used it as an excuse to accuse him of attempting to escape. On 27 September 1944 he is taken to Rahm's office. Rahm's deputy, Ernst Möhs and Benjamin Murmelstein, were also present. The indictment, which Möhs presented, led to Eppstein being shot in *Kleine Festung* immediately afterwards. A month after his wife was sent to Auschwitz.

Paul Eppstein was succeeded by Benjamin Murmelstein as *Judenälteste*. He was born in Lvov, and was a rabbi in Vienna. He was the only one of the three *Judenälteste* who was not murdered by the Nazis. His role and perceptions of his behavior in Theresienstadt is at the very least, controversial.

The French filmmaker Claude Lanzmann, who among other things is known for his Holocaust documentary *Shoah*, interviewed Murmelstein in

From a meeting of Ältestenrat in January 1944. Standing in the middle is the Judenälteste Paul Eppstein, who was shot in September 1944 in Theresienstadt. To the left of him in the picture is Otto Zucker, who was deputy Judenälteste, and on the right side Benjamin Murmelstein, the last of the three Judenälteste and the only one of them who survived. The photograph was, like the previous picture of Bauschowitz station, taken by Ivan Fric as part of the filming of the Nazis' propaganda film about Theresienstadt. (United States Holocaust Memorial Museum)

1975. It is a more than three and a half hour film, which was given the same title as the name Murmelstein used about himself, "The Last of the Unjust", a kind of sarcastic counterpoint to the title of André Schwarz-Bart's book *The Last of the Just*.

The conversation moves from Murmelstein's cooperation with Eichmann, already in 1938, about the logistics of the emigration of thousands of Jews, up to Murmelstein's role, first as number two in the *Ältestenrat*, and afterwards as *Judenälteste*. His rigorous work on both the embellishment of Theresienstadt, and the propaganda film about Theresienstadt for the Nazis, had, in his own words, the aim of showing the world that Theresienstadt existed. According to Murmelstein, it would have been impossible for the Nazis to exterminate the ghetto without it being a major international alarm signal. He also strictly enforced the rule that if anyone, for any reason, asked to be removed from a deportation list, that person had to get a substitute for the list, so that the SS quota was fulfilled.

Due to his many years of cooperation with and therefore close knowledge of Eichmann, Murmelstein offered to testify in the trial in Israel against Eichmann. His offer went unanswered. The Israeli prosecutor, Gideon Hausner, later said that he did not want a witness who had been Eichmann's partner!

Murmelstein's deep knowledge and understanding of Eichmann made him also strongly opposed to Hannah Arendt's description of Eichmann as an example of the "Banality of Evil". Murmelstein simply described Eichmann as a demon.

Gershom Scholem, a Jewish philosopher and historian, wrote in a letter to Hannah Arendt that all the survivors of Theresienstadt, whom he had spoken to, were of the opinion that Murmelstein deserved to be hanged by the Jews. When Murmelstein is confronted by Lanzmann with this statement, and in connection with the fact that Scholem also had spoken against the death sentence of Eichmann, Murmelstein sarcastically replied that Scholem was a great scholar, and he continues asking Lanzmann if he does not agree that Scholem was a little capricious, when it came to hanging.

After Theresienstadt's liberation by the Russians, Murmelstein was arrested by the Czech authorities and imprisoned in Pankratz prison for 18 months. The case against him was dropped, and he lived for the rest of his life in exile in Rome. He never set foot in Israel, probably fearing that he could have been murdered.

Benjamin Murmelstein's son has made a note, in Italy after the war, which in very concise form described his father's problems:

> In 1947, then Chief Rabbi Prato (who remained safe from 1939 to 1945), ignoring the role "not to pass sentence on your fellow man without having been near him" barred Rabbi Benjamin Murmelstein from community membership. Upon his death in 1989, then Rome Chief Rabbi Toaff, who also had denied Murmelstein membership, relying only on hearsay, ordered a "simple burial" with a grave on the cemetery hedge, not in the plot with his wife. He also forbade the "yzkor" prayer (for the dead) for "having him have part in the coming world".

Lanzmann's interview with Murmelstein became more and more fierce as the questions progressed. Lanzmann gets the clear impression that Murmelstein is both sincere and answers the questions truthfully even when very direct and uncomfortable. Lanzmann is in no doubt about his conclusion: the allegations against Murmelstein were unfair.

Our Arrival at SS Headquarters

In most descriptions in the literature about Theresienstadt there is a thorough discussion of the *Schleuse* (Sluice). It was here that the prisoners' first encounter with Theresienstadt took place.

The *Schleuse* was originally located in the Aussiger barracks, but was moved to the Hamburger barracks some time after the railway track from Bauschowitz to Theresienstadt was completed in the summer of 1943. The Aussiger barracks was still in use as *Schleuse* when the Danish Jews arrived at Theresienstadt in October.

In the *Schleuse* the prisoners were registered, searched and had all their luggage examined. It happened under the supervision of Czech gendarmes. The visitation work was done by a female prisoner. The *Schleuse* was a completely integral part of life in Theresienstadt. Everyone who came to the camp came through the *Schleuse* and were stripped of almost everything they had left.

The transport and name card I was given upon arrival at Theresienstadt. Although we were the only Danes who came to Theresienstadt at that time, we are registered as belonging to the fourth transport from Denmark. It was the group that came from Horserød camp on 23 November 1943. (Beit Terezin, Israel)

```
Am 25.4.1944 wurden von der Stapo Neustrehlitz(Mekl) die Jüdin
Rebekke K a t z n e l s o n, geb. 26.11.1917 in Kopenhagen und Toch-
ter, geb. 1941 im Getto Theresienstadt eingeliefert.
Katznelson hat freiwillig dän.Kr. 38,88 und 2 gold.Fingerringe mit
je einem Stein abgeliefert.
Der Betrag und die Ringe wurden an die Verwaltung abgeliefert.
(Vorg.: RSHA B.Nr. IV B 4-a-5446/42 g (1670)

                    Theresienstadt, den 25.April 1944

                          SS-Obersturmführer
Uebernommen:

SS-Hauptscharführer
```

Upon arrival at the Headquarters my mother had to hand over her rings and cash. But with German thoroughness, which is bizarre in a concentration camp where killings happened daily, she got a formal receipt.

Everything in the suitcases and bags were sorted into three piles. The best things were packed separately, after the SS had stolen what they wanted. That was, for example, jewelry, money and cigarettes. Those items were sent to the populations of bombed out cities in Germany. Second and third 'sorting' remained in Theresienstadt for possible local use. The completely useless things like residue of toothpaste, bits of pencils, half-empty matchboxes, flashlights without batteries went into the "shops" in Theresienstadt.

The word *Schleusing* had a special meaning in Theresienstadt. It meant "getting hold of" something, which in the optics of the prisoners was different from stealing. *Schleusing* was used only in connection with something taken from the prison guards.

My mother tells that we came to the Headquarters when we arrived in Theresienstadt, and not to the *Schleuse*. It was probably because we were the only ones who came at that time. She says:

> We came to one of the offices of the Headquarters. I was exhausted, tired and I started to cry. One of the Germans said that there was no reason to cry. After a while a man arrived, a nice gentleman. It was Eppstein, the former professor, now a prisoner in Theresienstadt. He was in command, you might say. He was responsible for the city, what

happened in the city and he was obviously accountable to the Germans for whatever he did. He looked very, very distressed.

He came to me and said that if I had some valuables on me, money or jewelry, I had to hand it over. It happened not only to me, he explained, it happened to everyone who came. Well, I had nothing special, for I had given most of my possessions to the Germans in Horserød camp. As far as I remember I had 38 kr. I gave the money and a gold ring to the Germans and I received a receipt to show that I had handed over the money and the rings, which were then put into a desk drawer.

He said that a young girl who was also from the camp would come and search me. The Germans noticed the clothes I had in the suitcase and said that I had too many things and that there was no reason for that. Nevertheless I was allowed to keep it.

All valuables had to be handed over and what was taken was carefully recorded, which can be seen from the receipt to my mother from the SS-Obersturmführer. After having been through the *Schleuse* the suitcase came back to my mother. When she got it back, the small hand-made blue boots with real leather soles that I had received in a package from my grandmother in Horserød camp, had been stolen. The boots had simply disappeared, just like many other things.

Then the young Jewish woman who had to body search me arrived. She did it very carefully. Far too carefully, I thought. She searched all my stuff and even put a finger into a jar of lotion. She was very persistent. When we had gone through all this and had answered some questions, they sent for someone to pick us up and take us to where we would stay.

My mother then said that

...it was rumored in the camp that we had arrived. My in-laws were in Theresienstadt, having been sent there from Camp Horserød. My husband, who had come from Sachsenhausen, was there too. I also met my father and my little sister. They had been arrested in their apartment in Copenhagen. My mother fled to North Zealand, where she had family members who were fishermen. She wanted to ask them to take them to Sweden. When she got back home, the Germans had been there and had arrested my father and sister. Then I met them all. It was obviously a fantastic reunion.

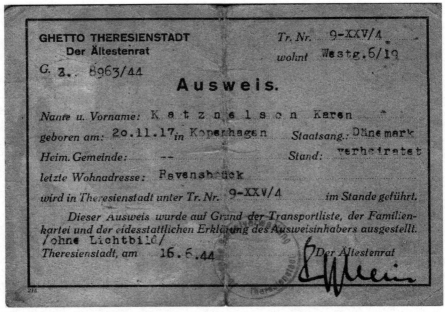

My mother's Ausweis (ID card) which she got a few months after our arrival at Theresienstadt.

I remember that I saw a lady sitting on a windowsill cleaning the windows, just like at home. Despite the condition we were in, it gave it a sense of happiness coming from Ravensbrück to Theresienstadt.

However, Ib and I were so ill that we were taken directly to the hospital, called the Hohenelber barracks. Theresienstadt was a city of barracks. I think there were four or five barracks [in fact there was, as we have seen, eleven]. It must have been a soldier's hospital. It was quite big, cold and not very nice. The prisoners who were there were ill, and the nurses and doctors, highly skilled people, were prisoners as well. It was to that place that Ib and I were taken.

My grandfather, who was at his workplace, was told that we had arrived. He immediately informed my father, who had the day off and was sleeping at his barrack. Obviously he immediately started looking for us. When he saw us, I was bleeding from my nose and mouth, and as a result of diptheria my mother could hardly see, nor could she walk straight or hold onto anything.

Descriptions of our Arrival at Theresienstadt

Even if there is some overlap between my mother's own story about our time in Ravensbrück and others' descriptions of our arrival at Theresienstadt, I feel it important to include them here, just as they are told.

One is Corrie Meyer's. She was with us in Ravensbrück until mid-January 1944. In her and her husband's book about Theresienstadt from 1991, she describes the condition we were in when we arrived. The other one is my aunt Annie, as she told it to my uncle Viggo during their visit to Theresienstadt in 1993. Corrie Meyer says that

> Annie Smaalann and Kate Hoffgaard came one evening and told us that Karen Katznelson and Ib had arrived. We hurried up to meet them, but when we saw her coming, supported by her father and her little sister Annie, we were terribly frightened. Skinny and with her mouth completely misshapen on one side of her face, she told us about the awful time she had had in Ravensbrück, after we had left.
>
> After six weeks in solitary confinement, as Ib remained at the *Revier*, she became ill with scarlet fever, diphtheria, and rheumatic fever, and as she could not tolerate the diphtheria serum, her face was completely distorted. Ib had, in addition to the diphtheria, also had scarlet fever and a severe bronchitis and then tuberculosis.
>
> She had been with Ib in the *Revier* for seven weeks, and the conditions there could hardly have been described in a way which would give a sense of the situation. Although the barracks building in which she stayed was only for infectious diseases (every illness was kept in a room apart from the others) the rooms were not sufficiently isolated. When one of the two thermometers had broken, the one left was used all over the barracks. No wonder that there was an outbreak of diphtheria in the scarlet fever room, and vice versa.
>
> The patients lay two and two in the beds and should, whether they had fever or not, wash themselves and go to the toilets, but the toilets were indescribable. Karen saw a 17 year-old girl's agony in the bed next to her own; she died in the evening, but they let her simply stay in the bed all night and a part of the next day.
>
> As Karen's health condition, like Ib's, was far from good (Ib still had both tuberculosis and diphtheria, and Karen a bad bronchitis), they were both hospitalized. Max was obviously very happy having his wife and child back, and he rushed around all day to bring them all the best he could get for them.

Although Karen suddenly got pneunomia, she got much better rather quickly, due to the good care she received. In late May, both were allowed to leave the hospital. Luckily her face, due to various treatments, was completely back to normal again. It was almost impossible to imagine what she had gone through.

My aunt Annie recounts:

> We were then told that Karen and Ib had arrived. She looked terrible. She had diphtheria and neuritis. Her mouth was completely pulled up on one side of her face. She was half deaf and could hardly see and had no feeling in her fingers or anything.
>
> I remember that she was wearing shoes with some strange laces. They were not shoelaces. Ib had sores all over his face and we could not get close to them to hug them, or anything. I remember that Karen and I were standing and looking at each other. It was as if one saw oneself again. Suddenly one could see that we looked a bit like one another, as strange as it sounds, for I don't feel that we do.
>
> Later I found out that she had had the same feeling. Ib was not able to speak Danish anymore. He could only speak German. Karen was immediately admitted to an epidemic department so that her diphtheria would not spread throughout the camp. She was admitted to the Hohenelber barracks, and her isolation meant one couldn't talk to her, as far as I remember. They must have had some kind of contagious disease. There must have been others too, but I do not know what kind of diseases they had. I don't know if it was tuberculosis. In any case she was in that hospital. We could only get in touch with her by standing in the courtyard and shouting. There was grating on the windows, but the upper windows were open, like a draught window. In the beginning she did not have the strength to answer us, so there was somebody else who shouted back to us for her. Finally she got out of the hospital and was declared free of infection. I don't remember how long she was in the hospital, maybe a month, I don't know. I did not see Ib. He must have been ... I can't say whether he was hospitalized with her or not.

My parents were well aware that my grandfather and aunt had been arrested on the evening of 1 October, however it is clear from my mother's letters from Horserød camp that they were not at all aware of the circumstances of the arrest and what had happened later on. "But I do not understand why

Annie and Dad have not come home", my mother wrote in the letter to my grandmother on 18 October 1943.

Of course my mother was interested in knowing about what had happened, as soon as she had the strength for it. For that story to be told we must now jump back about six months earlier to 1 October 1943, when the Germans started the action against the Danish Jews.

Note

1   *Ältestenrat* was a Council of Elders, the head of which was *Judenälteste* (Jewish Elder). It had nothing to do with age but was the German term for the structure of self-management.

8

Arrested Already: 1 October 1943

Why were they at Home? And why did they Open the Door?

I leave it here to my aunt Annie to tell about the events, as she told them to my uncle Viggo during their visit to Theresienstadt in 1993. She was 15 years old when she was arrested.

> On 1 October at 10 o'clock in the evening, during the curfew, we were listening to the English radio, the BBC. I had just eaten a bite of an apple, when the doorbell rang. Our front door was a door with glass in it. We lived on the ground floor on Cæciliavej (in Copenhagen). My father went out and opened the door. I heard someone say: "in the name of the Law, you are arrested Mr. Kermann".

The doorbell rang, and they opened the door! What would have happened if they had ignored the doorbell and had not opened the door? One possible answer can be seen as yet another example of the lack of enthusiasm by the Nazis in Denmark for a successful action against the Danish Jews. The head of Gestapo in Denmark, Karl Heinz Hoffmann, said after the war that he, at the final meeting before the action started, had argued that doors under no circumstances should be knocked down and that Jewish apartments should not be forcibly entered. Günther was opposed to this position, but Mildner and other senior security officers agreed with Hoffmann, and the result was that Günther, reluctantly, had to accept the order.

This explanation is actually confirmed in telegram no. 1208 from 5 October 1943 from Werner Best to the Foreign Ministry in Berlin. In the telegram he writes that "It is true that the security police's highest commanding officer had ordered that locked doors should not be broken down ..."

Annie goes on to recount:

> My mother had gone somewhere that I had not been told about. I thought to myself "what in heaven's name has he done, because

My aunt Annie. She came with my grandfather on transport no. 2 from Langeliniekajen in Copenhagen on 2 October 1943. (Private photo)

they've arrested him". And then a number of Germans with machine guns and pistols came into our flat. They said we should pack some warm clothes and food for 8 days.

I had no idea that something was going on. Nobody had told me anything.

I wondered where my mother was. She had gone to Nykøbing Zealand, where she had some relatives. I had no idea why she had gone there. It was only later I was told that she had tried to find someone who could take us to Sweden.

So we hurried up packing as much as we could. We took what was in the refrigerator. And my apple, I later was told, was still on the table with one bite taken from it, when my mother came back home. And we were gone.

I remember that I had just had a shower. We had a small stepladder in the bathroom, on which I had put my watch. When I went out to take it, one of the Germans followed me to see what I was doing. I just took my watch, but he stood there looking at me with his machine gun, or whatever it was he had in his hand.

We were then loaded onto a truck that was covered on top. We had to sit down on the floor. There was a bench at the end where the soldiers were sitting. We were driving and driving. The truck stopped, the Germans jumped off and came back. Many times they did not come back with anyone. But sometimes they came back with people they had arrested. Not many. I can't remember who they were. A married couple, I think, and a few others. The German soldiers, who were sitting at the end, said that I could come up and sit with them. I did not understand what they were saying, but my father said I should stay on the floor.

Then they got mad at him. So every time they jumped out, they stepped on his feet with their big boots.

When we finally stopped I thought, God knows where in the world are we? I realized that we were on Toftegårds Square, not far from where we lived. By then we had been driving for many hours and there were motorcycles and trucks on Toftegårds Square. Apparently it was a collection point. From there we continued to Langelinie, when they had finished arresting some more people. There were spotlights on the quay. It was so scary. It was dark and there was a big vessel. Then we were forced on board with our suitcases.

The first thing that happened when you came up the gangway was that you had to sign up at a table. My father had lit his cigar. There was an officer, and he hit my father in his head so that the cigar flew across the deck and he asked my father if he wanted to set the vessel on fire.

They probably had our names and we were forced down into the hold. There were some bunks, and we climbed up to the top bunk. There were bunks on top of each other, two above and two below all along on both sides. There was a narrow aisle in the middle where one could go, if one dared, get down from the bunk. There was a German officer who strutted around. He had a horsewhip. They shouted in the loudspeaker that the Aryan families, families where one part was married to an Aryan, should sign up.

My father tried several times to get down from the bunk. Every time he got hit, so he had to climb up again. He didn't succeed. He never managed to sign up. And then we sailed. I guess it was early morning. It was dark when we boarded, so it must have been at 5 o'clock in the morning or something like that.

And here the story goes back again to my grandmother's contact with Paul Hennig at Dagmarhus. We have already heard a part of the history about it in the chapter on our stay in Horserød camp. However, there are more interesting episodes.

Paul Hennig explained after the war that at 11 p.m. on 1 October, he received a telex message that Jews married to non-Jews should not be deported. He said that he quickly, and from memory, made a list of about fifty Jews whom, according to this provision, should not be deported to Germany. He also made a list for each command district of the Jews who should not be arrested, or if they were arrested, should be released immediately.

At 1 a.m. he drove to the vessel at Langelinie, got a table, and informed the already arrested Jews about the provision in the telex he had received. He urged them to get to him if they determined that the provision applied to them. Those who had documentation were immediately allowed to leave, while others were invited to come the next day to Dagmarhus with their documents.

My grandmother asked my grandfather, after the war, why he did not sign up while on the boat, when those who were married to non-Jews, were invited to sign up. He replied that he had tried to approach a Danish speaking civilian on three occasions. He said that he was in his bunk while he tried to address the person dealing with that issue, whenever he passed by. He happened to have my grandmother's birth certificate with him, but he was brushed aside every time he attempted to do so. He explained that the person was wearing a dark overcoat and a sixpence. Whether it was Hennig or not, he did not know.

Hennig explained that he did not remember speaking with my grandfather on the boat. Those he had spoken to had been called to the table where he was sitting. If one of those arrested had shown a certificate which stated that his wife was baptized, the question would have been examined. He did not remember what clothes he was wearing when on the boat. He did own a dark overcoat, and sometimes also wore a sixpence.

Hennig also explained that he remembered my grandmother, whom he had repeatedly spoken to in Dagmarhus. He could remember that she

My grandmother and grandfather. My grandfather was in transport no. 2 from Langeliniekajen in Copenhagen on 2 October 1943. My grandmother was not arrested. (Private photo)

explained that she was Aryan and married to a Jew, but that she did not live with the man when he was arrested. Had they lived together, the man had probably not been arrested. However, my grandfather explained in his statement that he and my grandmother lived with their daughter [my aunt] on Cæciliavej, and that it was only after the war that they had moved apart.

Hennig did not recall if she had filed any application for the release of my grandfather and aunt. He remembered that in the official register it was certified that my grandmother had converted to Judaism. She had, as he put it, 'been married to my grandfather by the Jewish rabbi, and he knew that for such a thing to happen, one is bound to educate children in the Jewish faith. If this situation had been clear, when the husband was arrested, Mrs Kermann should in fact also have been arrested according to the German regulations.'

My aunt then went on telling about the trip from Langelinie to Theresienstadt.

> We didn't get any food, only what we had taken with us. We were in the bunks. I had no idea how long we were sailing for. But I know that at one point we did not sail. The engines stopped, and then it was completely quiet, and there was a rumor that they would sink the boat with all of us on it.'
>
> But later I was told, I don't know by whom, that it was because they had to pass by a minefield. After a while the engines started again and we continued sailing. I had my period, which was very inconvenient and it was not at the time I should have had it. It was probably provoked out of fear. But I was lucky that on board there was a nurse named Selfa [Selde Diamant], and she had a bag with bandages or something like that. I asked her if she had something I could use, which she did.
>
> There was also a German on board, whom my father came to talk to. He was so gullible, my father. The German said that he was going back to Denmark. I really do not know how he got into a conversation with him. My father had brought all our ration coupons from home with him, for butter, coffee and everything, so my mother did not have anything. Then he asked the German if he could do him a favor and put them in a mailbox in Denmark to this and this address. The man promised to do so.
>
> At one point the German came to me and said that if I needed to go to the toilet, I should just tell him and he would accompany me to the deck. One of the young men overheard it, one of the Jews, whose name was Finn Leimann. He said that I should definitely not go with the German and if I had to go up he would accompany me. I was not really aware of why, but at some point I did need to go. He accompanied me and it appeared that there were German soldiers with German shepherd dogs on the deck. There were open privies

with a long plank, so there were not any places where one could hide. It was just about getting it done in a hurry, and then going back down to the hold again.

Then we docked at the port of Schwinemünde. There was a long line of train wagons for animal transports. We were loaded up into these wagons, which were meant for only 5 or 6 horses. We were about 40-45 people so it was crammed. I do not know how many cattle wagons there were. I have no idea. I was just forced up into one of them. Then the train started. In the wagon there was only a tiny little window through which some air came in. One could not open the door as they were locked. We had to shift between sitting and being near the window to get some air.

During the night there was a lot of shunting. Sometimes the door was opened so we could get out and relieve ourselves. There were no opportunities in the wagon for that. There was nothing.

They put some bread into the wagon. There were also two cans of jam. I don't remember if there was any water. We ate it. Unfortunately there were two brothers who were a bit crazy and one of them urinated in the jam at night, so we couldn't eat it any more. We had to get rid of it in a subtle way, without the Germans realizing.

There was a hole in the bottom of the wagon where one could see the railroad tracks. When the train was going, we stuffed jam into the holes. It disappeared so it looked as if we had eaten it. There was also an old lady, who was lying on a stretcher. I think she'd died but I'm not sure. There was not much room for us.

At one point, I got close to the window and stood and breathed there, and then someone said I should have a raw egg. It would strengthen me. I had never tried to eat a raw egg before. However, down it went. I swallowed the raw egg and then I fainted. It was obviously not something which strengthened me.

We were probably on the way for three days, because we were registered as having arrived on 5 October.

Hohenelber Barracks and a Children's Hospital

After having looked back at the events of 1 October 1943 and the following days with my grandfather's and aunt's transport to Theresienstadt, we return to my mother's and my arrival at Theresienstadt and us being hospitalized at the Hohenelber barracks immediately after our arrival. My mother repeated that she was very weak, that her hair fell out, and that she couldn't feel anything in her fingers.

Hohenelber barracks had served as garrison hospital even before Theresienstadt was transformed into a concentration camp. It was a fairly large hospital with big rooms and high vault ceilings. There was a well-equipped operating theater and five sorts of casualty rooms. In some of the rooms there were 40-50 patients.

Patients received a special diet called "Reko": soup, tea, a bun, which had only half the nutritional content of the usual ration of bread, a potato, which was more than usual, and every other day a bun of flour. However, the portions were, despite being prepared in the hospital kitchen, very small.

My mother and I stayed some time in the hospital in the Hohenelber barracks. "We were in a large hall near the window, and when someone wanted to get in contact with us, they were not allowed to come up because of the risk of infection. They had to stand below and shout. At the hospital there was also a Czech lady. She said that she had been very wealthy, but on the way to Theresienstadt she had thrown all her jewelry out of the window. 'Rather that than giving it to the Germans', she said."

The Hohenelber barracks, 1994. The Hohenelber barracks served as a hospital in Theresienstadt. It was there I was hospitalized much of the time we were in Theresienstadt. (Documentation Department, Terezín Memorial)

Sickroom in Theresienstadt. (Erich Hartmann, Magnum)

There appeared to be a bit of irony from other prisoners, because when they looked at the two year-old 'me', they said that I was a "schwerpolitisch prisoner" (politically difficult).

There was also an old man who came to the hospital every morning to assist. "I could hardly walk", said my mother, "so he helped me carry a basin filled with water. I gave him a bouillon cube. He was deeply grateful and was very interested in the fine aluminum foil wrapping. Less grateful was another fine Czech lady who helped me one day, as the old man had not come. I buttered a piece of bread for her, but evidently she felt it humiliating to accept it and said 'Ein solche geschäft machen wir nicht' (I don't want to engage in such a deal)."

My father added to my mother's explanation about how to get in contact with us by saying that "A woman lived above us. In the morning, before going to work, she came by and asked if she should bring something [for us]. She then gave it to a nurse."

My mother says: "Meanwhile my boy had fallen ill again, even more ill. He had tuberculosis. He was admitted to an orphanage, where you had orphans who also had tuberculosis, and whose parents had disappeared at some point and probably had been sent eastwards."

Meanwhile, when my mother had recovered somewhat, she was sent "home". Various information suggests that it was probably at the end of May

Letter dated 13 January 1944 from my grandfather in Theresienstadt, probably to my grandmother, stating that he does not know what has happened to my parents. He did not mention me!

1944, and "home" had been the West Barracks, where my grandmother lived, and there are indications that my aunt also lived there. These barracks are located to the right and the lower part on the Theresienstadt map, below the Jäger barracks.

While we had come to Theresienstadt and had been hospitalized, it was also clear that we had not arrived in Theresienstadt with all the other Jews from Denmark. A thorough investigation was going on in Copenhagen to find out where we were.

In a memorandum from 9 June 1944 to the Royal Danish Legation in Berlin, the Ministry of Foreign Affairs informed the Danish Legation that my mother and I, according to available information concerning the deportation on 23 November 1943, had probably been interned in the camp Ravensbrück near Fürstenberg, and that they did not have any knowledge as to where my father was. The Foreign Ministry asked the embassy whether it would be possible to obtain information about our whereabouts.

They had totally lost track of us and it is therefore no wonder that we initially did not get Red Cross food parcels as other Danes did, which raised problems for us.

There is yet another example suggesting that they had lost track of us. On 7 June 1944 Professor Richard Ege (Danish biochemist and nutritionist) wrote to the Director of the Red Cross, Helmer Rosting. He asked Rosting for help with some inquiries. One part of his inquiries was regarding my mother and me.

Ege wrote that "Both are assumed deported from Horserød camp in late November, but nothing has been heard from them since. It is certain that she has been in a camp (Fürstenberg) together with Mrs Hoffgaard, Mrs Meyer and Feldman, but when they left, she was apparently kept back because her son was ill. In a card from Theresienstadt on 13 January 1944 Isaac Kermann asks how it goes with Karen and Moses, her husband? Moses is believed to be in Sweden, but Karen Katznelson and her son Ib have been sent from Denmark without anybody having any contact with them." In other words, almost total confusion in Copenhagen regarding our fate.

I have not been able to find out exactly where in Theresienstadt I was at that time. In Theresienstadt there were several places where sick children were "kept". There was a large children's hospital behind the Magdeburger barracks on a corner not far from the moat, at the top right of the map of Theresienstadt. There were six rooms on the ground floor and seven on the first floor. If there was a need for more rooms, some buildings nearby could be used. The hospital could accommodate 106 patients. It has not been easy to find detailed descriptions of the children's hospital. The only thing I have found is in Philipp Manes' book *As If It Were Life*. The description in the

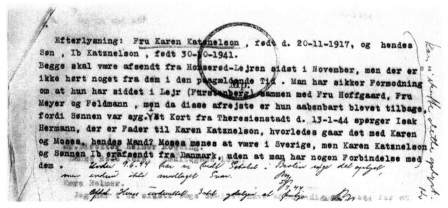

One of the "minor issues" appearing on Richard Ege's list of missing persons is about my mother and me. The authorities in Denmark, as late as June 1944, still did not know where we were.

book of conditions at the children's hospital is almost rosy, but probably has more color compared to other, gloomy descriptions in that book.

I was in a crib and urinated constantly due to problems with the kidneys. My mother did not have the strength to change me, and nobody else did it. My parents could visit me at the hospital. "When we came, he hid under the covers and would not talk to us. When we had to go, he began to cry. I was nagged by guilt over having taken him with us. I should have let him stay in Denmark", she said, and continued:

> My husband went to see him many times. I saw him too, but not so much because I had now been ordered to work in a *putzkolonne*, which meant cleaning. It was in a barracks in a filthy attic. And I was simply so exhausted because I had been so sick that I almost could not manage to go. There was a pump in the courtyard and an old zinc bucket. I had to fill it with water from the pump and carry it right up to the top of the barracks. One brush with the floor cloth and it became mud. And then down again for clean water. I could not, I did not have the strength.
>
> Luckily I got another job later. I was allowed to clean the hospital. It was somewhat easier. It could be done in the evening, which meant that I could be home during the day and visit the boy, who for a long time had been in a children's hospital. One day, when we came to see him, the entire children's hospital was empty. All of the children were gone. The nurses, doctors, who were also prisoners, were gone as well. It happened during the night. The only one who was left was my boy. They had left him alone.

My father added that "We had no idea what had become of them and what had happened."

"It was a complete wonder", continues my mother. "I can only attribute it to the fact that they had so much order in their system: He was Danish. The others had undoubtedly been taken to a transport. They had to reduce the number of prisoners once in a while."

And here it is worth recalling paragraph 3 in Werner Best's telegram to Berlin on 3 November 1943 after the meeting with Eichmann: "All deported Jews from Denmark shall remain in Theresienstadt ... "

The story about me being the only one was often retold. For a particular theme at the Jewish school in Copenhagen, my youngest daughter brought a page I had written about that story and gave it to the teacher.

The next thing that happened was that it showed up in Herbert Pundik's book from 1993, *Det kan ikke ske i Danmark: Jødernes flugt til Sverige i 1943*

(*It Can't Happen in Denmark. The Escape of the Jews to Sweden in 1943*).
Viggo Sjøqvist (former head of the archive at the Foreign Ministry) tells the
story as well, referring to Pundik's book, in his 1995 biography about Nils
Svenningsen. It is also mentioned in Arthur Arnheim's article in *Rambam:
A Journal of Jewish Culture and Research*, in 2003, although it was not
completely accurate. And finally, it appeared in an article by Danny
Rubinstein, based on an interview with Herbert Pundik, in the Israeli daily
newspaper *Haaretz*, from 25 April 2006. I wonder if a single sentence "At the
orphanage there was only one girl, a Danish Jew, left" in Robert
Fischermann's book from 2014 *At Forstå er Ikke at Tilgive: En Dansk KZ-
overlevers livslange rejse* (*To Understand is not to Forgive: A Danish
KZ-Survivor's Lifelong Journey*) is also another version of my story.

Glimpses of my Aunt Annie's Daily Life in the First Seven Months

My aunt Annie's telling of her story reflects the fact that she and my uncle
Viggo were wandering around Theresienstadt in 1993 without any fixed plan.
The memories came back to my aunt in disorder, triggered by associations
and questions from my uncle while they were walking up and down the
streets. It has been a puzzle to thematically structure her experiences from
the tape recording, making the themes consistent, giving a picture of daily
life, as she experienced and remembered it. I have adjusted her explanations
slightly, in order to paint a picture of daily life, and of the accommodations
under different circumstances, of the food, the work and the relationships
with others, of disease and of the "census", a story that has also been told by
others who experienced it.

My grandfather and aunt also came also through the *Schleuse*.

There we had to hand over everything we had, even the clothes. What
we had was examined. Clocks should be in one box and rings in
another box, and earrings and jewels and everything people had
brought with them. I had to hand over the clock I had picked up in
the bathroom, when we were arrested. I never saw it again.

We did not have much clothing. I think my father and I had one
suitcase together. It was not much. And in the suitcase were two
curtains from our living room, because when we were arrested they
said that we should bring a traveling rug with us. We didn't have one,
so my father took the curtains instead.

We were registered and were given "vouchers" for our meals. They
made cuts in the vouchers when one was given food. We also got the

yellow stars marked "Jew" that we always had to wear on our clothes. They had to been sewn onto our clothes, but we cheated a bit and used safety pins instead. That was considered very negatively by the elderly prisoners in the camp. They told us that we should be careful.

I was registered as a child and got a milk voucher after a short while.

Chief Rabbi Friediger and Klara Tixell recounted that they arrived to the Aussiger barracks on 5 October, where they slept the first night, all in one room on straw bags on the floor. The day after they were driven through the city, next to the West Barracks. These barracks were some elongated buildings outside the city. In the middle of a building there was a corridor, and on either side were five to six rooms with three story bunk beds each containing a straw bag. There was also a washroom and a toilet. Each room could accommodate 25-30 people. The men were placed in one side of the barracks, women and children on the other side.

On 12 October, late at night, the Danes were led into the city of Theresienstadt.

I have chosen to retell Annie's story about where they were placed, although it does not seem to be the same as the Chief Rabbi's and Klara Tixell's story about what happened soon after their arrival. Memory may have played a trick on her, or it may be that the unstructured interview, so to speak, scrambled her explanation. It might also be that she was placed differently than some of the others. There was a difference in how the interned were placed, depending on which transport from Denmark they had arrived on. Jytte Bornstein's story about it could also indicate that everyone was not in the same place. Despite the ambiguity, however, Annie's story nevertheless gives an impression both of the conditions there and how she herself remembers how it was.

> I think we were deloused in a disinfection institution, and then we were taken up to the attic of one of the barracks; the women in one barracks and men in another. I think I was brought to the Dresdener barracks. There were no bunks. There was simply nothing. There was just an empty floor in the long hall with a long roof ridge. I think I used one of the curtains from our living room at home that my father had torn down.
>
> As men and women went to different barracks, my father and I were obviously separated. I did not know where he was, and he did not know where I was. There was no one who took care of me. Everyone had more than enough to do in taking care of themselves.

I remember the first night. We lay there on the naked floor in that attic, and it was October. I don't know how I managed, but I ended up falling asleep. I remember I was lying beside Esther Tikotzki, also Danish. She must have been thirty-five years old, I think. It was difficult to judge. When we woke up in the morning, and I got up to fold the curtains, my legs just collapsed from under me, like jelly. So I fell. I had no feeling in my legs, and I don't know why. Perhaps because of standing up for so many days. I was conscious, but I simply just collapsed.

Some time passed and I tried again. This time I could stand. We had to go down and have food. We got black coffee, as far as I remember. A mug with black coffee. We must have been given a mug, a kind of tin cup and a kind of camping pot and cutlery. I don't recall that I had brought it with me. We were queuing for the coffee. We did not get any bread.

We had to climb up the stairs again, probably to the fourth floor of the barracks. Whether it was only the first night we were there, I do not remember. We then came down to another floor, where there were some bunks. There was also a mattress. There were no blankets, but there was a sheet.

I remember that I was again lying beside Esther Tikotzki. The next morning when we woke up, we could not understand why the sheets, which were white when we went to bed, were now completely dotted. We could not understand where it came from. It turned out that they were fleas. But as they had been overfed "by us" they were so drowsy that we could easily catch them. They could hardly move.

We stayed there for a long time because I can remember that as time passed, it became harder and harder to climb up to the third floor. We had no strength due to the hard work and poor diet. We got this famous coffee in the morning without bread. Black coffee. For lunch, I do not really remember anything other than we got something called knödel. It was a kind of a round, solid ball which was reminiscent of a potato.

Annie and Viggo's visit to Theresienstadt in 1993 was a detour from their holiday to Prague, and Annie compares the shape of the knödel in Theresienstadt with the shape of the potato they had had the night before, at a restaurant in Prague. She tells Viggo that that was why she had not been able to eat the potato they were served with the goulash the night before.

She continues telling that "the knödel must have been a kind of mashed potato with some fat, and then coffee. We always got coffee. In the evening it varied a bit, we got potato soup, where all the 'good' was at the bottom. It was the potato peel. And then there was something white. I don't know what it consisted of, some kind of beans, but not beans. I don't know what it was."

Annie also tells that their ration of bread was half a bread a week and fifty grams of margarine and fifty grams of sugar.

> It was not much. We had to manage it ourselves in a way so there was something for breakfast and lunch. There were no variations in the menu. It was the same every day. However, there could be a little variation in the knödel. Sometimes when we got potato soup for lunch, in the evening you could get something called a "buchte". It looked almost like a square, light bun with something that looked like chocolate sauce. It tasted fine, I thought. I don't think I ever saw any meat, I do not think we ever had that.
>
> The food was prepared in central kitchens, and one had to get there and stand in line with ones "voucher". There were a number of prisoners who poured the food with ladles so you had to hold out your bowl towards the pot. We had a kind of camping pot with a lid and then a mug. After you had the food, you had to go back to where you lived to eat it. It was something that had to be warmed up.
>
> As I already told, my father lived in another barracks. I could go and visit him. I think that I only visited him a few times. They also lived in a mess in an attic.

About a month after the Danes arrived in Theresienstadt, on the evening of 10 November 1943, it was announced that there would be a count of Theresienstadt's 50,000 prisoners. Everybody had to gather in the courtyards at 4 o'clock on the morning of 11 October, and we then walked to a valley outside of the town, to a place called Bauschowitzer Kessel.

There are several accounts of how young children were taken in prams or carried. Old people, up to 90 years old, and handicapped people were driven ahead. Only the sick, who were in hospitals, avoided being driven to the place.

How did my aunt Annie experience this event? She explains that "suddenly everybody was told that they should take what they had. It was mostly food. We had to gather at the end of the camp, everybody, and there were many."

My uncle Viggo, who apparently had not heard about the census before, asked if it was a pending evacuation.

Annie has apparently repressed what it really was because she replied:

> I can't tell, but everybody gathered into columns and was led out of
> the city. I do not know how many people there were in each column.
> We walked for a long time. There was something like a rampart, inside
> a fence, a huge area with a rampart around it. And on that rampart
> stood soldiers with machine guns all around, pointed down at us. We
> were marched up in columns and counted, and evidently they didn't
> tally up the right number.
>
> And then they started counting all over again. And they were
> getting different numbers every time. It took a long time to count all
> those people. I don't know how many we were, 35,000 perhaps or
> 30,000, 32,000, 40,000? I do not know.

It was out there at Bauschowitz Kessel, that Elias Levin, who was also from
Denmark, raised his face to God and in a state of great fear promised,
through his tears, that if he and his father and the rest of the family were
saved, he would, in gratitude, do a lot of work for the Jewish Community in
Denmark. That was a promise he kept. He has carried out a comprehensive
registration and publication of the inscriptions on the tomb stones at the
Jewish cemetery in Copenhagen.

Annie continues telling:

> There were people who died, and there were people who fell and could
> not get up again. I also remember that we were there during the night.
> Spotlights were lit, and there we stood as they continued to count.
> There were more and more who fell. Especially older people, of course.
> And I had no idea what the purpose was. We got more and more
> hungry and thirsty, and we could not move. We were not allowed to
> sit down as this could create disarray in the ranks. Suddenly it was all
> over, and we walked all the way back again.

Annie continued to tell about everyday life:

> I remember one day when I came up to visit my father, one of the
> young Jewish men who had come to Denmark in the thirties to learn
> farming was there. He had made a lovely rye-bread-and beer porridge
> in his pot with water and bread residues. He said I could eat some of
> it. It tasted simply wonderful. I almost think I can say that I've never
> had anything since which tasted so good.

At one point, I remember, we were moved to some barracks they had built. But as far as I know, it was only the Danes who were moved there.

It might have been the aforementioned West Barracks.

We were put together there, not family wise, or perhaps yes and no. The men and women lived apart, still in separate barracks. It was not one big room, but the barracks was divided into smaller rooms with a stove. And there were toilets and there was a sign "abortion" outside the door. I remember that I was so frightened when I saw it for the first time because I thought it was exclusively for those who had to have abortions. It turned out that it was the toilets.

At the new place there were double bunks, three on top of each other. In the corner there was a one-man bunk, also with three on top of each other and a little corridor in the middle, where there were some shelves, like bookcases, where one could have one's stuff.

After some counting she came to the conclusion that there were around 24 bunks in the room. She continued:

...a table and two benches. I do not know if we could sit there, all of us. We were never all there at the same time. Some went to work, and some had free time.

I knew some of those who I lived with. One of them was Miriam Gutkin, who lived with her mother. Her father lived by himself in another barracks, but they could come and eat together. There was an eternal struggle to get the food heated on the stove because there were so many of us there.

At one point there was a slightly older woman. She had a husband and a son. She got so upset one day because she had to wait and could not have her food heated on the stove. She took her pot of water and threw it into the glowing stove so we were almost killed, all of us. A spurt of flame came out. It was terrible.

I was in a double bunk with a young girl. She was a bit older than me. I was fifteen then. It's odd that I was with her as she had a sister, who was a little older. Where she was placed, I don't remember. I don't think she was in the same room as us.

Mrs Katznelson [my grandmother] lived in a room next door. Max's father [my grandfather] came and ate with her.

I can't remember how long we lived in that barracks, but it was a while.

I was employed in the laundry for a period. I pushed a cart with clothes that was rolled to a place that was outside the city. We had three shifts. One started at five in the morning, as far as I can remember. We met at the barrier. There was a gendarme, or some gendarmes who led us out there. I had to take the clothes on a cart, so they must have been dried at some point. The clothes that had been rolled were put together. There were numbers on them. One had to be careful not to get them mixed up. They were not our clothes, but the German's. One had to be quick. Our own clothes we had to wash ourselves with the ugly hand soap made of clay.

Annie recounts that one had to work quickly. My mother said that she once had a job laying carpets. They were very heavy, and as she was very weak because of her illness, she wanted to finish it quickly. She worked with a Czech woman, who said to her "*Langsam, langsam Sie arbeiten für die Deutsche*" (Slowly, slowly, you are working for the Germans).

Annie went on with her story:

I went from one barracks to another and back with the empty cart and brought a new load to be rolled. There was a gendarme at a house situated on a little rise. It was Christmas time, and there was snow. He stood guard. It must have been Christmas 1943. It was Christmas Eve, I was on my shift, and it was dark. There were lights in the wooden house and he had a small Christmas tree with lights. He had written with his feet in the new laid snow: "Merry Christmas" in German.

Since I had been running back and forth a few times, I was apparently the only one who pushed these carts at that time. The gendarme discovered that I had been aware of what he had written in the snow, so he stood with an apple when I came the next time. A large, red apple, which he threw over to me. I had to hide it, so that no one would discover it. He then must have wiped away the Christmas greeting. It was not there the next time I passed by.

That was my Christmas Eve. I got an apple. It was a big thing.

I do not know how we got up when it was time to go to work. Perhaps it was those who came home from the night shift who woke us up. I simply don't remember. We gathered in a column and were taken out, and back again. We were counted when we went out, and when coming back again. They did nothing but counting all the time. It was the Czech gendarmerie. They were so nice looking. Their jackets were red. Long jackets and boots. And I remember they had a slit in the back of their uniforms that could open up. And gold buttons on the front of the uniform. Or is it just an optical illusion because I did not see anything that was nice at that time.

A Czech special department of gendarmerie from Bohemia, numbering from 150 to 170 men, were the guards around Theresienstadt. In order to prevent contact between Jewish prisoners and the Czech guards, the SS ordered that the personnel should rotate periodically.

Annie also had other kinds of work. She was at some point in a so-called *putzkolonne*, which is what the cleaning team was called. "We started with the privies, and then we could advance to 'nicer' cleaning later on. There was supervision for everything we were doing."

Later, and until she came home with the White Buses, she got to work in the so-called "Glimmer" i.e. mica. Mica is a mineral silicate and it was cut into very thin slices for use in the German electronics industry.

Quite a number of Theresienstadt's women came to work in the Glimmer. It took place in the South barracks. The work there was so monotonous and tiring that the women forced themselves to sing to keep awake.

Annie said:

> We met at 5 o'clock in the morning, and then we went out. It was outside the ghetto. We were picked up and taken there. I cannot remember how long we walked. I have no idea about it. There were three shifts. I was not on the same shift all the time. Sometimes it must have been from 10 o'clock in the evening to 6 o'clock in the morning. We never had free time. We split the mica into paper thin pieces, which were then weighed in order to control how much had been made. We were sitting at long tables with a knife and on benches with no backrests. We sat there for eight hours at a time.

She continued with another story:

> As mentioned I had been registered as a child on our arrival at Theresienstadt. I was therefore told that I should go to the doctor and get an infant card. With that one could get one cup of milk a week. Apparently one had to go to the doctor to get it. At that time I could not say a word in German. I went to this doctor and neither could he speak any German. He was Czech. I went in and I got an injection in my arm, and then I left again.

I did not get my milk card. I tried once more and failed again. Twice I got an injection. The third time I was joined by someone who could make himself understood, and then finally I got the milk card. I do not know what I was vaccinated for. I have no idea. But it might have been doing something good!

Then I was ill with chicken pox and had to stay away from my work in the roller room. It was a terrible story.

I was in the barracks while everyone else went to work. I was completely alone. There was not any possibility to talk to anyone, and I was hungry. We had our bread in a backpack. I don't really know from where we got it. It was placed on a shelf. I was bored and I was hungry. There was a quarter of a loaf in the backpack. I cut very thin slices from that bread, so that my father would not discover it. But he found out anyway. He became so furious and completely crazy because I had cut slices from the bread.

I was there, alone with my chickenpox. Mrs Cholewa lived in the lower bunk, who had a lot of kids. They all had such beautiful, very curly hair. She had a couple of boys and a girl. Well, I noticed a fine-toothed comb. She was very eager to comb their hair. Every evening they were thoroughly combed, but I did not relate it to anything. Not until all the lice she had combed off of them walked up the bars of my bed and onto my sore covered head. They stayed in my hair under my sores. It was impossible to remove them.

They sent for a doctor who came and looked at me. He put me in the hospital. It was in one of the barracks. I really underwent a treatment! They washed my hair in a washbasin with ammonium chloride and tore my sores out with a fine-toothed comb. I had a towel on my head, and when I had to try to fall asleep at night, I just couldn't. I just sat up. It was terribly painful. It was burning like hell. The treatment lasted until they had managed to kill them all. The eggs were still there. They could not get them off. So they cut my hair, a kind of "short boy hair style", after which it was easier to handle the issue. I got the treatment again, and this time it was quite effective. I didn't have any sense of how long I was in that hospital, but I received my first Red Cross food package while I was there.

It must have been in the spring of 1944, I guess. The packages came with a name. But my father had not had any packages yet, by the time I got mine. There was sausage, butter, margarine, sugar. There were vitamin pills, green spinatins I think they were called. What else was there? Back then it was everything you could wish for. I can't remember the weight of the package, but it was quite big, as far as I remember.

I was there in the hospital and one night, when I could not sleep, I smeared a crispbread from the package with margarine, put sugar on it and ate it. It was simply delicious. Sometimes I took just a spoonful of sugar and ate it. There was a doctor and a nurse who had night duty. I also smeared a crisp bread, divided it into two pieces, and sprinkled them with sugar and gave it to them They were so happy for it. They had nothing to eat other than the daily, inedible diet.

Finally I got out of the bed. I was told that my father was in the hospital with pneumonia. I made him some food, crisp bread with sausage and probably also some cheese. I thought it might do him well.

I could leave the hospital to visit him and give him the food. Within a couple of days he got a package as well. Then he had his own package that he could eat from.

At last they had managed to get rid of the eggs on my scalp. I was released from the hospital and started working again.

She also talked about meeting my father, when he came to Theresienstadt from Sachsenhausen and Berlin in January 1944. "I remember that I hurried to the barracks where he was staying. I saw him there and I clearly remember that he had a cap on his head. As he saw me, I said 'hello Max', and he said 'hello Annie', then he took off his cap and it turned out that his scalp was partly shaven. I was shocked. He looked so funny. He did not know where Karen and Ib were."

The story now jumped forward to the spring and early summer months of 1944. My mother and I had arrived at Theresienstadt from Ravensbrück. We had been hospitalized at the Hohenelber barracks and the children's hospital with multiple diseases. My mother came out from the hospital and started to work, which leads us forward to the epoch-making event in Theresienstadt's history: the visit by a Red Cross delegation on 23 June 1944.

9

Red Cross and the Potemkin Façade

The Red Cross Delegation's Visit

It was a landmark event because for a period it changed Theresienstadt, or rather a small part of it, where the Red Cross delegation were taken, and because it improved conditions for some of the Danes, including us. The costs for others, however, were tragic.

One of the more remarkable achievements of Eichmann's visit to Copenhagen on 2 November 1943 was a commitment that Danish officials and the Danish Red Cross could pay a visit to Theresienstadt.

The day after the visit to Copenhagen Werner Best sent a telegram to the Foreign Ministry in Berlin, which mentioned that "... Eichmann stated that the Reich Security Main Office will make the following suggestion .... and within the foreseeable future, receive a visit by representatives of the Danish Central Administration and the Danish Red Cross. ... I ask for information about whether the Reich Security Main Office will proceed after Eichmann's proposal."

The visit was given the go-ahead, but the date was pushed back several times. There were many reasons for the postponement, the main one being that Theresienstadt should look presentable when the visit took place. Embellishment demanded time. One should be rather sure of the weather, that the grass was green and that the flowers would be in bloom. On 14 June the ready signal came from the Reich Security Main Office, and the visit was settled for 23 June 1944.

The fact that the Gestapo was opposed to the visit, and had therefore tried to prevent it, probably also played a role.

There are historians who believe that, to a great extent, it was due to SS leader Heinrich Himmler that the visit was considered important, and that the camp was to appear as a kind of model camp that the Germans pretended it to be. It may be because of him that the visit finally took place.

Heinrich Himmler 7.10.1900-23.5.1945

Himmler joined the NSDAP and SS in 1925 and soon got managerial tasks because of his organizational skills. In 1929 he became Reich leader of the SS. He then developed it into a powerful elite organization.

When World War II started Heinrich Himmler strengthened his power base. Special Einsatz Groups were established to implement the systematic killing of political opponents in the eastern European areas, and soon after the extermination of the Jews. He also established the Waffen-SS combat troops.

When Germany's success on the battlefields stopped, Hitler's response was to give Himmler additional power; he became Minister of the Interior in 1943, the year after the commander of the Replacement (Home) Army, and in 1945 he was – despite his lack of military experience – appointed commander of two army groups at the front. In the war's final phase Heinrich Himmler tried, through negotiations with Folke Bernadotte, to get the Western Allies to make a separate peace with Germany. This prompted Hitler to strip him of all power at the end of April 1945 and to order his arrest.

Heinrich Himmler committed suicide on 23 May 1945, after being captured by British forces.

Historians point out that, by that time, Himmler was trying to create a positive relationship with the Allies behind Hitler's back. That was the case during the negotiations on the repatriation of many prisoners in the concentration camps in early 1945.

In the second half of April 1944 the beautification operation of Theresienstadt started. The concentration camp, ghetto, city, or whatever you choose to call Theresienstadt, was being transformed into a Potemkin village. This meant that the daily written orders were illustrated. At the top was a picture of Theresienstadt, and there were small drawings at each section of the "messages". A competition among Theresienstadt's "inhabitants" was also organized. One could win two cans of sardines in oil and a piece of bread by suggesting new names for various streets.

In another regulation some of the previously-used names were also "embellished". Below the former names are mentioned in German and the "beautified" names in English:

Ghettowache was changed to Community Guard
Wach-und Ordnungsdienst to Security and Order Service
Ghettogericht to Court
Ghettobücherei to Central Library
Ghetto Theresienstadt to Jewish Settlement Area of Theresienstadt

In addition, the refurbishment of the houses that the Danes were to be moving into, along with the areas that the Red Cross delegation would pass by, was quite extensive.

The wooden partition between the "Aryan" street and the ghetto was the first to be demolished. On the "Aryan" street was, among other things, the *Kommandantur* (the SS Headquarters in Theresienstadt). The main square was transformed into a beautiful park with flowers and lawns and benches on the newly laid out paths. A fine music pavilion was erected on one of the corners, and a 30-40 man orchestra played there. Conducted by the German/Danish conductor Peter Deutsch, they would play cheerful music for several hours each day. The hospitals and old people's home were also improved, and the few stores also got a face lift.

The reverse side was tragic. To get the city to look less crowded, many prisoners were sent away in transports. It was most likely not completely clear to those interned in Theresienstadt where the transports were going to, but the fear that transports eastward could mean death was probably chiseled into the consciousness of each of them.

In September 1943 a family camp was established in Birkenau. Five thousand prisoners came to this camp from Theresienstadt. They were not exposed to the "usual" selection upon arrival, where the normal pattern was that prisoners fit for work were taken to one side while the others were taken directly to the gas chambers. The families were allowed to be together, they did not wear prison clothes, and they did not have their hair shaved off. In December 1943, another 5,000 arrived.

But almost to the day, six months after the first 5,000 arrived, they were murdered in the gas chambers in a single night. This pattern continued for a short period: a relatively normal life in a family camp and six months afterwards, certain death. The German's attempt to show Birkenau, as they had done with Theresienstadt, as being a model camp, was once again just an illusion.

Apparently the plan was that the International Red Cross delegation would also visit the family camp in Birkenau. Perhaps that plan was given up as unnecessary in light of the very positive report on the visit to Theresienstadt, which was written up by M. Rossel from the International Red Cross

The Red Cross delegation arrived on Friday 23 June 1944. The participants were the Swiss Dr. M. Rossel from the International Red Cross, Deputy Head of Department Frants Hvass from the Danish Foreign Ministry, Consultant of the Danish Health Authority Dr. Eigil Juel Henningsen and Dr. Heidekamp from the German Red Cross.

Frants Hvass (29.4.1896-21.12.1982) was head of the Foreign Ministry's Political-Legal department.

During the occupation of Denmark, he played a significant role in the political negotiations during the war. In October-November 1943 after the cooperation policy collapsed, he visited embassies in Madrid, Lisbon, Bern, Stockholm and Helsinki to brief the local Danish diplomats about developments in Denmark, which had led to the events of 29 August.

Hvass also participated in the Red Cross delegation that visited Theresienstadt on 23 June 1944.

After the visit to Theresienstadt, Hvass was a co-initiator of the White Buses that brought Nordic prisoners from German concentration camps into safety.

After the war, he became Permanent Secretary of the Foreign Ministry and later ambassador in Bonn.

As it was a Red Cross delegation it may seem surprising that it was the head consultant in the Danish Health Authority, Eigil Juel Henningsen, and not the head of the Danish Red Cross, Helmer Rosting, who participated. Rosting might have been excluded because he was suspected of having pro-German sympathies. Among several indications of that is a telegram Best sent to the Foreign Ministry in Berlin on 29 September 1943, in which he reports that Rosting on his own initiative had turned to him and suggested that "You should ... repatriate the Danish soldiers and confine all Danish Jews in the camps, which then became vacant .... However, one should not deport the confined Jews immediately and not at once, but announce that for each new act of sabotage, 50 or 100 Jews would be deported." But it is a telegram written by Best, so one cannot be absolutely sure that he reported Rosting's statements correctly.

It is interesting to note that the "replacement" of Rosting as member of the delegation may well have happened at the last minute, unless there was poor communication about the issue. A German note dated 20 June, only three days before the visit, listed Rosting as member of the delegation.

Rosting was arrested after the war, both on 6 and 7 May 1945, but was released both times. He suffered a nervous breakdown and committed suicide on 28 June 1945.

The Red Cross delegation was accompanied by the head of the Security Police in the Protectorate of Bohemia and Moravia, SS-standartenführer Dr. Weinmann. Also in the delegation was SS-Sturmbannführer Hans Günther from the Jewish Zentralstelle in Prague, and his brother Rolf Günther, who was a deputy to Eichmann in Berlin. Rolf Günther had been sent to Copenhagen during the action against the Danish Jews in October 1943. Moreover, alongside Rolf Günther was Eichmann's aide-de camp Möhs, detective inspector Renner from the Gestapo in Copenhagen, Legation Councellor von Thadden from the German Foreign Ministry and Dr. Heydekampf from the German Red Cross.

The head of the *Ältestenrat*, Paul Eppstein, gave a welcome speech to the delegation. The speech was obviously carefully prepared in several Council meetings and censored by Rahm.

The visit lasted a bit less than six hours. The delegation was of course only able to move along a carefully planned route.

It is too much to fully reproduce the rather extensive written reports Frants Hvass and Dr. Juel Henningsen prepared after the visit. However a few observations in the reports are worth noting.

Frants Hvass wrote that

> The overall impression of the city was good. There was order. ... The people had a fresh look and did not look undernourished. They were clean and well-groomed and seemed to be more well dressed than in the average German provincial town. They moved freely around within the city area and followed our visit with great attention. The large majority neither bowed or straightened up when we or the German officials and the commander of the camp passed them.

Hvass however, expresses reservations about a number of points, which gives the impression that he may well have been aware that he might not have been given a completely true picture.

Dr. Juel Henningsen also had a number of reservations, but wrote that "The city gives a bright and friendly impression. The streets are wide, there are numerous 'green areas' and large bastions. On the outskirts of the city and surrounding area are small gardens and fields."

On health care, he wrote among other things that "Among the doctors were a very large number of highly qualified specialists. Furthermore, there were numerous midwives, nurses, dentists and pharmacists. Because of the great need for nursing staff, special courses had been organized for women and they had been trained to assist the proper nurses."

He wrote further that "The nursing staff were nicely dressed in special dresses. Surgical nurses all in white; doctors had all white coats; the hospital had a special diet kitchen but also got food from the large communal kitchen, which was right next to the hospital. For patients not confined to bed, there was a green yard."

Hans Kirchhoff mentions in his book *Holocaust in Denmark* that the information in Rossel's report, in substance, is quite similar to the information in the Danish reports. In a 1979 interview with Claude Lanzmann, Rossel described Theresienstadt as an almost normal city. Despite being somewhat overcrowded, he had no sense that it was a Potemkin façade. He made no attempt to see behind it.

In the interview he also indicated that there had been ample opportunity during the visit for Jews to give him a hint, but he was amazed at people's servility and passivity, which obviously had provoked his interest. He explained this impression of "passivity" as due to the fact that the Jews in Theresienstadt were mainly prominent people, having sufficient means to ensure protection for themselves against being transported eastwards. Although later informed about the atrocities in Theresienstadt and the careful staging of the visit by the SS, Rossel maintained, in the interview with Lanzmann, that he, even today, would write exactly the same report without changing a single word. He accused the prisoners for not having given him a hint that the reality was fundamentally different from what he was shown.

To put it bluntly, it is amazing that even many years after the war and with the knowledge of the full extent of the Holocaust, he demonstrated no sense of understanding that as much as a wrong facial expression from the prisoners as the delegation passed by could have meant their death.

Juel Henningsen gave a speech to the Danish Theresienstadt Society on 17 April 1955. He was careful in expressing why he had been asked to participate in the delegation, and not Rosting, saying that "the Danish Red Cross, at that time, was not managed in such a way inspiring confidence that the organization was up to the task."

He also explained that before he left, he knew virtually nothing about Theresienstadt, but that from the three Mrs Schultzes (as noted they had been sent home from Theresienstadt in January 1944), who did not dare saying anything, he did get the feeling that the situation was bad.

It is most likely also correct when he explained that they were prepared to find us placed under very poor conditions, that the prisoners in Theresienstadt were malnourished, that they were dirty and poorly dressed, that the city was scary, and that there were mentally broken people, affected by terror and hopelessness.

He acknowledged that it would have been naive to think that the Germans wanted to show them anything like that, and noted that they did not see anything similar to the image they were expecting.

Posterity, both in Denmark and internationally, has frequently covered whether the representatives of the Red Cross had been completely duped during their visit, getting a completely distorted impression of the conditions, or whether their reports were written with the clear sense that a more true story could risk creating problems, not only for the Danes, but also with the Red Cross food supplies that were sent to the Danes.

In the literature there are examples of both points of view. To the Danish parliamentary committee established after the war, Hvass explained that he and Juel Henningsen were aware that a number of measures had been taken on the occasion of the visit. Rossel also explained in the interview in 1979 that an organized and pre-planned visit was surely orchestrated in a special way.

It seems quite unlikely that Hvass and Juel Henningsen would not have been aware that they were not given a particularly accurate picture of the situation. It also seems unlikely that they did not know that the writing of their reports after returning home would have to be done very carefully. They needed to be aware that too negative a statement could be counter-productive, and thereby cause irreparable harm. In addition, as Juel Henningsen said in his lecture at the Theresienstadt Society, that their impressions of the visit had to be weighed against the very negative expectations that they had beforehand regarding conditions in the camps.

The historian Bent Blüdnikow addresses the issue in an article in a historical journal of whether the reports reached the Allies and whether the content and form of the reports were instrumental in certain decisions. For example, whether the railway tracks to Auschwitz should be bombed. It is an extremely important and complicated issue, and a discussion about which is outside the scope of this book.

The criticism against the International Red Cross and its lack of action concerning the millions of Jews during the war has been massive. The Red Cross has previously covered itself behind the Convention of 1929, under which it was working. That Convention only gave a mandate to take care of military prisoners of war, and not to do something for people who were detained for political and racial reasons. The Germans claimed that the civilians interned in the camps were not covered by international law, but only German law.

On 24 January 2014 the International Red Cross expressed, on occasion of the International Auschwitz day, that the day also marks the organization's mistake in failing to help and protect the millions of people who were killed in the death camps. The organization publicly expressed its regret over its own powerlessness, and with regard to the errors that were committed in connection with the Nazi persecution and genocide.

My family's living condition improved as a result of the delegation's visit, but before I come to our life in the new house, it is useful to talk a little bit about the Red Cross food parcels.

Red Cross Food Parcels

One of the results of the return to Copenhagen from Theresienstadt of the aforementioned five people, who should not have been deported, was that in Copenhagen they became much better informed about the nutritional situation in Theresienstadt. It was with this knowledge that the content of the food parcels that were sent to the camp were made.

In late February 1944, the first packages of foodstuffs to Theresienstadt arrived. Hans Sode-Madsen writes in his book *Theresienstadt - og de Danske Jøder 1940-45* (*Theresienstadt and the Danish Jews, 1940-45*) that it was formally required that the packages be sent by individuals. In Theresienstadt reception of the packages had to be acknowledged, and it was possible to write a thank you to the sender. As family and friends, in many cases, had fled to Sweden, it was necessary to find "package sponsors". My parents also acknowledged the receipt of packages. The senders were in a few cases my uncle (mentioned in my mother's letters from Horserød camp) and my grandmother. Another thank you was sent to the acquaintance mentioned at the beginning of this book, who is the one who housed us for one night when we went underground at the beginning of October 1943. In a few other cases it is someone I never heard of.

One package normally contained: 1/4 kilogram of sugar, 1 kilogram of cheese, 1 can of sprats and 1 can of mackerel, 1 pc soap, ¼ kilogram of rye crackers, ½ kilogram of butter, 20 bouillon cubes, 1 kilogram of sausage, ½ kilogram of crispbread and 1 can of pork.

It is quite obvious that the standard package did not take into account Jewish dietary rules.

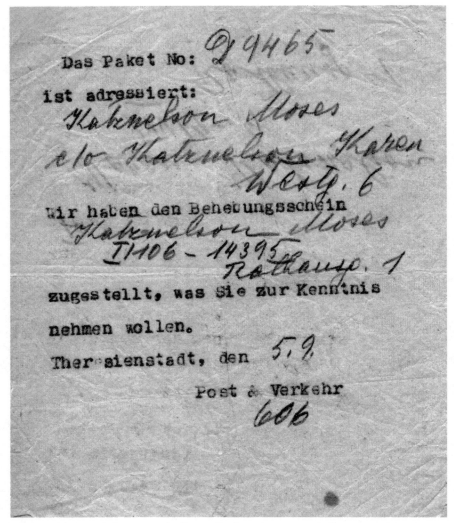

My father's acknowledgment in the "post office" in Theresienstadt for receipt of a package.

Elias Levin, who was very religious, wrote nothing directly about how he dealt with the content of the packages from the Red Cross, but about the food in general he writes that from time to time barrels of steaming hot food arrived that smelled delightfully of meat. One could not know, however, if it was horse meat, which is forbidden according to Jewish dietary rules, or whether the meat was tainted. He continued that it often happened that those

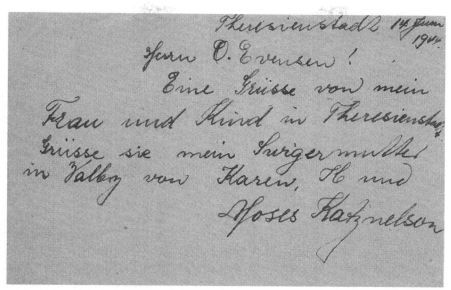

My father's postcard with a greeting to the person who sent us a package.

who had eaten from the barrels were later found in the latrines with diarrhea. They had destroyed their stomach and could not be saved. "We Orthodox Jews coped better, because we avoided eating meat", he wrote.

My mother and I should have been sent directly to Theresienstadt from Ravensbrück, along with the other Danes who came from Horserød camp. But as we were not sent to Theresienstadt with the others, our Red Cross packages were quickly taken away because in Copenhagen they did not know where we were. So, while the Danes in Theresienstadt received packages from February 1944, my mother and I only got packages from the end of June, a few months after we had come to Theresienstadt. It is from that time that I have a receipt for a package, written in my mother's handwriting.

After the long stay in Ravensbrück, despite the food we at some point got from other Danish women prisoners, we were severely malnourished. It was, therefore, a big problem that we did not receive any packages until the end of June. We had to share a bit from our family member's packages. And in fact, there was not much to share.

For the same reason Corrie Meyer did not get any food parcels at the beginning, so she turned to Rabbi Friediger and managed to get something from the surplus packages. Corrie suggested to my father that he go to Friediger and ask for help. The packages in surplus were packages that were sent to Danes who had died before Copenhagen knew about it. They had not stopped sending the packages. When he asked Rabbi Friediger for a bit of food for me, Friediger got very angry and called him a *schnorrer* (a not very polite Yiddish word for a beggar), and my father did not get any food. It was therefore something of a surprise to me when I read Friediger's remark in his book about Theresienstadt from 1946, that "if the addressee had died or departed with one of the transports, I received these packages, and with my friend Axel Margolinsky I distributed them to the sick and those who never got packages. We could thus spread the joy, which was indescribable, and for us, who usually delivered the packages to those people, it gave great satisfaction."

Even among the prisoners in Theresienstadt, there were social differences between people, and quite evidently we did not belong to the "important"!

In January 1945, a petition was allegedly made against Friediger's high-handed package distribution. My father says that Friediger's son also opposed his father's administration of the food packages, which many found quite unfair. There is another example, identical to my father's story, about a young woman who was deported with her parents. She was convinced that she could not get anything from these extra packages because she was a "Russian Jew". My father says that my grandfather was a little snobby and that he tried, unsuccessfully, to prevent my father from signing the petition.

My mother said that "strangely enough – I do not know how it could be – I was no longer terribly hungry. It was as if the hunger had gone, that we had become accustomed to it. I was thirsty and I only thought about malt beer. I don't know why, I never drank malt beer at home. The only thing I thought of was malt beer."

My father had a somewhat similar observation. Years after the war he used to say that the severe cold in Sachsenhausen was much worse to endure than hunger in Theresienstadt.

My parents' comments about hunger is undeniably something contradicted by most reports from other Danish prisoners, who clearly were not able to "get used" to the hunger.

Annie said that "I can remember that there was also dried milk and porridge oats in the Red Cross packages. One day I managed to escape from work and we were sitting in my bunk at each end, Karen and me. All the others were at work. Karen and I were alone in the entire barracks, and I served porridge oats with milk and sugar. There we sat enjoying the moment, telling each other what had happened in the past period."

The embellishment of parts of Theresienstadt ahead of the Red Cross delegation's visit meant that some of the housing conditions were improved. This gave some of the Danish Jews, though not all of them, better living conditions, including us.

Rathausgasse 1

Our improved housing was on the ground floor in Rathausgasse 1. It was our new "home". In the literature on Theresienstadt, it is often said that the Danes moved to the "beautified" houses in early June 1944. In other places it is said that it happened just before the delegation's visit on 23 June. Let us look at the evidence that I have about when it might have happened.

To find out when my family and I moved into a room in Rathausgasse 1, the postal receipts from the Red Cross food parcels are a good source. The receipts for the packages we received indicate where we stayed in May and June, before and after the delegation's visit. They have the following addresses:

On 22 May my father lived in Hauptstrasse 55/1
On 5 June my grandmother lived in West Gasse 6-10.
On 14 June my father lived in Hauptstrasse 55/1
On 25 June my grandmother lived in Rathausgasse 1.

These addresses show that my grandmother did not live in one of the military barracks at the beginning of June, but in the West Barracks located in the lower right corner of the map of Theresienstadt, below the Jäger Barracks. Probably in barracks no. 6, room no. 10.

My father was living at Hauptstrasse on 14 June. It was the Hannover barracks, where they slept in three-storey bunks. He said that "where I lived, it was neat and clean, without fleas and lice. Up in the attic there were lice. But our Room Elder took care of our room, opening the windows to let in some fresh air. He cleaned and washed the floor every day."

On 25 June we were registered in Rathausgasse 1, in one of the four beautified "Dane-houses". It suggests that we only moved to the "beautified" room immediately before the visit of the Red Cross.

The move to Rathausgasse 1 meant that our family was now together, although the space for us was very small. We had a room of a bit less than 20 square meters. There were two bay windows facing the street with a window bar in the middle, where we had a mirror. There were no bunks, only single beds. There was also a wardrobe which was for all of us. Of course there was almost no floor space, so we had our things under the beds.

My parents and I lived in our room, as well as my grandparents, my grandfather and my aunt. In the room on the first floor, among others, 8 year-old Jytte Bornstein lived, who wrote the very moving book *Min Rejse Tilbage (My Journey Back)* with drawings and text from Theresienstadt. She also writes about Rathausgasse 1 in the book.

About our new home Annie said "there was brand new furniture, which had just been made. It really smelled of new wood. There were new beds and a new wardrobe. It was all new and the wood smelled." She also told that the delegation passed by while "we were having a nice breakfast, with eggs, the first we had seen in all the time we had been in Theresienstadt. And then they asked if we were ok. We said yes, and did not dare to answer otherwise."

She went on saying that she didn't have anything in the wardrobe, which made my uncle Viggo ask her if she only had the clothes that she was wearing. She replied that she had received a package from her mother with some clothes. "Of course there was not much privacy in the room and we had to dress and undress in front of others. But I don't think one thought much about it. We did not walk around naked. It was not that bad ... I don't really know what to say. I think I remember something with a makeshift curtain across the room. Whether it is true or not, I am not sure."

My mother also remembered the visit by the Red Cross delegation.

> We got orders that we should look nice. We were then settled into the house. They [the Red Cross delegation] walked around, and how much of an impression they got of it as a showcase, and how much seemed hidden behind the facade, I really don't know. I guess they saw through it, more or less. At least one got the sense that somebody out there was paying attention to us. Everybody else in the camp felt comfortable about it. There is someone from the outside who knows where we are and is paying attention.

In light of the comment made by my mother, there is reason to once again return to the Red Cross visit. Among Theresienstadt's 35,000 to 40,000 prisoners there were many different views about the Red Cross visit and the comment from my mother is obviously the feeling she came away with.

The German Rabbi Leo Baeck, who was also in Theresienstadt and survived, wrote about the ghetto after the war and his view was completely different. He stated that most prisoners only felt pain and disappointment over the visit, and that the delegation seemed to believe completely in the façade that was set up for them. As only the ground floors of the houses could be seen from the street, SS had ordered the majority of those who lived on the ground floor up to the upper floors, which became totally overcrowded. Baeck writes that the impact of the visit on the prisoners' morale was appalling, and that they felt forgotten and abandoned.

Annie told a little more about our Rathausgasse home.

There was a toilet, a privy, out in the yard. And then there was a sink, I remember, along the staircase, where we tried to wash our clothes with the soap we were given. It was a lump of clay, which dissolved in no time. We washed the best we could but it was not good. It had to be done.

There was a shared bath. I was there once in the beginning, when I took a shower. But later we did not dare to use it because we had heard rumors that gas was used there. Instead we used a stand-up bath from then on. One can't say that we were terribly clean.

There was a stove in the room. We got coal from the railway track. There was a turn on the tracks and that was where the coal fell off as the wagons were open. We went out with buckets to pick it up. There was a lot of talk about going out and picking up coal. Even Ib, that little "man", was also out with a small bucket collecting coal and potatoes. What else did we use for the stove? I don't really remember. Whether it was peat, I can't say. I did not care much about it.

The story about coal has an extra twist that really illustrates the situation with so many family members, under these special circumstances, living in the same small room. My mother said that my father was out at night collecting coal from the railroad tracks. When he came back to our room, he poured it into a metal bucket and that was obviously rather noisy.

This annoyed my grandmother terribly as she had to get up at about 4 o'clock in the morning to go to work. She had received a postcard from my aunt (my father's older sister), who was in Sweden. She managed to escape in October 1943 with her family. My aunt asked how she (i.e. her's and my father's mother) was. My grandmother replied, "I've Moses, then you know how I am." When one hears the tone of voice of my mother telling that story, it is quite clear that my grandmother's answer to the postcard definitely wasn't meant as a nice one.

My mother is also rather sarcastic when mentioning that story, because she tells another story about my father from the time in Horserød camp, after my grandparents were sent off to Theresienstadt and we were held back. The only thing my mother says about my father was that he could only think about how he wanted to leave (to Theresienstadt!) in order to help his parents. This triggered a vehement argument between my parents, because my mother could not accept that he obviously was more interested in his parents than his own wife and son. "Well, he really deserved my mother in law's remark on that postcard", she says.

Annie continued:

> The old Katznelson and his wife [my grandparents] lived by the end
> wall of the room. There was a covered up door in which there were
> some shelves where she kept many things, behind a curtain. There was
> a kind of curtain in front. I don't know if she had made it herself
> because she got some packages from Marie [my father's sister] from
> Sweden which contained amazing things. They simply contained
> everything. I tend to believe that she saved Karen's life because she
> brought everything to the hospital when Karen was hospitalized. So
> somehow, Karen overcame all of what she had of illness and weakness.
> She was simply so ill. It was unbelievable that she recovered.

Somewhere in Rathausgasse 1, behind our room, there was a kitchen where
we could warm up our food. The food had to be picked up from one of the
15 kitchens that were spread out over the city.

My mother recounted that they sometimes also warmed the food on the
stove in our room. When the cooking pot was on the stove, it often happened
that there was a bedbug crawling and then "splash! It would fall straight down
into the pot".

About picking up the food, Annie said:

> We had to stand in line for our food. I remember that I blissfully had
> eaten my lunch and was about to go to work again. I was standing in
> front of the mirror in our room combing my hair. Then my father said
> "go and pick up my food". I "belonged" to the children's kitchen, as I
> was registered as a child. The adult's kitchen was in a different place
> from where we children got our food. But the food was the same as
> far as I remember, except for the cup of milk we got once a week. It
> was almost impossible to get home with that cup, before everything
> had fallen out. I don't really know what the difference was.
>
> But in any case, he wanted me to go and pick up his food. That
> meant I would stand in line once again to get it. I told him that he
> should go and pick it up himself. I was 15 years old and I had also been
> at work. I did not want to stand in line once again to get his food. That
> resulted in him beating me and slapping me in my face and he hit my
> neck so that I slammed my forehead into the mirror. He told me that
> I should not be cheeky.
>
> At one point I was in line for food at the children's kitchen. No, it
> must have been at the adult's kitchen, because I was talking to a girl in

front of me. Apparently, because of my age, I now belonged to the adult's kitchen. In any case I stood there speaking German with the girl in front of me. We chatted while waiting for our turn.

Suddenly somebody tapped me on my back. I turned around and it was my German teacher from Carolineskolen [the Jewish school in Copenhagen], who looked amazed at me and said: "I did not believe my own eyes, that it was really you Annie, standing there and speaking German like a native. I tried to teach you that for so many years without success. And now we have only been here 3 or 4 months, and now you manage". One just had to learn it, otherwise one couldn't get on, and then you just got injections!

Annie explained further that

> ...old Mrs Katznelson and I ... we were not on the same work shift. So when I had to sleep late in the morning and she would start her shift at 5 o'clock in the morning, she woke me up and said "Oh, Annie, comb my hair." She had such a beautiful hair that was put up. It was silver gray.
>
> She was sitting on her bed, and I stood doing her hair, very nicely. She looked as if she just had left from a hairdresser. It was rather easy to comb. And she had hairpins, which she perhaps had brought with her from home. The hairstyle was quite nice. So that was what she required of me when she had the morning shift, and I needed sleep. But I did not reflect much on it. I was young. I just did it.

At one point it happened that my grandparents got a room on the first floor of the house. Whether they had it for themselves, I don't know. My mother said that she was somewhat angry about it because it had happened in a strange, hush-hush manner. They were replaced in our room by two people that we had no special relation to. They moved into our room. It was Chaim Leib Brudzewsky and his 20 year-old daughter Miriam. His wife had probably managed to escape to Sweden, while his mother came to Theresienstadt, where she died.

Annie said that "Brudzewsky would go to work early in the morning. It annoyed my father, for when Brudzewsky opened the door to the wardrobe it creaked, and he also stomped around on the floor."

At one time, my grandfather got quite interested in a Czech lady in Theresienstadt. Since my grandfather had apparently quarreled a lot about Brudzewsky making noise in the morning, he replied that my grandfather should reflect a bit. When Brudzewsky got up in the morning, he went to meet his God, while my grandfather went out to meet "another". "Which one is better?" he asked. "He really got that punch", Annie says.

It may seem strange that there could be these kind of relationships between the sexes in a concentration camp, and that one, in many ways, could live a relatively "normal" life. In fact Norbert Troller, in his book *Theresienstadt: Hitler's Gift to the Jews*, has a whole chapter on *Love and Sex in Theresienstadt*. It is too far afield from the scope of this work to closely consider Troller's theses, but he talks about the burning need, also in a concentration camp, for prisoners to be liked and cared about. It was important to share the few hours that life in the camp allowed with a person who meant everything to you. The loneliness, if one was separated from a girlfriend or a spouse, was also significant. In addition to the need to have someone to share concerns with. "Who can condemn?", he writes. Any day a transport to the east could suddenly and forever bury feelings and the object of one's love.

As incredible as it sounds, there was also a thriving cultural life in Theresienstadt. Philipp Manes was German who considered himself more German than Jew. He was deported to Theresienstadt in 1942, where he organized about 500 lectures. He described his many activities in his book *As If It Were Life*, where he also described that the children, to a certain extent, were educated, although there was a prohibition against it. The Danish Chief Rabbi Friediger also gave lectures.

It is important to recognize and emphasize Norbert Troller's finding "that Theresienstadt was not much more than a transit station on the way to the extermination camps in the east", and that practically all of those who gave lectures and entertained in different ways ended up in the gas chambers. Philipp Manes arrived at Auschwitz on a transport on 28 October 1944. It was the last transport from Theresienstadt to Auschwitz, with 2,038 prisoners. It arrived on 30 October. About 240 men and 140 women were selected. Many of them were sent to other camps, and the remaining people were gassed. They were the last victims in the gas chambers, which were destroyed shortly after.

When asked whether she participated in some of the cultural activities, my mother replied: "No, we did not. We got about 1,000 books from home, from the Red Cross. I, along with Cilla Cohn, were asked to hand them out to the Danes who wanted to borrow books. The two of us were responsible for the 'library'. I also borrowed some books. I cannot remember what kind of books they were." The books came as a result of a request made to the Red Cross delegation during their visit. The books, however, only arrived in February 1945.

It is important that neither Norbert Troller's nor Philipp Manes' considerations overshadow what Theresienstadt really was. The counting of the number of prisoners who came in transport and prisoners who died in Theresienstadt, speaks its own language.

Theresienstadt was not much more than a transit station on the way to the extermination camps in the east. Despite the relatively good conditions compared to most other camps, one has to try and imagine how it was having constant fear of being selected for transport, or to be taken to *Kleine Festung* and risk death for a minor offense, and the total uncertainty about one's destiny. On the top of that, the nutrition was poor, everything was filthy and there were many diseases.

Lawyer Morits Oppenhejm, who was one of the so-called prominent prisoners, said that "The suffering in Theresienstadt is indescribable. People are forced to work as slaves almost without getting any other food than half tainted potatoes."

My mother, in one of her interviews, also described the feelings of despair, helplessness and fear that characterized the prisoners, even if there also was a kind of "normal" daily life. She said that "if you are not constantly thinking about what is going to happen tomorrow and not thinking about hunger, then there was a kind of daily life. Thoughts about home and about the past languished into something unreal. I could not have the thought that we would never come home again."

"We could not sleep at night", my mother recalled. "We itched. One day my husband said that now we have to try to do a thorough cleaning and try to find out where all the vermin was coming from. We separated the beds. At the bottom there were boards with cracks and there were bed bugs in thick layers. We got a bucket with Lysol and scooped them into the bucket." In the wardrobe my father had his hat, a real "Anthony Eden hat" with a brim. Up in the brim there were dead bed bugs in large numbers.

Some of the "daily" events, were described by Annie, and not my mother, who remembered the following about my grandfather.

> He also got Karen, when she arrived in Theresienstadt, to wash his underwear. Apparently he got the idea that he now had a maid. She had still not recovered completely and was still rather weak. She was standing there rubbing his underwear with the poor piece of soap. She did not refuse to do it. I think she must have had a kind of respect for him in one way or another. I guess in the end she told him that she had enough to take care of with a child, so he had to do it himself.

My uncle Viggo thought that my father should wash his father in law's underwear, for he says "Max should have done it", which gives Annie the clue to tell a bit about my father.

Max was so busy organizing. He was good at it. He could get everything, simply everything from "fraudulent activities". He worked with shoes and made footwear. For whom? Probably for the Germans, I believe. He managed to get something out of it one way or the other. Incredible that he dared. He could have risked ending up in *Kleine Festung*. But he did dare. I don't know how it worked. But he was good at it. And my dad also did it. He was tailoring and repaired things. I do not think he made anything for me, but for others, and then he got some extra bread, from which I also got something.

A few other episodes also give a picture of my father's 'activities'. He worked in a shoe barracks with my grandfather.

My father was walking with two "special" bags. In them were a number of shoe repairs he had made "privately". This was not allowed, and the bags and their contents were confiscated. My grandfather, who did some work for a director, told my father that if he apologized to the director and said he would never do it again, he would get the bags back. "Like hell I won't", he replied, and was roundly told off by his father. He didn't get the bags, but in the evening my grandfather came back with them.

One day, my father was off work and was at the square in the middle of town. He suddenly noticed the head of the camp, Rahm walking together with Eichmann. "I fled into the nearest gate", he says. "I did not want them to ask me what I was doing and why I was not at work."

My grandfather worked for a small shoemaker who had a workshop. Suitcases were made of leather at that time. Bags from those who had died were cut open, and the leather could be used to repair the shoes. One day when he was alone, he cut up a suitcase. He found 250 marks between the lining and the leather. He gave the money to the shoemaker and got half a loaf of bread. My father told him that it was ridiculous to have given him the money, as he could have gotten much more if he had simply kept it.

My father had been given a German transport number when he came to or left Sachsenhausen in November 1943. That fact nearly put him on a transport to Auschwitz which almost surely would have meant his death. He was on the list of prisoners three times that should be on a transport. He ran around from office to office, all night, to get his name off the list. He sought help from Rabbi Friediger, who was very angry at him to be disturbed at night. A German prisoner, who had met my mother and I when we arrived at Theresienstadt, managed in some way or another to get him off the list. Was a bribe needed or not? I do not know, but my father was always good at wriggling out of trouble.

At this point it was mid year, 1944, and there is reason to look over some official writings from that summer.

A somewhat unexpected document dated 16 July emerged. In that document my parents declared, in front of Judge Julius Moritz, that after their arrival at Theresienstadt they had lived as husband and wife and that they did not want a divorce. Judge Julius Moritz was one of the so-called prominent prisoners. He died a few days before the repatriation with the White Buses.

My mother said that the reason behind the divorce was that she had hoped that she and I could avoid being deported and could remain in Denmark, as she was only a half-Jew. In one way or another my parents must have been told that a divorce petition had been filed on 4 February, and what the underlying idea had been.

The document is signed by both of them. It must have been considered an important legal document because the Danish Legation in Berlin wrote on 4 September to the Foreign Ministry in Denmark, that they had received the declaration on 25 August, with a verbal note from the German Foreign Ministry.

Finally, on 8 August 1944 my grandmother received a message from the Foreign Ministry saying that my mother and I were in Theresienstadt. In the draft letter to my grandmother, B. Dons Moeller of the Foreign Ministry added, in his own hand, that he, from the Foundation of 1944, a couple of days ago on the basis of a received letter, had learned that my mother lives in West Gasse 6 (the West Barracks). He also added that there was no mention of me. There was also an error, unless the message had been several months underway, for on 8 August we lived in the beautified house in Ratthausgasse 1.

There may also have been a communications error between the Foreign Ministry and the Danish Red Cross. In the Red Cross' Weekly Information Bulletin no. 7, dated 12 March 1945, there was a list with names and data (prisoner numbers?) on Danish nationals who were in the concentration camp Ravensbrück, Fürstenberg in Mecklenburg. That list also included my mother's name and mine, along with the other Danes, who came with us from Horserød camp. That list was made more than half a year after the Ministry of Foreign Affairs received the confirmation that we were in Theresienstadt. At the time the list was made by the Red Cross, the other Danish Jewish women and children had left Ravensbrück 14 months earlier, and my mother and I, 11 months earlier.

We now return to one of the interviews with my mother, in which she is asked whether we had relationships with other prisoners. She answers:

Ekstraktefskrift. $20 \ D \ 43/3/70$

DANSK RØDE KORS.   F o r t r o l i g t.

Ugemeddelelse Nr.7.

12.Marts 1945.

. . . .

. . . .

3. I Koncentrationslejren Ravensbrück.

Nedennævnte danske Statsborgere befinder sig i Koncentra-

tionslejren Ravensbrück, Fürstenberg i Mecklenburg:

Andersen, Lilli	1.8.04	94305
Berg, Else	3. 3.13	94306
Dahl, Karen	21. 3.04	94307
Frederiksen, Gerda	1. 5.24	94308
Hansen-Holm, Dagmar	5.12.01	94309
Hansen, Johanne	12. 6.90	94310
Ibsen, Marianne	14. 1.11	94311
Klitgaard, Kamma	9. 9.12	94313
Jensen, Gerda Eva	9. 7.17	94312
Lauridsen, Else	25. 1.15	94314
Nielsen, Ellen	15.10.88	94315
Smaalann, Annie	22. 9.30	25079
Meyer, Kornelia	6. 8.10	25076
Meyer, Olaf	16.12.40	25078
Meyer, Peter	14. 2.39	25077
Hoffgaard, Karen	12. 9.96	25071
Hoffgaard, Lillian	3.12.20	25072
Hoffgaard, Kate	25.10.28	25073
Katznelson, Rebekka *x)*	26.11.17	25074
Katznelson, Ib	30.10.41	25075
Pedersen, Astrid	18. 1.01	25693
Kristensen, Emma	9. 7.24	19554
Fischer, Hansen	5. 5.24	26110
Døssing, Ellen	29. 8.13	84445
Weng-Seidemann, Anna	5. 8.96	36818
Sandøe, Sunneva	4. 4.98	75510
Storm, Karin	28. 2.04	25068
Sørensen, Klara	2. 3.15	25069
Henriksen, Anna	26. 4.07	25692
Erdmann, Paul Julius	8. 7.20	D8419 Bl. 2 Re
Holmgaard Bergholt, Jørgen	15.12.18	D8502 Bl. Re
Hansen, Børge Stendahl	11.11.14	D8488 Bl. 1 Re
Jacobsen, Henry Werner	12.11.21	76450.

. . . .

. . . .

x) ~~xxxxxx~~ identisk med Karen Emmy

Katznelson f. 20/11 1917, Moder til

Jb Katznelson

On the Red Cross list from 12 March 1945 – almost a year after we came to Theresienstadt –
all the Danish Jews are listed, including my mother and I, who came to Ravensbrück. It
demonstrated some of the difficulties with the registration in the camps, in which were the
Danish prisoners. Such lists were fundamental when the White Buses came to repatriate the
Danish prisoners in late 1944 and 1945.

Yes, we had, in a sense. We could not avoid meeting each other. Some lived close to where we lived and some lived elsewhere. We often saw each other during the day but everyone lived his own life and had enough to do managing the situation.

Life went on and the days passed and we were struggling with all the problems we were facing. It sounds strange, but in a way, we also had a kind of everyday life. However, we also had the great advantage of being Danish and were not selected for transport. But when it happened to other people we were very, very shocked, the mood was depressed and the people in the camp were crying. We gradually got to know other prisoners: Czechs, Germans, Dutch. There was always the risk that they were going to be listed for transport. You might have become friends with someone, and then they had to leave.

I remember our *hausäldeste* [house elder] where we lived. It was an elderly couple, Mr and Mrs Lustig were their names. He was taken out for transport and she was not. I must say it was hard psychologically, very hard, when someone so close to our house was on the list.

Mrs Lustig was an elegant, confident woman. "Ich bin Innenarchitektin", she said. She taught us to put the carpets, we used during the night, together.

Jytte Bornstein, who lived above us in Rathausgasse, also remembered Lily and Karl Lustig. She also described the situation when Karl Lustig was selected for transport. She wrote that "the day he left with his little bundle of luggage, the two small people walked as I had always seen them walking, holding hands. She followed him to the assembly point. She would be with him as long as possible." After the war Jytte received information that upon arrival at Auschwitz, Karl Lustig had been taken straight to the gas chamber.

My mother continued her story and noted that

> ...about the transports, we at least knew that where they were going was worse than Theresienstadt. That there actually were gas chambers. There were rumors about that as well. I remember, it was also bad, it was while I was hospitalized in Hohenelber with Ib, the doctor was taken out for transport. We were in a very large room. We were close to the window. He came from the door and walked through the great hall, slowly shuffling, stooped. He was such a nice man. He came straight to our bed, patted Ib on the head and then left. He definitely knew what was going to happen.

There was another little ... well, she was also a doctor, a female doctor, she was hunchbacked, very deformed. She sang for us occasionally with a voice so wonderful. She had a voice ... even amid all the misery ... I enjoyed hearing her singing. She also went on transport. There were many moving intermezzos, even if we were not directly involved in them. Just knowing that these people disappeared was terrible.

It is important to dwell on these horrific transports. Theresienstadt, which was meant to have less than 10,000 inhabitants, was soon completely over-populated with up to 50,000 prisoners. On average there were 40,000 prisoners in the camp. The process was then that the German leadership of Theresienstadt ordered the *Ältestenrat*, based on certain criteria, to select a certain number of thousands who should be sent in transports to the east, which was certain death.

The criteria could be, for example, 5,000 men aged 18 to 55. The next time it could be the family members of those 5,000; women, children, brothers, sisters, then invalids and the ill, etc.

The *Ältestenrat* was required to make the decision and chose names from family members, friends, acquaintances, or unknown Jews, for the list of those to be led to certain death in the gas chambers of Auschwitz-Birkenau. No wonder that in connection with this unbearable task, a situation arose of increasing bribery as a way to, perhaps, preserve life, if only for a short period.

This usually took place in the middle of the night, when the *hausäldeste* would distribute the list of names. The list was a duplicated note, on which one could read when you had to go on a transport, where and the time by which you had to sign up. The name, address and transport number was on a long yellow strip.

H. G. Adler, who has written the most detailed and comprehensive book available on Theresienstadt, calculated the number of people who came in transports, and how many transports left the camp. The numbers clearly illustrate that Theresienstadt was no more than a transit camp on the way to the killings in Auschwitz-Birkenau. That was a fact, even if the Germans used euphemistic names for Theresienstadt.

1942 first half of the year	16,001 people came in 16 transports
1942 second half of the year	27,870 people came in 19 transports
1943	18,328 people came in 10 transports.
1944	25,995 people came in 18 transports, or, a total of 88,194 people.

Added to this horrible statistic we can add the approximately 34,000 who died in Theresienstadt. All in all the number who did not survive was more than 122,000, of the roughly 155,000 people who at one point or another passed through Theresienstadt.

Approximately 15,000 children under 15 years passed through Theresienstadt. All but about 100 were killed.

There was also a "thinning" of the over-populated city ahead of the Red Cross delegation's visit. Figures for the number of deportees prior to the visit is, in various histories, set between 10,000 and 17,500, depending on from when you count.

Such statistics are horrible. Statistics and counts easily blur the feeling that behind every single number is a person of flesh and blood, people with their own hopes for life, with relationships with parents, spouses, lovers, children, family and friends and acquaintances. At a memorial service Lord Jonathan Sachs, the Commonwealth's former Chief Rabbi, used the image that if one minute of silence were to be kept for each of the 6 million murdered Jews, the silence would last for almost 12 years! It is a powerful illustration of how many 6 million are.

Forty-eight Danish children from infants to 15 year-olds arrived at Theresienstadt, and all survived.

I will not get into speculations about guilt and responsibility, but it is difficult not to note that the Danish cooperation policy helped the Germans, which meant that they did not have to allocate many resources to Denmark, and could use them elsewhere. Furthermore the Red Cross delegation's visit to Theresienstadt to assess the Danish Jew's situation meant that others were sent on transports eastward so that Theresienstadt was not too crowded when the delegation arrived. And as will be recounted, the rescue with the White Buses in late 1944 and 1945 also came at a price for others.

10

A Drawing and the Artist

On 19 February 1945 a pencil drawing of me was made in Theresienstadt. The drawing is now on the wall in my son's home. The Jewish Museum in Copenhagen has a copy of it. "It was a young Dutch girl who made it" my mother told me. The signature on the drawing only shows that it was drawn in Theresienstadt by the RMG.

I have never been particularly interested in the slightly sparse signature, but it's more of the mystery that I look so healthy, which is in stark contrast with the information contained in various medical records about me after the war. The explanation is probably that the artist only had a rather short look at me in February and then made the drawing on the basis of the photo shown in the section "My Mother and my Five Months in Ravensbrück".

At one point I received an email from Silvia Goldbaum Tarabini Fracapane, who had previously received a copy of the drawing. Silvia received a Doctor of Philosophy degree for her dissertation about *Experiences of Persecution, Deportation and Ghetto Life. Danish Testimonies about Theresienstadt*. Silvia wrote that:

> I have found out who made the portrait of you. It's a Dutch artist who I think is still alive. Her name is Rose-Marie Gompertz. After the war she married and her name is now Rose-Marie Sterenberg-Gompertz. I actually have drawings of another child (Rachel Wallach, born in Theresienstadt), also made by her.

I searched online and found Rose-Marie mentioned on a Dutch website for an art gallery in Marum, a small town in the northwestern part of Holland.

I rang her and we had a good conversation. She was naturally very surprised to suddenly to get a call from Denmark about a drawing she had made 68 years ago. She could not remember the actual drawing, nor did she when I sent her a copy of it. She told me that she had been making drawings all her life and that in Theresienstadt she made portraits as soon as she managed to get some paper. Because of the amount of drawing activity, and because it had happened almost 70 years ago, it was no wonder she didn't remember the drawing of me.

We agreed that I should visit her, and in September 2013 my wife and I went to Holland.

Rose-Marie, who was called Riete, had moved to a nursing home in Drachten shortly before our visit. She could hardly see with one eye and only had 30 per cent sight in the other, but even though she was clearly marked by her age, she boldly told us about her experiences in the Dutch resistance movement, until she was arrested and deported to Theresienstadt in the fall of 1944.

We had the opportunity, briefly, to have a look inside her home, which had not yet been packed up. On a shelf in the kitchen was the copy of the portrait of me that I had sent her. It was quite moving to see it there.

She was 93 years old. My mother had always referred to her as a young Dutch girl, but she was only three years younger than my mother. Riete mentioned that for many years after the war she gave talks in schools about her experiences during the war, and there had also been several interviews with her in Dutch newspapers.

She was a warm, lively and charismatic personality that, according to a friend of hers, could have been an angel on Earth, if any such existed.

Riete at the nursing home in 2013. She sits in her wheelchair and looks with a magnifying glass at a copy of the drawing she made in Theresienstadt on 19 February 1945. The drawing can also be seen on the cover of this book. (Private Photo)

In Riete's official documents during the war, she was cataloged as 55 per cent Jew. Her four Jewish grandparents were baptized, and her father had also been baptized as a child. She was also baptized, did not feel Jewish, and did not have much knowledge of Judaism.

Riete belonged to the group of Dutch Christians, who would be referred to as "the baptized Jews" or "Protestant Jews", and for a long time that group was protected in the Netherlands and later in Theresienstadt, from further transports.

The family lived in Naarden before the war. The father was a kind of representative for the baptized Jews in contact with the Jewish Council. As happened to all Jews in Holland, Riete's family was moved to Amsterdam, where it was easier for the occupying power to control the Jews. When her father became ill and died in 1943, her mother lost her protection as a Protestant Jew and was taken to Westerbork.

> **Westerbork** was initially a refugee camp in the Netherlands, where German-Jewish refugees were placed before the war. In July 1942, the camp's status was changed to a transit camp, from where Jews and Gypsies were sent east.

That same year Riete's sister and her husband were arrested by the Dutch security service. They were convinced that their documents were not genuine. The security service contacted the municipality of The Hague, and it was determined that they were 100 per cent Jews. The security service was very proud of this result, which prompted Riete to ask them how much they received in payment per Jew. The answer was 15 guilder (about €130 in 2017 money). They were placed in a theater in Amsterdam, where the Dutch Jews were taken before being transported to Westerbork. However, the Jewish Council managed to smuggle them into a Jewish kindergarten on the other side of the road.

Riete was involved, quite early on, in illegal work, and used the cover name Lisbeth. It was her skill at drawing that was useful. She worked intensively forging papers and passports. She was stopped several times when walking around Amsterdam.

On several occasions she had been shocked to see Jewish families with children being dragged onto the street and detained and had wanted to intervene. She had come to the conclusion, however, that if she did she would have been arrested, and that she was more useful in continuing her secret work.

When she was stopped, she was always saved by having documents proving that she was a Protestant Jew. Once it was close to going all wrong. She had some illegal passports and papers inside her blouse, but she managed to get to a toilet where she tore them all into small pieces and flushed them away.

In April 1944 her group was betrayed, and she was arrested and deported to Westerbork, where her mother also was.

Riete told me that it was a kind of relief to be arrested, making it easier for her to bear the guilt she felt by not helping when children were dragged out onto the street and arrested.

Despite the fact that Westerbork was a concentration camp with all that followed, Riete thought it was going to last. The worst thing was that they often had to say goodbye to someone who was going to be transported to the east. They knew it was serious, but the full consequence was not clear to them.

In September 1944, Riete and her mother, together with approximately 4,900 others, were sent away. The transport was a train intended for animals. During the few days the journey lasted they sometimes got a little water and bread, and there was only one bucket that could be used as a toilet.

In Theresienstadt they were placed in an attic. The beds were made of straw, filled with fleas and lice. She was made to work two eight-hour shifts a day. On one of the shifts, she worked in Glimmer. My aunt Annie also worked in the Glimmer.

Riete did not think that the Germans used the mica for anything. It was just accumulated and stored. Although she may have been on the same shift as my aunt Annie, they probably never had any contact with each other. According to Riete, they lived in very separate groups in Theresienstadt, and she was with the Protestant Jews. She did not have special contact with the Danes. There must have been some contact, because she made that drawing of me.

In her second eight-hour shift, Riete worked with distributing food. She ladled soup into bowls. Sometimes a person did not have a bowl, and they would pour the soup into a bag they had made of newspaper. She smiled when she talked about this work because it allowed her to get some extra food, as there was often something left in the buckets.

Later she loaded boxes of ash onto trolleys. The boxes would then be thrown into the Eger river, a tributary to the Elben river, in order to hide what had happened. There was a name on each box. Thousands of boxes were thrown into Eger. The boxes were carried hand to hand from the trolley to the river. Once, a girl down the line broke down in tears. She had seen a relative's name on a box.

Riete managed to get some paper from the administration, which allowed her to draw portraits. She said there were a lot of writing tools in Theresienstadt. She was not sure if she remembered correctly, but would not rule out that she used some of the tools she had used in her illegal work for drawing at Theresienstadt.

Rite never made drawings to get paid with food or other sought after items, but I wonder if my mother didn't give her a slice of bread for drawing me, even if Riete had not asked for it.

In addition to the drawing of me, some of the drawings of children are kept at the Ghetto Fighters House in Israel. There are also some drawings of Rachel Wallach, privately owned, who was born in Theresienstadt to parents who were deported from Denmark.

Shortly before the liberation, Riete was made to build barracks. She was convinced that their purpose was for gas chambers. Several others corroborated this.

Even though she had no special contact with the Danes, Riete was very much absorbed by the event of the Danes being picked up by the White Buses. She said she was very happy that the Danes could leave and waved goodbye to them. She mentioned a rumor in the camp that one of the buses had been bombed on it's way through Germany.

About three weeks after the Danes left Theresienstadt, the camp was liberated. Riete was still moved by talking about the events shortly before the liberation by the Russians. Towards the end, the Germans brought a steady stream of Jewish prisoners to Theresienstadt from other concentration camps, and they were almost human skeletons. It was impossible to give them injections, as there was hardly any meat between the skin and the bones. She was also very malnourished and had typhus.

Riete said that she would never forget that period, even though she was never beaten or tortured and had not seen anyone else treated that way. "Many others experienced much worse things than me" she said. "I was lucky but I have to be honest. I was a coward and I did not take any risks."

She was convinced she did not end up in Auschwitz because she belonged to the group of Protestant Jews. And she was convinced that if the war had lasted a little longer they would all have ended up in the gas chambers. Riete died on 30 December 2014. 107,000 Dutch Jews were deported to the concentration camps. Only 5,000 survived. Less than 5 per cent. The Netherlands had the highest death rate of Jews in Western Europe.

11

The White Buses – The Myth that is Hard to Knock Down

It was in light of the imminent German collapse that both Danish and Norwegian officials, by the end of 1944, started to consider how it would be possible to bring Danish and Norwegian concentration camp prisoners home from Germany.

The very dismal picture towards the last months of the war include, among other things, comments from Hitler made at a secret cabinet meeting on 24 February 1945. According to the Free German press service in Stockholm, Hitler told Himmler, at that meeting, that on his specific orders, all prisoners in labor camps, prisons and in concentration camps should be murdered.

Himmler, however, was playing a double game. He was interested in establishing contact with the Western Allies, through Sweden if possible, to agree on a separate peace agreement to save Germany from total defeat.

Several months before the cabinet meeting in February Himmler stopped deportations to Auschwitz and, behind Hitler's back, had given instructions to cease the definitive eradication of the Jews, and that approximately 600,000 Jews should be released and taken to Switzerland. Part of a deal was that Germany would get trucks and tractors.

In January 1945 an agreement was made that 1,200 prisoners were to be released and transferred to Switzerland every other week, and that 5 million Swiss francs would be transferred to a Swiss bank after each transport.

The first 1,200 were transferred from Theresienstadt to Switzerland on 7 February 1945. It could not be kept secret, and coverage of it in the Swiss newspapers, stating that the deal had been concluded, was not completely accurate. Hitler was furious when he learned about what had happened and all further releases were stopped. German radio announced on 16 March that all Jews should be murdered.

The first Danish transport of prisoners from the concentration camps took place in December 1944, when the prisoners from Buchenwald were taken to the Camp at Frøslev[1]. The benevolent attitude of the Germans only allowed the prisoners to be taken to the camp at Frøslev. These transports were planned and implemented entirely by Danish efforts.

On the Swedish side Count Folke Bernadotte was given complete responsibility for Swedish rescue operations in Germany. He therefore became a key figure in the many negotiations with the Germans about the possibility of getting the prisoners home.

Count Folke Bernadotte was the Swedish king's nephew and had many high level contacts. He was self-assured, a good dealmaker, and was gifted linguistically, achieving fluency in English, German and French. In 1943 he became Vice-President of the Swedish Red Cross, and when the president, his uncle Prince Carl, surpassed 80 years old, it was natural that Bernadotte became the operational leader of the Red Cross's activities.

The myth about Bernadotte and the transport of the Danish Jews in the White Buses has been alive since the end of World War II, and probably still is.

The concept of the White Buses in the postwar era has often become a sort of synonym with the home transport of the Danish Jews from

My mother in front of one of the White Buses. It was placed in Ravensbrück in connection with the celebration of the 50th anniversary of the camp's liberation in 1995. (Still image from film. Private photo)

After the war, my mother sent flowers to Count Folke Bernadotte as a thank you for our rescue with the White Buses. She later received this thank-you card from him.

Theresienstadt, although the White Buses also brought a significant number of the other Danish and Norwegian prisoners home.

After the war, in gratitude of our return home with the White Buses, my mother sent flowers to Folke Bernadotte, who acknowledged it with a thank-you card for her on which he had written: *Thank you very much for the beautiful flowers. I send my best wishes for a Happy New Year. (Signed) F Bernadotte*

On 9 April 2005, the Danish Queen was invited to a memorial in the Swedish Gustav Church in Copenhagen, to mark the 65th anniversary of the German occupation of Denmark. The Bernadotte action with the White Buses was at the center of the event. My mother was also invited. She proudly gave the Swedish ambassador a book I had written to my children in 2003, in which there was also a picture of Bernadotte's thank-you card. What she had forgotten was that my description of the White Buses in the book was based on Johannes Holm's book *Sandheden om De Hvide Busser (The Truth about the White Buses)*. That description completely peels away the myth of Bernadotte and the Jews' transport home from Theresienstadt.

That present to the ambassador was perhaps not particularly well placed, but in light of the historian and lecturer at the University of Gothenburg, Sune Persson's lecture at the event, in which he stated that Denmark's role in the rescue campaign was far greater than previously assumed, the present was perhaps not as awkward as I immediately imagined.

This book is primarily about my family's arrest and deportation. That is why it is ours and the other Danish Jews' rescue from "Hitler's Hell" that should be the focus of this chapter.

It would be too simplistic not to mention that there were many other Danish prisoners in the concentration camps, about 5,500, and it would be unreasonable not to mention the efforts that Folke Bernadotte made in connection with the transport of these prisoners, even though it did not directly lead to the rescue of the Danish Jews and, incidentally, came at great cost to other prisoners.

We will take a closer look at this before returning to my parents' report of what happened when the White Buses lined up in Theresienstadt on 13 April 1945 and on how they experienced the home transport.

The evaluations of Bernadotte's efforts have been very varied. Only six weeks after the end of the war he published his book *Last Days of the Reich: The Diary of Count Folke Bernadotte*, which was translated into several languages. In the book he describes his actions in an immodest way, and recounts the international praise for his efforts.

A couple of years passed and a new book was published which completely removed the halo from Bernadotte. The author was Felix Kersten from Estonia, who was Himmler's indispensable private doctor and masseur. He was a kind of go-between for Himmler and Bernadotte during the negotiations about the relocation of the prisoners from the camps. In his memories from 1947, he emphasizes his own significant role in the operation of the White Buses and rates Bernadotte's role very negatively. The well-known English historian H.R. Trevor-Roper, who in 1947 was famous for his book *The Last Days of Hitler*, picked up the thread from Kerstin, whom he gave credit for the success of the rescue operation, mentioning Bernadotte as a "transport officer, no more". He also suggested that Bernadotte refused to bring the Danish Jews to Sweden.

That prompted the Swedish Ministry of Foreign Affairs to publish a press release stating that it was Bernadotte and nobody else who led the operations in 1945, and that Swedish officials, who had been present at the negotiations with the Germans, had witnessed Bernadotte's tremendous interest in rescuing as many Jews as possible from Germany to Sweden.

The Danish doctor Johannes Holm wrote *Sandheden om De Hvide Busser* (*The Truth about the White Buses*) in 1984. The reason was that Frants Hvass, who in 1945 became Permanent Secretary of the Ministry of Foreign Affairs, had invited all who held leading positions in "The Danish Relief Corps" to a private dinner. It was the first and only time that they all met after accomplishing the rescue of prisoners from the camps. They agreed that the Swedes ought to be accorded a good deal of goodwill, especially Bernadotte personally, concerning the implementation of the rescue transports. They agreed that no one in the Relief Corps would attempt to demystify what had happened. They would keep their mouths shut about what had happened in the spring of 1945. That agreement was kept until 1984, when Holm wrote his book.

In his book Holm explains what really happened, when it comes to the myth of Bernadotte's efforts to rescue the Danish Jews.

Sune Persson, who emphasized the Danish effort in his lecture at the Swedish church, wrote *Vi Åker till Sverig: De Vita Bussarna 1945* (*We Are Going to Sweden: The White Buses 1945*) in 2002. It was an attempt to clarify all the circumstances surrounding the rescue operation. He wrote that the criticism of Bernadotte was unreasonable, and that it was Bernadotte personally who was the undisputed leader of the entire operation. It was Bernadotte who led the crucial negotiations with the German leaders and that he was the one who conveyed Himmler's offer of a separate German surrender on the western front. However, the context here is the rescue operations in general, not the special action to get the Danish Jews home from Theresienstadt.

The book was published in English in 2009 and contains new material in relation to the 2002 edition. The book is called *Escape from the Third Reich: Folke Bernadotte and the White Buses*. The British author and former senior diplomat at the United Nations, Brian Urquhart, wrote in the preface to the English edition that Persson's conclusions come as close as we can get to providing a correct and fair representation of this famous and unique humanitarian operation.

One can really question that statement. Among other things, I have found several factual errors in the book about the Danish Jews in Theresienstadt. Furthermore, it would be quite strange if on this issue, of all issues, we would now know the definitive truth and interpretation of such complicated events.

Persson's analyses have been the subject of serious criticism by other researchers. The historian Ingrid Lomfors has, among other things, emphasized that there was a lot of silence about a very dark, seamy side in the relief efforts. "There was a barter of human life" she says, claiming that the White Buses were offered to the Germans for their use at the end of March 1945, in order to forcefully move 2,000 French, Russian and Polish prisoners from Neuengamme to Braunschweig, to make room for Danish and Norwegian prisoners. The commander of Neuengamme, Max Pauly, wanted the weakest prisoners taken away from the camp before the Allies reached it.

The move ended in a humanitarian disaster, because those who were moved were the most vulnerable in the camp. This piece does not fit into the Swedish history's heroic picture, says Ingrid Lomfors. She also claims that until the end of the war Bernadotte was involved in the bartering of human life and that the government in Stockholm gave directives on which prisoners of this or that nationality should be brought to safety in Sweden.

Heated discussions often end with declarations painted in black or white.

To get a better understanding of what happened, it may be useful to quote a passage from the historian Hans Kirchhoff's book *Holocaust in Denmark*. He describes the events in this way:

> The episode caused turmoil at that time, but it's ethical and moral dilemma was then forgotten and was well hidden in the national narrative. Lomfors asks indignantly the question of whether the Swedish Red Cross became SS's opponent or helper? The answer must be both yes and no, as is often the case when dealing with evil. And then you might ask if the alternative to following the commander had been to stop the whole action!

Just a couple of years before Persson's book was published, Lomfors and Persson were in heated debate. Persson held the view that it was more important to note what Bernadotte actually did than the perception about his motives during his many discussions with the Nazis.

There were Danish non-Jewish prisoners in Buchenwald, Neuengamme, Sachsenhausen, Ravensbrück, Dachau, Mauthausen and several other camps. In each case difficult negotiations took place with the Germans to get permission to take the prisoners out of the camps. People higher up in the hierarchy often held different positions on these issues than officials in the lower echelons. The disputes between the SS and the Gestapo did not make it easier for the operations to be approved.

The situation during the period from the first transports home in December 1944 until April 1945 was both kaleidoscopic and chaotic, with disputes between Swedes and Danes as well.

The logistics were also difficult. Transport equipment and personnel were needed and not least people who were willing to drive through a Germany on the edge of collapse, with bombed cities, broken roads and constant bombing from the Allied forces.

The Soviet troops moved forward from the East and approached Berlin rapidly. The Allied forces moved forward from the West, crossed the Elbe river, and established a bridgehead less than 125 kilometers from Berlin. At

Dresden there was only approximately 80 kilometers between the two fronts and at Berlin, only about 100 kilometers. There were extensive daytime and nighttime air bombardments.

It was through that narrow corridor that our transport from Theresienstadt had to go.

The fishermen's efforts to bring the Jews to Sweden in October 1943 was naturally focused on after the war. They, as well as all the many other helpers in the rescue operations in October 1943, deserve all the honors and thanks they have been given. On the other hand, it is as if the hundreds of people, be it drivers, car repairers, nurses, dispatch riders and other assistants, who put themselves at great risk to get prisoners out of the concentration camps in the last months of the war, have not been granted a similar place in history. They are not to be forgotten.

Johannes Holm, who played a central role in the planning and execution of the home transport, writes that the myth should be disclosed, and that we should expand our thanks for our home transport from Theresienstadt. He also writes that it was largely credited to a small group of Danish officials headed by the Permanent Secretary of the Social Affairs Ministry Hans Henrik Koch, that the attempt to get us home was made.

The castle in Friedrichsruhe became a sort of collection point, depot and starting point for transports to the concentration camps in Germany. It is located 30 kilometers southeast of Hamburg and was owned by Otto von Bismarck, who was married to a school mate of Folke Bernadotte.

During the last hair-raising days before the final decision was taken to bring the Jews home and obtain the necessary permits from the Germans, Hans Sode-Madsen wrote that on 8 April, in the Swedish camp, it seemed as if there was no plan to bring the Jews home from Theresienstadt. On the Danish side it was considered important that the Jews were taken out of the camp, and it was made clear to the Swedes that it was a matter of urgency, because the battles in Germany made the "corridor", through which our transport had to travel, narrower by the day.

Bernadotte stated that he discussed the transport of Danish Jews with SS brigadier Walter Schellenberg, who told him that because of resistance in the RSHA, an attempt to get the Jews out would have a negative impact on the transports of other Scandinavian prisoners.

Folke Bernadotte gave in to the German argument. The Swedish Ministry of Foreign Affairs also believed that it was too risky to try and bring the Jews home from Theresienstadt. The assessment also allegedly concluded that the distance to Theresienstadt was longer than for most of the transports that had previously been carried out, and that the 'corridor' through Germany had become much narrower.

In this context, it should also be noted that the historian Trevor-Roper, who, in connection with a new version of Kersten's memoir from 1956, maintained his previous accusations against Bernadotte, but now in a somewhat milder form. He admitted that there was no basis for believing that Bernadotte was anti-Semitic, but that he had used anti-Semitic language in his refusal to get the Jews home from Theresienstadt.

Much has been said, negatively, about Bernadotte's attitude towards bringing us home from the concentration camp, as well as about his motives. It is not well documented that Bernadotte had such distasteful motives, and it is obvious that he and the Swedish Ministry of Foreign Affairs had a point. A transport to Theresienstadt was significantly more complicated than any of the others, both because of the long distance to Theresienstadt and because the Germans offered much greater resistance when it came to the release of Jews, rather than of non-Jews.

According to Johannes Holm, the Danish camp was dismayed by Bernadotte's and the Swedish Ministry of Foreign Affairs' decision, and in a state of desperation it was decided, if needed, to make a purely Danish transport. Unfortunately, the crucial permission by the Gestapo in Berlin was still missing. Johannes Holm, who in Friedrichsruhe was the representative of the Danish Health Authority, and a helpful Obersturmbannführer Rennau, who was Himmler's liaison officer in Friedrichsruhe, went to Berlin to solve the problems.

Thanks to a persistent effort, whose main ingredients were food, cigarettes and schnapps in abundant quantities, the necessary papers were obtained. In addition to the immense relief of the Danes, it was one thing as to what Bernadotte and the Foreign Ministry in Stockholm considered to be diplomatically wise, and something else as to what the Friedrichsruhe action group decided to do.

One problem was that the Danish equipment was not in a good enough condition to safely drive approximately 2,000 kilometers to and from Theresienstadt. The result was that the transport was carried out with Swedish equipment, Swedish management, and a combined Swedish-Danish crew.

Hans Sode-Madsen wrote that when the buses and trucks passed by the castle in Friedrichruhe, there was a telephone call from the Swedish Ministry of Foreign Affairs with an order to stop the expedition. Arvid Richert, the Swedish ambassador to Berlin, now stationed in Friedrichruhe, answered coldly that this was not possible, as the column was already on its way, which was a white lie. Captain Harald Folke who was the leader of the column, was ordered to proceed immediately.

There is slightly conflicting information about the number and type of vehicles involved. One of the prisoners mentioned in his description that it was a column consisting of 35 buses, a truck with gasoline drums, 2 motorcycles, a field kitchen, a caravan to transport the sick and a 72-man crew. Hans Sode-Madsen claims there were 23 buses, 6 trucks, a field kitchen, a rolling workshop, a crane car, 3 passenger cars and 3 motorcycles, all gas driven.

Whether one or the other statement is correct, it illustrates that it was quite an extensive column that was going to drive through an area of intense bombings from allied aircraft. There was no guarantee that the aircraft would avoid hitting a bus, even if it had a white roof with a red cross painted on it. And with a truck carrying gasoline, an air attack could have been catastrophic.

Friediger tells that on 13 April he was asked to the *Kommandantur* together with the *Judenälteste*. "With my heart up in my throat, I went up to the *Kommandantur*. There were three gentlemen there: the commander, a higher SS officer and an unknown man in a dark blue uniform."

In relation to the myth about Bernadotte's efforts in rescuing the Danish Jews, it is interesting that Friediger, in an interview after the war, said that Holm said that he had come on behalf of Bernadotte. In his book from 1986, Johannes Holm wrote about the exactly same event that he told Friediger that he was representing Deputy Permanent Secretary Hvass and thus the Danish Ministry of Foreign Affairs.

How did my parents experience the event? My mother's story also starts on 13 April. "I heard about the White Buses for the first time on the day we had to pack. There was excitement in our group. People came running and said: 'There are some buses, we're going home, we're going home'. Of course, at first one didn't believe it. But gradually the whole ghetto was in excitement."

As explained, my grandfather was very careful with his work as a shoemaker. He was a man who was proud of his craft. For my grandfather it did not matter if he made boots for the Germans. It just had to be excellent craftsmanship.

My father recounted that he rushed to my grandfather and told him that he should drop everything, "we're going home". No way. My grandfather wanted to finish his job!

My mother continued saying:

> First, we were very unhappy that we had to leave all the others behind. What would happen to them now? All the other prisoners said: "Now our security is leaving because the Danes were our security". There was also some trade in food going on between the prisoners. We don't have potatoes so they got some of our sausages or something, and then we got their potatoes. We exchanged that way. And one had a really

good friend he or she got some food once in a while, a piece of bread with sausage. It was to the benefit of the whole ghetto that the Danes got packages.

As we were leaving our rooms, windows and doors were besieged with people who wanted some of what we were leaving behind. Things were also handed out. It was difficult ... it was very sad to leave the ghetto and see all the people who were left behind standing and waving. It was very moving. I remember I cried bitterly.

We were waiting two days at the Jäger barracks where bunk beds were set up. The buses had difficulties in getting through. The war was about to end. In the morning we were registered. The first thing they said to us when we got into the bus was: "We must hurry up because the Russians and Americans are meeting, so the war is just over our heads. There is no time to waste".

But one thing the Germans ordered was that there should be curtains for the windows. We were not allowed to take them away. We were not allowed to look out when we drove through Germany, which we of course did. It was a horrible sight.

Then we went into these White Buses. It was just paradise. It was difficult to imagine that we were going home. The drivers were Swedish. They had chocolate and cigarettes. There were Swedish drivers who were completely fearless and carefree. We still had some fear in our minds, however, but suddenly we saw these German officers who were now completely different, more human. I'm pretty sure that they wished to leave with us.

The young Swedish drivers wanted to get something from Theresienstadt. They got a yellow star, the ones we had to wear on our clothes, and then we got a piece of chocolate. My sister Annie had a broach made in Theresienstadt and she gave it away for a piece of chocolate. She was annoyed about it ever since.

Sven Meyer said that the house elder came with a list of the names of those who should go to the *Schleuse*. On the list were only the names of Corrie, Peter and Olaf. Sven's name was not on the list and in order to get that sorted out he went to the administration in Theresienstadt. He said that there was obviously a specific order that those from Sachsenhausen were not included in those who were about to go home. He then contacted Friediger who apparently "fought like a lion" to solve Sven's problem and he ended up getting the permission.

It is unclear what my father did, who was in the same situation as Sven. What he said was: "I was not supposed to go home. They closed the last door [it is not clear whether it was in the barracks or if it was on the bus] and then I jumped into the car in which there were only two Germans. It was the caravan for supply stuff."

His story 50 years after the event is probably not completely correct. Silvia Goldbaum Tarabini Fracapane believes that he was in the last carriage with the others who did not have Danish transport numbers and the foreign women who were married to men in the Danish group. It is also a bit difficult to imagine that he could just jump into a car and then be allowed to get out of Theresienstadt. Had it been so easy, how could one prevent other prisoners from doing the same?

The trip to Denmark was through Dresden, Potsdam, Kyritz, Pritzwalk and Schwerin.

They were all looking out of the windows of the bus, even though it had been forbidden to do so. My mother continues: "Everything was rubble, everything. Miserable people. Someone spat at the bus as it went by. It was a long trip. It was also strenuous. In the buses everyone was stuffed into limited space. So some had to sit on the benches in the middle, benches without back rest. It was hard because the trip took 5 days. So from time to time we had to change seats in order to get a back rest."

Was it the pain of driving for so long or failing memory after the many years that passed which made the trip a little longer in my mother's mind than it actually was? The departure from Theresienstadt was on 15 April, and at 7 a.m. on 17 April, the buses crossed the Danish border.

She continues:

> At night we had to lay down on the ground in a forest while the canons thundered over our heads and the ground wobbled. Everything was chaos around us. We could not continue until everything had "calmed down".
>
> The next day we continued toward Denmark. We came to Padborg and were received with porridge oats and got a shower. People there were sweet, loving and kind to us. I was so dirty that the soap foam was dark brown when it ran down from me.'
>
> After a few hours of rest the column continued to Åbenrå, where we got lunch packages and milk from the Red Cross. The trip continued to Haderslev, Kolding and Odense. Here we had dinner, and we stayed overnight as well.
>
> I was in a clean bed with my boy next to me. I think that would be the happiest day of my life.
>
> The next morning on 18 April, we continued to Copenhagen, where we arrived at noon.

Driving through Denmark was really a triumphal trip. People were standing on the streets. They waved Dannebrog flags[2]. They shouted welcome and where do you come from, have you really been so far away? They were such happy moments. One had a lump in the throat all the way. We were not allowed to stay in Denmark because the war was still not over. We came to Sweden where there was a bit of confusion. The Swedes did not really have control over the situation.

Then a person came along. They called him "Landfiskalen". He said, and our nerves were a little upside down, "Now you have to take it easy because you are in Sweden". And happily we were.'

Before moving on to our stay in Tylösand, Sweden, let us just hear how the now 15 year-old Annie Smaalann experienced coming back and being reunited with her mother. She was disappointed when she came to Malmö because none of her family members were at the quayside, and no one could give her information about them. A little later, however, her mother and grandfather appeared.

She was taken to Strängnäs in Sweden. In the beginning, her relationship with her mother was problematic. "A little girl was sent away and a grown up returned home. My mother could not figure it out", she said. She went on saying that she was "dragged around" even if all she wanted was to be allowed to be alone. "Misunderstood kindness", she says.

Notes

1   The camp at Frøslev was in the Southern part of Jutland not far from the German border.
2   Dannebrog is the name of the Danish flag.

12

Beginning a New Ordinary Life

Tylösand

> We were taken to different places. Families were split up. Some came to one place and others to another place. Well it really didn't matter. At some point we would get together again. I came with my boy, my sister and my mother-in-law to a seaside hotel called Tylösand. It was closed for the winter. We were accommodated into some small barracks buildings on the grounds. We had our meals at the hotel.

The confusion resulted in my father ending up in Strängnäs, a camp barracks in the middle of the countryside not far from Stockholm.

On 4 May the message came that Denmark was a free country again.

My mother said that

> The message was heard on the radio from BBC while we were all gathered in the large dining room at the hotel. Everyone was sitting with their ears close to the radio. Everyone was happy and dancing happily.
>
> But I was not. I was so sad thinking of all that had happened. My mind was full of thoughts of that. I was not part of that joy. I really was not. I felt that everything had been so terrible, so I could not feel any ... of course it was wonderful that there was now peace. I was away from home and my mother was at home and my sister. But of course it was good to come home again.

A further impression of her mood comes from the letter she wrote to my grandmother on 7 May:

> Dear little mother.
> I am sitting here in my room and think of you and all my loved ones in Denmark today when the war is finally over. It is impossible to understand that we soon will see you again and that I can now write

a proper letter for you – not just 30 words every second month on an open card.

Yes, there will be something to talk about once we get home. We have seen and experienced so much that it is unbelievable that we are still alive. I have my own private little story with Ib. We were left alone in a concentration camp in Germany for 5 months and arrived as the last Danes at Theresienstadt. Both of us were seriously ill but due to the Danish and Swedish packages we both got better again in the course of the summer. Yes, I've actually put on more weight than at home. The climate down there was very healthy when we left.

On 13 April it was already a beautiful summer. It was really a day, can you imagine, when we got the message to pack. We were so paralyzed that we could not even be really happy. It all happened over the course of two hours and even if we had talked about how it would be if we ever would come home we could not understand it when it really happened. The journey home was an adventure and the reception in Denmark no less, especially in Jutland. People were throwing flowers, chocolate and cigarettes into the windows of the buses. The Dannebrog was everywhere and everyone shouted "Welcome home to Denmark". Believe me it went straight to the heart and it was painful to leave Copenhagen, but it was probably the best for us. It was not without pain to live in Denmark, I can understand.

Now that we listen to the radio and read newspapers for the first time in 18 months, we can gradually get a sense of the situation that has become quite different in the 1½ years we have been away. Now we are in quarantine in a magnificent hotel near Gothenburg, "Tylosand Havbad" where we are having a good time. However, it was not good that Malmö organized it so badly that several families were split up. Half of us had to go to a camp near Stockholm and now Max and my father-in-law are there while my mother-in-law, father, Annie, Ib and I are here in Tylosand, but now we are hopefully becoming truly free people and can enjoy it together.

How is Lea and Børge's boy doing? I hope it was not anything serious with him. You can believe Annie and I am excited to see him. He will be a real playmate for Ib. He often speaks about you mother and he has repeatedly said "Was it my grandmother who ran after the bus in Denmark". Now he speaks Danish but last year he could only speak

German. He had been in the hospital for so long that he could not understand what we said to him as only German and Czech were spoken.

I could continue page after page but I will finish now and if you will write to me mother, then send the letter to Marie Aizen[1], Göteborgsvägen, Alingsås, for we will probably not be here much longer.

Now many loving greetings and kisses to you little mother, Lea, Børge, their boy, Mr and Mrs Petersen and everybody we know from father, Annie, my mother-in-law, Ib and yours Karen

On the reverse side there was a PS.

PS. I would have had Annie to write a few words on this side but now I hear she has cycled to the city, even if it is forbidden, but the soldiers have left their guard and several of the young people have taken advantage of it. Here the shops are full of light and there is delicious chocolate, real cacao, lots of American movies and so on. It is like coming to a wonderland after the mess we have lived in. We all need to let ourselves go. Annie is probably in the cinema today. She has met a young man, a cook from the hotel, a Swede, and she has had all nationalities. Germans, Czechs, Dutch, Danes, Swedes. She is going from one to the other but that is probably not very serious. We have so often talked, Annie and I, mostly in the W.C. – it was the only place we were alone. So often we said to each other: "God knows what they are doing at home now. Are they in Toftegaards bio[2] tonight or are they sitting and having coffee together?" It was so strange to think that life was on its normal course and we were so far apart. Well, Annie must write a letter herself to you mother as I now will post this letter to you. Let us soon get together.

Even if I had been close to dying in the camps another dramatic episode occurred in Tylösand.

'One day something happened. It nearly went wrong once again for Ib. I had borrowed an electric heater, a small one, which was standing at the end of the bed. Next to us was a woman with her children. And then there was a little playmate playing with Ib in our room while I was up getting food. I had barricaded the bed so he could not fall out.

I had put a chair outside the bed. When I got home I heard crying. I said "Why are you crying?" I opened the door. The duvet was filled with smoke. There was fire in the bed and he could not get out because of the chair I had placed. The carpets at the end of the bed were both smoldering and burning.

I dropped the tray with food and everything and got him out. I asked "how did this happen?", I asked him, "who's been in here, what

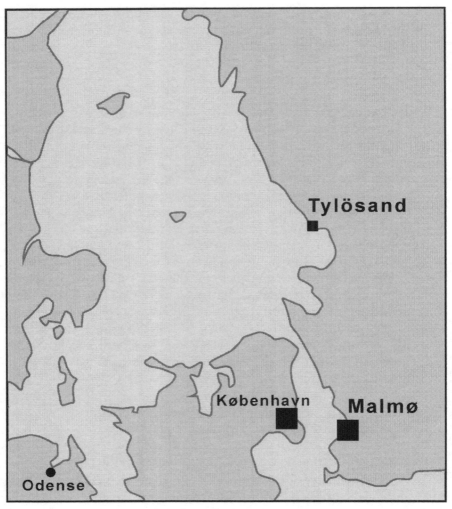

Map with Tylösand marked. The White Buses brought us to Sweden where we stayed at the Tylösand seaside hotel.

happened?" He just smiled and shook his head. I did not really get anything out of him.

So of course I removed the heater when I left the room. I still had to have him lying in bed. I did not dare to say anything about it at the hotel. I was afraid ... yes I do not know what would have happened ... but they would probably have been quite upset. We might not have had any other blankets. What do I know? We did not talk about it at all.

It was difficult to get the permission to go home. The Swedes would not really let us go. We were quarantined. We were tested for diseases and for vermin and so on. It took 6 weeks before we were allowed to go home. Finally we got the permission and then the journey had come to an end and a new life was about to begin. We had to reestablish our home and find some work. We were well aware that Denmark had had a hard time, but our time in the misery was at least over.

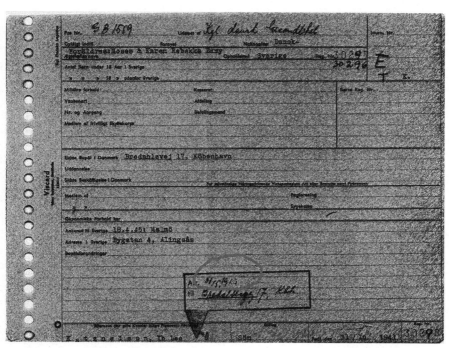

Document from the Danish Legation in Sweden with the mark of my departure from Sweden on 31 May 1945.

On 20 April 1945, a note was filed in the Ministry of Foreign Affairs stating that Moses Katznelson, Karen Emmy Katznelson and Ib Katznelson had been transferred to Sweden on 18 April 1945 and that their relatives had been informed via the Danish Red Cross.

From the central register of the Danish Refugee Administration in Sweden, documents were issued for my parents, myself, my grandparents and my aunt about our departure from Sweden on 31 May 1945. It is also clear from the documents that at the time of our return we stayed with my father's sister and brother in Alingsås. They managed to escape to Sweden in October 1943. Our return was to our address before the arrest, Bredahlsvej 17, Copenhagen.

After the War

In the *Schleuse* in Theresienstadt on 25 April 1944, my mother had to hand over her rings and 38.88 kroner. A formal receipt was signed by both a SS-Obersturmführer and an SS-Hauptscharführer. It is really amazing that she got the rings back after the war via the Ministry of Foreign Affairs.

Our apartment on Bredahlsvej was totally in order when we came back. When we went underground in October 1943 my parents had given the keys to some friends. They had rented the apartment out to a wholesale meat dealer in Copenhagen. He had his own house but did not want to live there because he had to heat it up with peat which he did not want to do. When the war was over he moved out and back to his own house and we were able move into our own flat.

Then ordinary days began again, so much so that when my mother went down to the kiosk on the corner, the first thing the man said was that my mother had an unpaid bill of 18 kroner!

A somewhat tragic-comic remark was also made by my aunt when my mother, some days later, went to the cinema with her. She had not been in Theresienstadt. Their tickets were cut by the man at the front door, which made my aunt say: "Imagine, he has been standing here and cutting tickets for 1½ years, while you've gone through all that."

The liberation government, formed immediately after the end of the war, was quick in making decisions. Mogens Fog, who had been a prominent member of the resistance movement, became Minister for Special Affairs. He tabled a bill already in September 1945 about compensation to the victims of the occupation.

The bill, which came into force on the 1 October 1945 provided for compensation to Danish citizens who "have suffered injuries or sickness whereby their business capacity is temporarily or permanently deteriorated ... "

It does not seem obvious that I, as a 4 year-old, could get some compensation according to that law, but at least it was based on that law that my parents had me medical examined. The first medical report about me after the war is from January 1946, and it is based on some medical examinations from June 1945.

The doctor found visible signs of an encapsulated double-sided tuberculosis, that I was not quite healthy, and that I should still be under medical observation, especially to keep an eye on the pulmonary tuberculosis. There were also a number of other observations from the study that are not completely legible and very "medical", but my health situation was not good.

It was also requested that my parents get a statement from a former co-prisoner confirming my stay both in Ravensbrück and Theresienstadt.

In addition to the more official medical examinations, I was also frequently seeing doctors because of my general weakness. On one of the occasions I saw a pediatrician who treated me quite rudely. When my mother remarked that I was not well and that I had gone through so much, he replied that there were also many Danish children (I was Danish!) that had had hard times. He pricked my ear without any warning to take a blood test, causing me to spontaneously kick him in the crotch and say "fuck you". It led to a hard slapping in my face. I fell and hit some test tubes which fell on the floor. The nurse who was about to pick them up, was told she should not do it as "the mother should pick everything up".

As my mother said, by the autumn of 1945 I had learned a lot of bad Danish words, although my language was still characterized by both German and Czech, which had been the languages I had been surrounded by.

I was perceived to be malnourished and weak to such an extent that in 1946, 1947 and 1948 I was admitted, each time for three months, to Princess Margaretha's Kystanatorium,[3] not far from Hornbæk.

I have my first memories from these stays. The treatment at the sanatorium had probably consisted of fresh air and good, nutritious food. A single event, however, about the food, made its mark on me.

I remember the junket. I would not eat it. I simply could not get it down. We children sat in a giant room in a semi-circle and ate while the foster mother[4] was sitting at a kind of teacher's desk to monitor if we were eating everything. I did not. So when the other children were allowed to go out I was placed in the middle of the big room all alone, with the foster mother sitting there a step above the floor where I was sitting. I was forced to sit there until the junket was eaten.

Since then, I have been largely unable to eat and drink milk products.

A few years ago I was in Hornbæk to have a look at the sanatorium where I spent three months of my childhood on three separate occasions. The huge room was not very big. It was actually quite small. But of course a child does not have the same perception of size as an adult. The room had grown bigger and bigger in my memory.

I still remember my despair during the first evening meal at Hans and Margrethe Moes, the forest ranger at Kalø, whom I mentioned in the Prologue. Before I left home that summer in 1949, I had been told by my parents, in detail, how to behave. And whatever I was served I should be grateful for. Basta!

By my plate on that very first evening meal was a very large glass of milk. What to do? To me it was like a glass of medicine, and medication that tastes badly you try to take it in as quickly as possible. And that was what I did with that glass of milk. I drank it in one gulp. The effect was catastrophic or at least I felt it that way. Sweet Margrethe said that she could see that I really liked milk and poured a new even bigger glass up for me.

Since that time, knowledge and a sense of education has fortunately developed. Why was it me, at the sanatorium, who was asked to sit at the bedside of a very ill little girl, and was asked to sing the song "In a Bed at the Hospital"? I do not know.

It is a song that can be sung in a very, very sad way. The origin of the song is unclear, but it may have been written in 1903 by a nurse at the Blegdam Hospital's tuberculosis ward, after one of her patients died. I still remember the melody and the first verse, and the episode is still clear in my mind:

> In a hall in the hospital,
> where the white beds are,
> was a little weak-chested girl
> ill and pale with golden hair.

The evenings and nights at the sanatorium were both the best and the worst for me. When I lay under the duvet entirely alone, I felt protected in a way from the wickedness of this world. But at the same time I remember the wind's whistling in the plantation between the sanatorium and the sea. It provoked a strong longing for my parents from whom, as in the time in Ravensbrück, I was once again separated from. It was scary and creepy. Even today I can recall the sound and the feeling.

The economic situation during my childhood was tight, and it wasn't logistically or economically easy for my parents to visit me at the sanatorium.

I actually have no recollection that they ever came. But I remember that my uncle Bernhard came. It was he who managed to escape from Gestapo on Amager Strandvej when we were arrested on 4 October 1943. On Sundays all the children at the sanatorium went to the fence, close to the road outside. There they could see when their relatives came to visit.

I was there as well, Sunday after Sunday. At least that's how I remember it, although every Sunday was probably not a visiting day.

One Sunday when all the children had been reunited with their visitors, I was left at the fence completely on my own and outside the fence was a man. He was also alone. It was my uncle Bernhard. I could not recognize him nor he me.

I have a note from the Central Office for Special Affairs for Greater Copenhagen. It was the institution that took care of the victims from the war. The note shows that in August 1947 my father received 340 kroner to cover convalescence, board and travel expenses. It is also clear from the note that the amounts (there were also other amounts than the 340 kroner) also included me. I guess that the 315 kroner for convalescence and the 23.70 kroner, generously rounded up to 340 kroner, concerned me. So maybe my parents had visited me, even though I have no memory of it.

The correspondence with *Direktoratet for Ulykkesforsikring* [5] continues: 1945, 1946, 1947, 1948, 1949 ....

In March 1949, the Directorate wrote to my parents that they wanted to have me (once again) medically examined by the pediatrician Axel Friedlænder.

That was definitely too much for my mother. She replied (with emphasis) that she absolutely did not want to see Dr. Friedlænder again, and that the Directorate previously had said that they would decide on the matter regardless of having received her personal remarks about the state of my health. She, like Dr. Friedlænder, had lost patience with the eternal writing and writing during almost four years, and that she would have the issue settled now regardless of the outcome.

Of all days, the rejection of her request for compensation for me was on the date of liberation – 4 May 1949.

My whole childhood was clearly influenced by the events during my first years of life. I was in no way to get too far away from home. It was only because of an extremely strong effort from my class teacher in elementary school that was I able to continue in year 6 in a gymnasium as far as 7 kilometers away from home, and not in the school on the other side of the street.

The same protective thinking was probably behind the fact that I think I got the shortest possible religious preparation for my bar mitzvah.[6] The preparation took place "in the center of Copenhagen" far away from home! Nor should I speak too much about getting a Jewish education. And I should not mention that I had been in a concentration camp.

The tense day, at least for me, was the Sabbath closest to my 13th birthday, according to the Jewish calendar. I was terribly nervous, even though I only had to do the minimum possible for the bar mitzvah ceremony of saying a prayer for the Torah. My nervousness got even worse because at the start of the service, I was told off by the then Chief Rabbi Marcus Melchior.

It is the tradition that the Rabbi, who was the renowned Marcus Melchior, at the end of his sermon from the pulpit, talks very personally to the bar mitzvah boy. My guilt was that I had not told Marcus Melchior what had happened during the first years of my life. He felt – quite naturally – that it should have a central place in what he would say to me.

Marcus Melchior was an excellent preacher and orator so I suppose that he nevertheless managed to include something about my childhood in his personal remarks to me. I do not remember.

We moved apartments and I attended a grammar school. But my past was hidden in silence. My school mates were aware that I was a Jew, probably because I was exempt from religious education, but nobody took special notice of that. None of them had any knowledge of my 18 months in a concentration camp.

I also kept quiet when I went to the draft board. I was terrified by eventually being enrolled in the military. However, I had got a medical certificate from my parents and when they at the draft board saw that, I was rejected with the remark: 'You have experienced enough'.

I started at university and had a career in government administration which resulted in a number of international activities. When I was a young professional at international meetings, where German participants were older than me, my first thought was always guessing their age and then adding the number of years that had passed since the war and, depending on the outcome of the mathematics, I started to wonder what the person had done during the war.

Yascha Mounk writes in his book *Stranger in My Own Country* that three out of five leading bureaucrats in the German ministries during the 1950s were former Nazis. Fortunately, I did not know that statistic at those meetings. Apart from the episode I mentioned in the Prologue of this book, they are thoughts that I always kept inside of my head.

During a visit to Israel in the early1990s, my wife and I went around in a rented car. At one point we by chance noticed a road sign to Beit Theresienstadt. It turned out to be a museum in Kibbutz Givat Chaym. I had no idea of it's existence, but despite the lid I had put on the events at the start of my life, we decided to visit it.

Our Arrival at the Kommandantur

It turned out that the museum kept originals of the transport notes on the prisoners in Theresienstadt. They quickly found mine. (See the copy of the transport card in the chapter "Our Arrival at SS Headquarters"). Suddenly everything became very clear and concrete and I broke down. When my parents and I visited the Theresienstadt museum in 1995 my father wanted to go down to the basement where they had copies of the same transport card. I refused to go with him. I remembered too well how I felt about it in Israel. The atmosphere between my father and me on that occasion was not so good. He thought my behavior was stupid.

I celebrated my 75th birthday inviting my children, their spouses and our grandchildren for a prolonged weekend in Prague. It seems strange to visit Theresienstadt on such an occasion, but my children had wanted to do it for a long time, in order for them and their children to hear the story, while having me showing them the various places in Theresienstadt.

In the Ghetto Museum it was moving to enter the room where the names of the 15,000 children who perished as a result of their stay in Theresienstadt were painted on the walls. It was shocking to discover that my name was on the wall as well, but with a small printing error on the date of my birth.

One of my grandchildren, 8 year-old Noah, insisted that I had to demand that they delete my name immediately. When I said to him that from an aesthetic point of view it would be a bit strange to have a blank spot in the text on the wall and that they probably wouldn't do it, he insisted that they then had to repaint the wall.

It is now more than 70 years since the events during the war. In all the years since there have been psychological and physical repercussions. These are things I have tried to keep under lock and key in my private chest of drawers. But in the last 15 to 20 years awareness of the events has become stronger and stronger.

In an interview in Jyllands-Posten[7] a couple of years ago, I said that I was working on a project: gathering the knowledge I had about the fate of my family during the occupation. I said that there were two reasons for doing it. One reason was that I wanted to pass the story on to my children. At the same time I felt that I might get rid of the story by writing it down. However, I acknowledged at the same instance that it was probably nonsense, and that I would never get rid of it.

The project developed into this book. And no, it has not helped. Actually I am unsure whether it has had the opposite effect.

WOLFGANG ALEX 22.3.1932·KAMIENIECKA FEJGA 1933·KAMMERMANNOVÁ HANA 20.3.1935·
NDLEROVÁ JOSEFA 10.7.1928·KANE MEJSZE 1936·KANN ELSE 1.8.1929·KANN SIMON ADOLF
ONIST CHAIM 1932·KANTOR KAREL RUDOLF 16.3.1930·KANTOROVA MARTA 14.2.1929·KANT
PETR 7.3.1941·KANTURKOVÁ VĚRA 4.6.1931·KAPACZEWSKA MATLA 1931·KAPACZEWSKA SON
LAN CHANA 1936·KAPLAN SYMCHA 1932·KAPLAN MERA 1938·KAPLAN CHAIM 1932·KAPLA
M 1933·KAPLAN ARCIA 1932·KAPLAN HIRSZ 1931·KAPLAN MATEL 1930·KAPLAN MASZA 19.
DE CLARA 23.3.1936·KARATSCHUN SAŠA 14.5.1933·KARPEL ERVIN 30.10.1935·KARPELES MII
LESOVÁ IRENA 30.12.1930·KARPELESOVÁ HELGA 4.2.1933·KARPELESOVÁ HANNA 10.2.1939·
OVÁ HANA ERIKA 4.1.1930·KARPOWICZ BENJAMIN 1932·KARSOVÁ ALŽBĚTA 23.4.1929·KAS
JT 8.2.1937·KASZEWSKA RACHELA 1932·KASZEWSKI MEJER 1931·KASZMAN CHOMA 1933
10.1928·KATZ OTTO 16.5.1930·KATZ JIŘÍ 4.3.1933·KATZ MORIC 30.5.1927·KATZ PAVEL 9.1.1
KATZ KAREL 27.5.1929·KATZ TOMÁŠ 28.3.1932·KATZ JOSEF 14.10.1935·KATZ JINDŘICH
ANUŠ ERICH 15.1.1929·KATZ JERRY (JESSY) 17.3.1936·KATZ FRANTIŠEK 10.6.1927·KATZ PA
ZMANN INGE 16.5.1933·<u>KATZNELSON IB 30.1.1941</u>·KATZOVÁ JOLANA 1.5.1934·KATZOVÁ
INA 23.10.1932·KATZOVÁ MARKETA 22.3.1939·KATZOVÁ LUCIE 22.2.1939·KATZOVÁ HAN
IDER JIŘÍ 26.8.1936·KAUDEROVÁ SÁRA 2.12.1942·KAUDERS HANUŠ IVO 17.12.1929·KAU
OVA EVA 1.6.1927·KAUDERSOVÁ EVA 14.6.1931·KAUFLEROVÁ DAGMAR 13.3.1937·KAUFI
NJAMIN 13.4.1929·KAUFMANN ROBERT 8.11.1932·KAUFMANN PETR IVAN 18.12.1940·
FMANN JIŘÍ 26.9.1929·KAUFMANN JAN 7.1.1930·KAUFMANN LEOPOLD 5.4.1928·KAU
UFMANN THOMAS 20.8.1933·KAUFMANNOVÁ EVA 3.2.1936·KAUFMANNOVÁ DOR/
NNOVÁ ALICE 7.6.1930·KAUFMANNOVÁ HERTA 12.8.1933·KAUFMANNOVÁ LENA 8.3
VA BEJLA 1931·KEIL MANFRED 15.2.1930·KEIZER ALFRED 30.3.1940·KEIZER MARIAN
IN PAVEL 15.12.1930·KELLNER EDGAR VIKTOR 7.9.1943·KELLNER KURT 3.6.1927·KE
KELMAN LUTZ 30.3.1938·KEMENYOVÁ EVA 25.2.1936·KEMPLEROVÁ VĚRA 19.9.1934
BERNHARD 18.6.1936·KERN KAREL 5.5.1928·KESSLER JIŘÍ E. 18.4.1938·KESTLER PA
RTA 3.11.1937·KESZTENBAUMOVÁ LIANA 12.5.1935·KETTNER JIŘÍ 14.3.1930·KIEN
CHE SIOMA 1936·KINDLEROVÁ DORIS 18.4.1932·KINCHE MAJA 1933·KIRSCHH
ZANA 2.8.1932·KIRSCHNEROVÁ EVA LIANA 8.2.1932·KIRSCHNEROVÁ EVA 15.7.1

A wall in the Ghetto Museum on which the names and dates of birth of the perished children are painted. My name was also on the wall, by mistake. It was not a good experience to see my name there.

Nevertheless it has had one positive effect. I have dared to tell the story to young people under the umbrella established by the Danish Institute for International Studies, about genocide, in which schools can "borrow" an expert or an eye-witness to give a lecture. My experience is that the young people are far more absorbed by a personal story than by a lecture about even a captivating topic. I hope I manage to give coming generations an idea about what anti-Semitism, racial hatred and intolerance to others can lead to. But the process is tough.

I can only give the lectures by creating the same distance to the events, mentally, as my mother did when she spoke in Hvidovre Club for Elderly people. When I give lectures I feel that Corrie Meyer's and my aunt's descriptions of my mother's and my arrival at Theresienstadt after the stay in Ravensbrück are so important that they should be read out directly. It is emotionally too hard for me and I cannot, in that context, manage to "simulate" distance to the story. I often have to ask someone in the audience to read it aloud for the students.

After one of the lectures a few of the students came to me and asked if I was still a believing Jew. Even though they were only 15-16 years old it seemed that they were aware that after the war there were Jews seeking to eradicate their Jewish identity. I responded a little inaccurately to the question of whether I was a believer. I hardly know! But one thing has been clear to me for many, many years. Not least as a Holocaust survivor I have a special obligation to contribute to keeping Judaism alive – both as a religion and a culture. My participation in the weekly Sabbath service is important to me. It is a part of me. I have also tried to pass down a Jewish identity to my children and grandchildren.

The recent trends of anti-Semitism in many places in Europe, especially in France and England and now also in Germany and some Eastern European countries, are deeply disturbing. It has also shown its ugly face in Denmark. As mentioned, my school mates were well aware that I was a Jew. On my question about this to a couple of them recently, one of them replied that I never "flagged" it and that I was completely integrated in the group and on an equal footing with all the others. He added that he was shocked now to know that "you had to spend 1½ years of your life in a KZ camp". I have never felt any form of anti-Semitism myself. Nor have I ever heard that which my parents sometimes heard that "we do not like Jews, but we like you".

There is an increasing challenge and obligation for all of us to show tolerance to others, regardless of ethnicity and religion.

Justice – Not Vengeance

Before leaving this story let us review what happened in the trial of the man who fired the shot that killed Rena Madsen – Hans Michael Diehl – and the two informers Kaj Ernst Pedersen and Heinrich Christian Vanseløv. There was also Paul Hennig, who so zealously made sure that most Jews who were arrested were sent to concentration camps. And finally, the judgment of Werner Best.

Justice – Not Vengeance is the title of Nazi hunter Simon Wiesenthal's memories from 1989. The title is quite right when you look at the postwar litigation which is directly related to the story in this book.

Considering how fast the people involved in the persecution of Jews made terrible decisions, it is eye-opening to read the thick stacks of documents that were used as a basis in the postwar trials, which have been central to the story in this book. The Danish judiciary largely sought justice, not vengeance.

And yet. Maybe a little qualification is called for.

The developments in the verdicts of the City Court, the High Court and the Supreme Court, and the subsequent early releases might indicate that vengeance played a bit of a role in the first sentences, which were significantly harder than the sentences carried out later, in the appeal cases.

Hans Michael Diehl, who was also accused of crimes other than the action at Syrefabrikken, was given a life sentence in 1947 in the City Court. The sentence was appealed and the High Court reduced it to 20 years in prison.

Kaj Ernst Pedersen and Heinrich Christian Vanseløv, who had also been involved in several other criminal cases, both received sentences of 16 years in the City Court. The High Court sentence was reduced to 12 years.

On 10 September 1952, the King approved the release of all three, and the remaining part of their sentences were nullified.

In Nordre Birk's Criminal Court Paul Hennig was sentenced to death on 19 June 1947. Half a year afterwards the High Court changed the sentence to life imprisonment, a verdict which was confirmed six months later by the Supreme Court. He was released in 1956.

In sentencing Werner Best on 20 September 1948, it was stated that, according to the available information, the risk of an action against the Jews had become imminent around 1 September 1943. The court also stated that there was not conclusive evidence to assume that an action had already been decided, when he sent the telegram of 8 September 1943, in which he proposed the action. The Court came to the conclusion that the telegram was assumed to have caused the decision to start the deportation of the Danish Jews and that Best had ordered his staff to make preparations for it.

The Court determined, however, that Best had also been active in limiting the unfortunate consequences of the action. This actually turned out to be the case, but that he may well have been motivated more by concerns about the consequences of the actions on policies he carried out in Denmark.

The Court concluded that the deportations undoubtedly were against international law and Best was thus found guilty and was sentenced to death.

The sentence was appealed, and the High Court revised the sentence 18 July 1949. The High Court accepted Best's statement that before he dispatched the telegram on 8 September 1943, he had been informed that the Jewish action had already been decided, which is why he was acquitted for having taken the initiative to begin the deportation of the Danish Jews in October 1943. This was a clearly different assessment than the City Court's.

An additional mitigating circumstance was that the Court accepted the claim that Best had approved that one of his employees – Duckwitz – warn the responsible people in Denmark of the action, and that it may be assumed that it was due to his influence that the deported remained in Theresienstadt.

The sentence in the High Court was clearly much more lenient than the death penalty from the City Court. It was changed to 5 years in prison, of which the 4 were already considered having been served.

The mild sentence gave rise to so much stir that the matter came before the Supreme Court. Here the sentence was changed to 12 years in prison.

Werner Best was released and expelled from Denmark in 1951.

Notes

1 My fathers elder sister who managed with her family to escape to Sweden.
2 A cinema.
3 A sanatorium at the sea side in North Zealand.
4 Probably a kind of nurse.
5 The government institution for handling issues with former prisoners of the camps and members of the resistance movement.
6 A bar mitzvah is in a way similar to the Christian confirmation.
7 A Danish newspaper.

In 1955 my mother's encapsulated tuberculosis from Theresienstadt broke up.

In the 1960s, both my parents got disability pensions. They could not manage to work any more. The psychological after-effect of their stay in the camps had become too intense.

In the early 1990s, my father's encapsulated tuberculosis from Theresienstadt broke up.

On 7 June 1996, my father passed away.

On Friday 6 February 2009 my mother was hospitalized in Gentofte Hospital with a very weak heart function. She had just had a pacemaker implanted. She said to me "Ib, here you are sitting feeding me in the same way as I fed you in Ravensbrück". Those were the last words she said to me. A few days later she passed away.

In October 2013, I gave a talk about our experiences during the war for an audience in the museum of Horserød camp. When I finished one of the participants asked me if, in spite of everything, I thought I'd had a good life after all.

I could, and still can, answer that positively.

13

Acknowledgements

Several people have been very helpful with inspiration and comments while I have been working on this book. Some of them are mentioned here.

What triggered the first thoughts of writing about the events in connection with our deportation was a call from a good acquaintance of mine, the former head of the archives in the Foreign Ministry, Otto Schepelern, who suddenly called me one day and said that he had by chance seen a file with my name on in the archives. On the basis of that I wrote a small private book *Fra Ljubonitschi til Prinsesse Margarethas Kystsanatorium* (*From Ljubonitschi to Princess Margarethas Coastal Sanatorium*), in 2003, which was primarily meant to be a book for my children.

I really got much deeper into information about what had happened when I received an email from Silvia Goldbaum Tarabini Fracapane who worked on a Doctorate on *Danish Testimonies about Theresienstadt. Experiences of Persecution, Deportation and Ghetto Life.* In the mail was an attachment of a copy of *EkstraBladet* from 19 November 1945, which is extensively discussed in this book.

It was obvious that there should be a follow-up to the story in the article in the form of a trial of the two informers. At that time I lived in London and was a board member of the European Bank for Reconstruction and Development (EBRD), appointed by the Danish government and representing Denmark, Ireland, Lithuania and Macedonia. It was therefore an invaluable help that another good acquaintance, the then attorney general of the government Karsten Hagel-Sørensen, offered to find the material on the trial in the National Archives, go through it, and send me copies of the many relevant pages.

During the writing I have been in regular contact with Silvia. I am deeply impressed by her thorough research, vast knowledge and focus on how the prisoners experienced being in Theresienstadt. She has been an invaluable source of information that she has been willing to share with me, and in responding to my many questions. I cannot thank her enough.

I am also grateful that the historian and associate professor Hans Kirchhoff has taken the time to read my manuscript thoroughly and contribute with corrections and suggestions based on his extensive knowledge of the occupation. Several of his books have been rich sources for the parts in my story that are not based on my parents' and my aunt's stories.

A big thank you should also be extended to the historian Sofie Lene Bak who more than any has contributed to the research on the Jewish action in 1943 and the postwar period for the many who had to leave their homes. Her comments have been extremely useful and her suggestions for expanding certain pieces of information in the book that may seem to lack context, have led to the expansion of the notes in the book. Hopefully it has made parts of the book more informative.

A thank you also to the historian and journalist Bent Blüdnikow who in his many articles on the subject has pointed out some more broad and international perspectives on the events of that time than I had realized in my first draft.

The journalist Niels-Birger Danielsen, whose biography about Werner Best has given me a lot of useful knowledge, has been helpful with comments on my manuscript.

Also a big thank you to my good friend from my youth Ingelise Lytzen-Andersen, who totally uninvited embarked on the great work of a thorough proofreading (the Danish version) and the removal of the many fill-in-words in the quotes. I also want to thank Joshua Burgess who did a lot to help me with the first English draft translation of the book.

Let me also thank Aage og Johanne Louis-Hansens Fond and Helga Melchiors Familiefond for their generous financial support which has made the publication of this book possible.

Last but not least, I would like to thank my wife Merete, and my children Noemi, David and Hannah for their patience. Not only for the many years when these events, although not very noticeable on the surface, have affected me and nevertheless been noticeable to them, but also for the period in which I researched the subject of this book and been temporally and mentally almost totally absorbed by getting the many events on paper.

Timeline

1940

9 April — Denmark occupied by Germany.
The Danish Government pursues a 'Cooperation policy' with the Germans

1942

5 November — Werner Best is appointed German Plenipotentiary in Denmark.
Erik Scavenius becomes Prime Minister and Foreign Minister. His cooperation with Werner Best was and still is considered very controversial

1943

28-29 August — Resistance and sabotage are increasing. German ultimatum to the Danish Government that capital punishment for participation in sabotage is implemented.
This is not accepted by the Government which then resigns. The 'Cooperation policy' continues by the Permanent Secretaries

31 August — Gestapo breaks into the office of the Secretary of the Jewish community and takes over the jewish ministerial protecols containing information about the Danish Jews

8 September — Werner Best recommends to Berlin that action is taken against the Danish Jews

17 September — Gestapo takes files about the Danish Jews from the community's office

1 October — Action against the Danish Jews is launched. The community warned by a German diplomat. About 7,000 Jews escape to Sweden. Ib and his parents go underground

2 October — 281 arrested Jews are transported to Theresienstadt

4 October — 25 Jews assembled in Syrefabrikken prepared to be sailed to Sweden - including Ib and his parents - arrested as Gestapo raids the place

4-5-6 October — Ib and his mother taken to Western Prison and further on to Horserød camp

13 October — 175 Jews interned in Horserød camp then transported to Theresienstadt

23 November — 19 Jews, including Ib and his parents, transported by train from Horserød Camp probably to Theresienstadt

24 November — Apparently because of bombing of the rails the transport is stopped North of Berlin. Ib and his mother are taken to the concentration camp Ravensbrück. Ib's father is taken to the concentration camp Sachsenhausen.

1944

10-11 January — The Danish Jews in Ravensbrück and Sahsenhausen are taken to Theresienstadt. Ib and his mother are held back in Ravensbrück

23 April — Ib and his mother are transported from Ravensbrück to Theresienstadt

23 June — The Red Cross delegation visit Theresienstadt

1945

15 April — Ib and his family and the other Danish Jews leave Theresienstadt with the White Red Cross buses, and arrive in Denmark 18 April and are then taken further on to Sweden

4 May — German troops in Denmark capitulate with effect from next morning

31 May — Ib and his parents return from Sweden to their home in Denmark

Bibliography and Archival References

Adler, H.G., *Theresienstadt 1941-1945. Das Antlitz einer Zwangsgemeinschaft*, 1955.

Bak, Sofie Lene, *Ikke noget at tale om. Danske jøders krigsoplevelser 1943-1945*, 2010.

Bak, Sofie Lene, *Da krigen var forbi. De danske jøders hjemkomst efter besættelsen*, 2012.

Bak, Sofie Lene, *Jødeaktionen oktober 1943. Forestillinger i offentlighed og forskning*, 2001.

Barfod, Jørgen H., *Helvede har mange navne*, 1994.

Berenstein, Tatiana, *Yad Vashem Studies*, 1986 Volume XVII.

Bernadotte, Folke, *Last Days of the Reich. The Diary of Count Folke Bernadotte*, 2009.

Bertelsen, Aage, *Oktober 43, Oplevelser og tilstande under jødeforfølgelsen i Danmark*, 1961.

Blum, Jacques, Bøggild, Eva, Enoch, Yael, Fracapane, Silvia Goldbaum Tarabini (ed.), *Jødeaktionen i Danmark oktober-43*, 2010.

Blüdnikow, Bent, *Min fars flugt. Jødiske skæbner i oktober 1943*, 2013.

Bornstein, Jytte, *Min rejse tilbage*, 2013.

Danielsen, Niels-Birger, *Werner Best. Tysk rigsbefuldmægtiget i Danmark 1942-45*, 2013.

Eisenberg, Alex, *Theresienstadt elegi*, 1993.

Feig, Konnilyn G., *Hitler's Death Camps. The Sanity of Madness*, 1979.

Fischermann, Robert, *At forstå er ikke at tilgive. En dansk kz-overlevers livslange rejse*, 2014.

Fosmark, Johannes (ed.), *Danske i tyske koncentrationslejre*, 1945.

Friediger, M., *Theresienstadt*, 1946.

Georg, Anders (ed.), *I tysk fangenskab*, 1945.

Hansen, Ole Steen, *Bombemål Berlin*, 2014.

Hjortsø, Thomas, *Den dyre flugt. Pengenes strøm under redningen af de danske jøder i 1943*, 2010.

Holm, Johannes, *Sandheden om de hvide busser*, 1984.

Jerichow, Anders, *Oktober '43. Danske jøders flugt til Sverige eller deportation til Theresienstadt. Kildesamling*, 2013.

Katznelson, Ib, *Fra Ljubonitschi til Prinsesse Margarethas kystsanatorium*, 2003 (private print).

Kirchhoff, Hans, *Samarbejde og modstand under besættelsen – en politisk historie*, 2004.

Kirchhoff, Hans, *Den gode tysker G.F. Duckwitz. De danske jøders redningsmand*, 2013.

Kirchhoff, Hans, *Holocaust i Danmark*, 2013.

Kreth, Rasmus og Mogensen, Michael, *Flugten til Sverige. Aktionen mod de danske jøder oktober 1943*, 1995.

Kulka, Otto Dov, *Landscapes of the Metropolis of Death*, 2014.

Larsen, Dennis og Stræde, Therkel, *En skole i vold. Bobruisk 1941-44. Frikorps Danmark og det tyske besættelsesherredømme i Hviderusland*, 2014.

Levin, Elias, *Mine erindringer om mit ophold i Theresienstadt*, 2001.

Lidegaard, Bo, *Landsmænd. De danske jøders flugt i oktober 1943*, 2013.

Manes, Philipp, *As if it were Life. A WWII Diary from the Theresienstadt Ghetto*, 2009.

Meyer, Corrie og Sven, *Theresienstadt – det iscenesatte bedrag. Erindringer fra nazisternes "mønster"-lejr*, 1991.

Melanie Oppenhejm, *Menneskefælden. Om livet i Theresienstadt*, 1981.
Mounk, Yascha, *Stranger in my Own Country*, 2014.
Nielsen, Poul, *Kun et nummer. 18 måneder i kz Sachsenhausen*, 2016.
Oppenhejm, Ralph, *Det skulle så være. Dagbog fra Theresienstadt*, 1966.
Persson, Sune, *Escape from the Third Reich: Folke Bernadotte and the White Buses*, 2009 (translation into English of the Swedish edition from 2002, updated with new material, *Vi åker till Sverige: De vita bussarna 1945*).
Pundik, Herbert, *Det kan ikke ske i Danmark. Jødernes flugt til Sverige i 1943*, 1993.
Sandfort, Paul Aron, *Ben*, 1997.
Sjøqvist, Viggo, *Nils Svenningsen. Embedsmanden og politikeren. En biografi*, 1995.
Sode-Madsen, Hans (ed.), *Dengang i Theresienstadt. Deportationen af de danske jøder 1943-45*, 1995.
Sode-Madsen, Hans, *Theresienstadt – og de danske jøder 1940-45 med Jo Spiers upublicerede tegninger*, 1991.
Sode-Madsen, Hans (ed.), *I Hitler-Tysklands skygge. Dramaet om de danske jøder 1933-1945*, 2003.
Hans Sode-Madsen, *Reddet fra Hitlers helvede. Danmark og De Hvide Busser 1941-45*, 2005.
Stensager, Anders Otte, *Kvinderne i Ravensbrück. Danske skæbner i en tysk kz-lejr*, 2011.
Trevor-Roper, Hugh, *The Last Days of Hitler*, 1947.
Troller, Norbert, *Theresienstadt. Hitler's Gift to the Jews*, 1991.
Yahil, Leni, *Et Demokrati på Prøve. Jøderne i Danmark under Besættelsen*, 1967.
Weiss, Helga, *Helgas dagbog. En piges beretning om livet i en koncentrationslejr*, 2013.

Articles in Magazines

Arnheim, Arthur, "Opgøret som udeblev", *Rambam* nr. 6 pp. 16-26, Selskabet for dansk jødisk historie.
Arnheim, Arthur, "Hvorfor danskerne i Theresienstadt slap for at blive deporteret", *Rambam*, nr. 12 pp. 126-129, Selskabet for dansk jødisk historie.
Berenstein, Tatiana, "Forløbet af den mislykkede jødedeportation", *Rambam* nr. 2 pp. 101-110, Selskabet for dansk jødisk historie.
Blüdnikow, Bent, "Moral og internationalisme i debatten om jøder og Danmark. En personlig historiografisk beretning", *Historisk Tidsskrift* 115:2, pp. 452-504.
Fracapane, Silvia Goldbaum Tarabini, "Myter og misforståelser om deportationerne til Theresienstadt", *Rambam* nr. 17 pp. 56-65, Selskabet for dansk jødisk historie.
Fracapane, Silvia Goldbaum Tarabini, "Wir erfuhren, was es heisst, hungrig zu sein. Aspekte des Alltagslebens dänischer Juden in Theresienstadt", Andrea Löw/Doris L. Bergen/Anna Hájková (eds), *Alltag im Holocaust. Jüdisches Leben im Grossdeutschen Reich 1941-1945*, Schriftenreihe der Vierteljahrshefte für Zeitgeschichte, München, 2013, pp.199-215.
Hoffgaard, Sven (interview), "Falskmøntner hos Hitler", *Politibladet* nr. 8.
Juhl, Gittel, "Mit liv i Danmark og Theresienstadt", *Rambam* nr. 20, pp. 83-94, Selskabet for dansk jødisk historie.
Kreds af Danske, "Til Kamp mod Stikkerne" (Hans Michael Diehl is mentioned): *Frit Danmark* nr. 11, 1. ågang, marts 1943.
Lomfors, Ingrid "Varför gör Sune Persson narr av min ansats", reaktion på Persson, Sunes, "Skev bild av Folke Bernadotte", *GU Journalen*, december 8/2000 (Nyheter från Göteborgs Universitet).

Melchior, Marcus (interview) "De danske jøder var blevet advaret", *BT*, 2. oktober 1945.

Melchior, M., "Mindedage", *Jødisk Samfund*, 5 April 1946, nr. 3.

Munkholt, Cherine, "Ellen W Nielsens historie", *Nyt fra lokalhistorien – nyhedsblad for Dragør Lokalarkiv*. Nr. 13, 2001.

Rohde, Ina, "Berenstein og Duckwitz", *Rambam* nr. 2, pp. 111-112, Selskabet for dansk jødisk historie.

Stensager, Anders Otte, "Hoffgaard", *Rambam* nr. 17, pp. 37-44, Selskabet for dansk jødisk historie.

Sterenberg-Gompertz, Rose-Marie (interview), "Het ergste was het afscheid nemen, telkens weer", *Groningen Dagblad* 12. April 2000.

Sørensen, Klara, "Gode og mindre gode minder, Dagligliv i Vester Sottrup, Besættelsestiden i Odense og Ravensbrücklejren", *Årsskrift for Sottrup Sogn*, 1988.

Archive Material

National Archives, Auswärtiges Amt, Inland II, pakke 220.

National Archives, Københavns Byret: 23. Afdeling for Retsopgørssager: Sag nr. 23-418-1946.

National Archives, Statsadvokaten for Særlige Anliggender: UK-sag nr. 2084 vedr. H (i pk. 99).

National Archives, Kriminalpolitiet i Københavns Amts Nordre Birk, Rapport til sagen mod Paul Reinholdt Edgar Hennig.

National Archives, Udenrigsministeriets sager 120.D.43/3/53 og 120.D43/3/70 om Lise Katznelson og Karen Emmy Katznelson med flere.

National Archives, Den Danske Flygtningeadministration i Sverige, Centralregistret.

Royal Library, Astrid Blumensaadt, note med titlen "Børn i Ravensbrück".

Written Testimonies

"Alfred i Strängnes til hr. P.M.G", 22. *April 1945* om hjemtransporten med De Hvide Busser, http://www.emu.dk/sites/default/files/56.%20Brev%20fra%20Alfred%2011.4.45.pdf

Heningsen, E. Juel, *Indtryk og erindringer fra mit besøg med den danske kommission i Theresienstadt*, Foredrag i Theresienstadtforeningen 17. April 1955.

Löb, Gerhard: *Afhopperen i Roskilde*, www.folkedrab.dk/sw92175.asp.

Madsen, Jens Egon Christian, *Fra Kerteminde til Det Kongelige Theater – og ud i verden*, www.aabakken.dk/slaegten/madsen_egon.html.

Klara Tixell, *"Danske børn i Theresienstadt"*. *Erindret og beskrevet af Klara Tixell i 1950*, www.theresienstadt.dk/sw85032.asp.

Filmed and Oral Testimonies

Christensen, Annie: Samtale med sin mand Viggo Christensen: Båndet samtale fra Theresienstadt med titlen "Fortæl det til dine børn", 1993.

Danske børn i nazistisk fangenskab, 2009, Minerva Film, Dansk Institut for Internationale Studier, Holocaust og folkedrab.

Faden, Annie: vidnesbyrd til USC Shoah Foundation Institute Visual History Collection, Interview Code 24897.

Horserødfilmen: http://videnskab.dk/kultur-samfund/dansk-scoop-i-holocaust-forskning.

Katznelson, Karen: Vidnesbyrd til USC Shoah Foundation Institute Visual History Collection, Interview Code 23917.

Katznelson, Karen: Filmet foredrag ved Hannah Katznelson i Hvidovre Ædreklub, 2003.

Katznelson, Karen: Båndet interview ved Silvia Goldbaum Tarabini Fracapane, juni 2007.

Katznelson, Karen: Filmet interview ved David Katznelson, November 2010.

Katznelson, Karen og Max: Filmede samtaler i Sachsenhausen, Ravensbrück og Theresienstadt ved David Katznelson, April 1995.

Katznelson, Sjaje: Båndet interview om hans barndom, September 1982.

Katznelson, Sjaje: Båndet interview med Jan Katlev, 8.Marts 1982.

Lanzmann, Claude: DVD, "The Last of the Unjust", samtale med Benjamin Murmelstein, 2013.

Lanzmann, Claude: DVD, "A Visitor from the Living", samtale med Maurice Rossel, 1997.

Dissertation

Wedderkopp, Maj: *Velkommen til Helvede! Danske kvinders overlevelsestrategi i koncentrationslejren Ravensbrück 1943-45*, 2013.

Electronic Media

Sode-Madsen, Hans, Theresienstadt og de danske jøder, www.theresienstadt.dk/ sw84947.asp.

Den Store Danske, Gyldendals åbne encyklopaedi.

Wikipedia.

Various information about shtetler in Belarus.

- www.kehilalinks.jewishgen.org/bobruisk/summary/lubonich.html.
- www.kehilalinks.jewishgen.org/bobruisk/summary/kovchits.html.
- www.jewishgen.org/yizkor/bobruisk/bysktoc1.html.

Index

Action against the Danish Jews, ix, 4,
9, 18, 20, 24, 27, 29-30, 32-36, 38,
40, 42, 50, 52, 59-60, 64, 84, 162,
168, 218, 222

Âltestenrat (der Juden) (Council of
Elders), xi, 130-133, 141, 168, 186

Andersen, Alsing (Defense Minister),
36, 38

Andst (Police Commissioner), 54

Arend, Hannah (*Banality of Evil*), 134

Arnheim, Arthur (Danish historian),
71, 154

Auschwitz(-Birkenau) concentration
camp, viii-x, xii-xiii, ixx, 8, 35, 90,
106, 113, 129-130, 132, 166, 170,
180, 182, 185-186, 192-193

Baeck, Leo (German Rabbi), 176

Baranowski, Hermann (Camp
commander), 111

Barracks in Theresienstadt, (Aussiger,
131-132, 135, 155), (Bauhof, 131),
(Dresden, 131, 155), (Genie, 131),
(Hamburger, 127, 131, 135),
(Hannover, 131, 175),
(Hohenelber, 131, 138, 140, 148,
149, 163, 185), (Jäger, 131, 151,
175, 202), (Kavalier, 131),
(Magdeburger, 130-131, 152),
(Sudeter, 131)

Bauschowitz, 125-127, 131, 133, 135

Bauschowitzer Kessel, 157, 158

Belzec concentrations camp, x

Ben Adam (Jewish honorary title), 36

Berenstein, Tatiana (Polish historian),
32-33

Bergen-Belsen, concentration camp, 8,
128

Berlin, x, 6, 16, 21, 24-25, 29, 30-31,
34-35, 88-89, 110, 112-113, 117,
120-122, 125, 142, 153, 163, 168,
198-200

Bernadotte, Folke Count, 165, 194-201

Best, Werner (Top German authority
in Denmark), 20-26, 28-36, 69-70,
84-85, 108, 129, 142, 153, 164,
167-168, 217-219

Birkenau concentration camp (see
Auschwitz-Birkenau)

Blumensaadt, Astrid (Prisoner in
Ravensbrück), 91, 105-106

Blüdnikow, Bent (Danish historian
and journalist), 33, 170, 222

Bobruisk, vii, 11-12, 14-16, 18

Bornstein, Jytte (*My Journey Back*), 73,
155, 175, 185

Bovrup (Catalogue over members of
the Nazi party), 6, 7

Bratteli, Trygve (Norwegian Prime
Minister), 115

Braumann, Panchars, 121

Brudzewsky, Leib, Miriam, 179

Buchenwald concentration camp, 111,
193, 198

Buhl, Vilhelm, (Danish Prime
Minister), 20, 36

Bunke, Erich (Head of Gestapo department for issues concerning Jews), 72
Burger, Anton (Head of Theresienstadt), 128
Bøg-Jeppesen, Børge, 41-42

Chelmno concentration camp, x, xii
Cholewa, Edith, Sulamith, 53, 61, 162
Clauberg, Dr. (Nazi camp doctor), 90
Clausen, Frits (Danish Nazi leader), 6
Copenhagen, vii, ix, 2, 9-11, 16-18, 22, 25, 27-29, 32-33, 35-38, 42, 44-45, 49, 51-52, 55-56, 58, 60, 65, 69, 73, 84-85, 89, 113, 124, 129, 137, 142-143, 146, 151-153, 158, 164, 168, 171, 173, 179, 188, 195, 203, 206, 210, 213-214
Czechoslovakia, Czech, viii, xi-xii, 86, 126-129, 131, 134-135, 149-150, 160-161, 179, 185, 207, 211

Dachau concentration camp, 99, 198
Dagmarhus (Nazi headquarter in Copenhagen), vii, 29, 47, 49, 51, 54-58, 60-62, 64-65, 77, 82-84, 101-102, 108-109, 129, 145
Danish Anti-Jewish Leage, 64, 75
Danish Legation, embassy (in Copenhagen, 32-34), (in Berlin 72, 109, 151, 183), (in Helsinki, 167), (in Bern, 167), (in Lisbon, 167) (in Madrid 167), (in Sweden, Stockholm, 209)
Danish Parliamentary Committee, 170
Danish Refugee Administration, 210
Danish Relief Corps, 196-197
Danish Resistance (Museum), 42, 84
Danish Theresienstadt Society, 169-170
Denmark, xii, 1-2, 4-5, 9-11, 16-22, 24-27, 30-31, 33-35, 40, 42, 56, 66,

69-70, 72-73, 76, 85-87, 91, 100, 103, 106, 121, 124, 135, 142,147, 151-153, 155, 158, 170, 183, 187-188, 192, 195, 203-206, 209, 217-219
Deutsch, Peter (German/Danish conductor), 2, 166
Diehl, Hans Michael, 10, 56-59, 217-218
DNSAP, Danish National Socialist Party, 6
Duckwitz, G.F. (German diplomat), 29, 32-36, 40, 218
Dutch, 66, 114, 126, 185, 188-190, 192, 206, 207

Edelstein, Jakob (Judenälteste), 132
Eger (river; Ohre in Czech), xi, 127-128, 191
Eichmann, Adolf, 35, 69-70, 128-130, 133-134, 153, 164, 168, 182
EkstraBladet (Danish newspaper), 47, 52-53, 55, 89, 221
Elbe, river, xi, 191, 198
Eppstein, Paul (Judenälteste), 132-133, 136, 168

Feldmann, Salomon, Klara, 10, 72, 89, 100, 112, 120, 123
Fischer, Josef (Community's librarian), 28-29
Fischer, Ragna, 91, 93
Folke, Harald (Captain), 200
Fric, Ivan (photographer), 126, 133
Friediger, M (Danish Chief Rabbi), 25, 27, 130, 155, 173-174, 180, 182, 201-202
Friedlænder Axel (Doctor), 213
Friedrichsruhe Castle, 200
Frit Danmark (Danish illegal paper), 56

Frøslev internment camp, 64, 193, 204
Fürstenberg, x, 90, 151-152, 183

German-Soviet Non-Agression Pact, 31
Germany, viii, x-xi, xviii, 1-3, 5-6, 16,
    19-21, 26, 31-32, 40, 63, 66-69, 71-
    73, 76-77, 82, 84, 86, 88, 90-91, 98,
    128, 136, 145, 165, 192-194, 196,
    198, 200, 202, 206, 217
Gestapo, ix, 4, 7, 20, 28-30, 35, 48,
    49-52, 55-56, 58, 60, 64, 69, 72, 94,
    109, 120, 125, 128, 142, 164, 168,
    198, 200, 213
Gestapo-Juhl (Juhl, Hans Wilhelm
    Adolf), 85
Ghetto Fighters House, (Israel), 192
Ghetto Museum (Theresienstadt),
    215-216
Ghettowache, 131,166
Glimmer (Mica), 161, 191
Grosse Festung (Big Fortress), 128
Grothen, Julius, 121
Günther, Hans (German major in
    Reich Security Main Office), 132
Günther, Rolf (Deputy to Eichmann in
    the RSHA), 130, 168
Göring, Hermann (Hitler's deputy), 30

H, 10, 44-51, 77
Haindl, Rudolf (Scharführer), 132
Hanneken, Hermann von (German
    General), 22, 24-26, 32, 34
Hansen, H.C. (Foreign and Prime
    Minister), 26, 33
Hedtoft, Hans (Prime Minister), 33-34,
    36
Heidekamp, Dr. (German Red Cross),
    167
Heller, 10, 72, 86-87
Hencke, Andor (German Deputy
    Secretary), 34

Hennig, Paul, vii, 28-29, 64-68, 70, 75,
    82-83, 108, 121, 145, 147, 217-218
Henningsen, Eigil Juul Dr. (Consultant
    of the Danish Health Authority),
    167-170
Henriques, Arthur (Lawyer, Secretary
    of the Jewish community), vii,
    28-29
Henriques, C. B. (President of the
    Jewish community) 29, 36
Heydekampf, Dr. (German Red
    Cross), 168
Heydrich, Reinhard (Protector of
    Bohemia and Moravia), 20, 30,
    128
Himmler, Heinrich (Reich leader
    of the SS), 30, 35, 164-165, 193,
    196-197, 200
Hitler, Adolf, 2, 20, 25, 30-31, 34, 128,
    165, 193, 196
Hoffgaard, Sven, Karen, Kate, Lillian,
    10, 66, 68, 72, 89, 94, 100, 109,
    112, 114, 117-118, 120, 139, 152
Hoffmann, Karl Heinz (Head of
    Gestapo in Denmark), 142
Holm, Johannes (*The Truth about
    the White Buses*), 195-196,
    199-201
Holm, Per (Lawyer), 77, 83, 108-109
Horserød Camp, vii-viii, x, 9, 25, 27,
    37, 40-41, 49-50, 53, 61-69, 72-76,
    78, 80, 82-85, 87-89, 112, 121, 124,
    135, 137, 140, 145, 152, 171, 173,
    177, 183,
Horserød Museum, 219
Hvass, Frantz (Deputy head of
    department in the Danish Foreign
    Ministry) 72, 167-168, 170, 196,
    201
Hvidovre Club for elderly people, 5,
    45, 48, 76, 216

Jewish Museum, Copenhagen, vii, 73, 131, 188
Judenälteste, 130, 132-133, 141, 201

Kaindl, Anton (leader of Sachsenhausen), 112
Kaltenbrunner, Ernst (SS-Obergruppenführer), 35
Katznelson, Gisse, Sjaje, Bernhard, 9, 44, 48-51, 58, 61, 159, 178-179, 213
Katznelson, Karen, Max (Moses), Ib, viii-x, xiii-xv, xvii, xix, 3, 9, 61, 64, 76-77, 79-82, 113, 116, 124-125, 138-140, 152, 159, 163, 174, 177-178, 181-182, 185, 206-207, 210, 219, 240
Kermann, Itzko (Isak), Yrsa, Annie, 6, 9, 77, 139, 141-143, 147, 152, 154-158, 160-161, 163, 174, 176, 178-181, 191, 202, 206-207
Kersten, Felix (Estonia), 196, 200
King Christian X, 19, 20, 31,
Kirchhoff, Hans (Danish historian) (*The Holocaust in Denmark*), 22, 29, 34-36, 69, 84, 121, 169, 198, 221
Kleine Festung (Small Fortress), xi, 128, 132, 181-182
Koch, Hans Henrik (Permanent Secretary of the Social Affairs Ministry in Denmark), 199
Kommandantur (SS headquarter in Ravensbrück, Theresienstadt), 99, 166, 201, 215
Kovchitsy (Shtetl in Belarus), vii, 11, 12, 13
Kristensen, Emma Florentine, 104, 105
Kulka, Otto Dov (Otto, Kulka)

(*Landscapes of the Metropolis of Death*), viii-xv, xvii-xix

Lachmann, Karl (Vice President of the Jewish community), 29, 36
Langelinie (Harbor in Denmark), 64, 124, 143-147
Lanzmann, Claude (*Shoah, Holocaust televison serie*) xvi, 132, 134, 169
Lomfors, Ingrid (Swedish historian), 197-198
London (surname), 10, 72, 86-87
Lubonichi (Shtetl in Belarus), vii, 11-14
Lustig, Mr. and Mrs, 185
Löb, 10, 72-73, 86-87

Madsen, Jens Egon Christian, 58, 60
Madsen, Rena Pfiffer (Regina, Rena), 52-53, 57-60, 217
Majdanek concentration camp, x, 90, 120
Manes, Philipp (*As if it Were Life*], 152, 180
Margolinsky, Axel, 174
Mauthausen concentration camp, 117-118, 198
Melchior, Marcus, Chief Rabbi, 1, 38, 44, 214
Meyer, Corrie, Sven, Peter, Olaf (*Theresienstadt, The Staged Deception*), 9, 10, 66, 68, 72, 84, 87, 89, 93, 96-97, 100, 109, 112-114, 116-117, 120-121, 123, 139, 152, 173, 202, 216
Mica (see Glimmer)
Mildner, Rudolf (SS-Standartenführer), 24, 34-35, 108, 142
Ministry of Foreign Affairs (Denmark), 26, 28-29, 36, 72, 77-78, 108-110, 121, 154, 167, 183, 201, 210, 221

Ministry of Foreign Affairs
  (Germany), 33, 35-36, 69-70, 72,
  120, 142, 151, 164, 167-168, 183
Ministry of Foreign Affairs (Sweden),
  196, 199, 200
Mohr, Otto Carl (Danish ambassador
  in Berlin), 69-70
Murmelstein, Benjamin (Judenälteste),
  132-134
Müller, Heinrich (head of Gestapo), 69
Möhs, Ernst (Rahm's deputy), 132, 168

Nagel (German official), 83
Nass (German criminal secretary), 56,
  58
Neuengamme concentration camp,
  197-198
Nielsen, Ellen W, 90-92
NSDAP (National Sozialist Deutsche
  Arbeiter Partei, National Socialist
  Labor Party), 30-31, 165
Nuremberg Laws, German, 11, 31, 66-
  67, 74-75, 82, 108

Occupation, German, vii, xvi-xvii, 4-5,
  8, 19, 21-22, 26-27, 30, 33, 40, 63,
  65, 85, 110, 167, 195, 210, 215, 222
Operation Bernhard, 117

Pankratz prison, 134
Pedersen, Kaj Ernst, 10, 54-56,
  217-218
Persson, Sune (University of
  Gothenburg), 195, 197-198
Politiken (Danish newspaper), 84, 104
Prague, ix-x, 6, 126, 130, 156, 168, 215
Prato (Chief Rabbi), 134
Protestant Jews, Dutch Christians,
  Baptized Jews, 190-192
Putzkolonne (Cleaning squad), 153,
  161

Rahm, Karl (SS Sturmbannführer,
  Head of Theresienstadt), 128-129,
  132, 168, 182
RAM (the Minister for Foreign
  Affairs), 35
Rathausgasse 175-176, 178, 185
Ravensbrück concentration camp, x,
  xiii, 1-5, 8, 42, 53, 55, 86, 89-91,
  93, 95-96, 98-109, 111-112, 124,
  129, 138-139, 151, 163, 173, 183-
  184, 188, 194, 198, 211-212, 216,
  220
Rdel Zipf concentration camp,
  117
Red Cross delegation (visit), 2, 129,
  163-164, 166-169, 171, 174-176,
  180, 187
Red Cross food parcels, supplies, 151,
  162, 170-175, 206
Red Cross, 64, 70, 88-89, 91, 129 152,
  164, 169-171, 180, 183-184, 194,
  198, 201, 203, 210
Rennau (Obersturmbannführer), 200
Renner, Fritz (Criminal assistant,
  Gestapo in Copenhagen), 29, 64,
  82-83, 168
Renthe-Fink, Plenipotentiary in
  Denmark, 20
Revier, viii, 95, 99, 102, 104-108, 116,
  120, 139
Ribbentrop (German Foreign
  Minister), 25-26, 30-31, 34, 69
Richert, Arvid (Swedish ambassador),
  200
Ritzau (Danish news agency) 27, 37
Rose-Marie-Sterenberg Gompertz,
  RMG, Riete, 188-192
Rossel, Maurice (International Red
  Cross) 167, 169-170
Rosting, Helmer (Head of Danish Red
  Cross), 152, 167-169

RSHA (Reichssicherheitshauptamt, Reich Main Security Office), 30, 70, 128, 130, 132, 164, 199

SA (Sturmabteilung), 30
Sachsenhausen concentration camp, x, xiii, 1-5, 8, 38, 85-86, 88, 111-113, 116-120, 129, 137, 163, 174, 182, 198, 202
Scavenius, Erik (Danish Prime Minister and Foreign Minister), 20-21, 23, 26
Schellenberg, Walter (SS-brigadier), 199
Schleuse (Sluice) (Schleusing), 131, 135-137, 154, 202, 210
Schultz, 83, 89, 108, 110, 120, 121, 170
Seidl, Siegfried (SS-Hauptsturmführer), 128, 132
Shell House (Gestapo Quarter in Copenhagen), 51, 65, 109
Shtetler, vii, 12, 13, 18
Singerowitz, Michael, 10, 72, 112, 118, 120
Smaalann, Annie, 9, 51, 60-62, 72-73, 87, 89, 94, 100, 139, 204
Sobibór concentration camp, x
Socialdemokraten (Danish newspaper), 16, 83
Sode-Madsen, Hans (*Theresienstadt and the Danish Jews, 1940-45*), 171, 199-201
South barracks, 161
SS (Schutztaffel, the protections corps), 20, 30, 35, 65, 67, 90-91, 112, 114, 116-118, 126, 129-130, 136-137, 169, 198, 201, 215
SS Headquarters, 130, 135-136, 215
Stauning, Thorvald (Danish Prime Minister), 19
Stockholm, 26, 35, 167, 193, 198, 205, 206

Strängnäs (City in Sweden), 204-205
Stutthof concentration camp, viii, xiii
Suhren, Fritz (Commander of Ravensbrück), 91,93, 111
Sundby (hospital), 58
Suskowitz, Carl, 10, 72, 112, 120, 123
Svenningsen, Nils (Permanent Secretary of the Ministry of Foreign Affairs), 25-26, 28-29, 36, 68-69, 84, 154
Sweden, vii, ix, 1, 4, 9, 25, 40-45, 47, 51-54, 56, 58, 60, 71, 73, 87, 109, 137, 143, 152, 171, 178-179, 193, 196, 198-199, 204, 208, 210, 219
Syrefabrikken, 44, 46-49, 52, 54-58, 60-61, 72, 218
Sørensen, Klara (Resistance movement), 88-89

Thadden, von (Legation Councellor German Foreign Ministry), 69, 168
Theresienstadt, viii-xiii, xvii, ixx, 1-6, 8-11, 27, 40, 53-55, 61, 63, 69, 70-72, 82, 85-86, 100, 106, 108-109, 116, 120-121, 123-124, 126-139, 142, 147-157, 161, 163-167, 169-171-177, 179-193, 195-197, 199-200, 202-203, 206, 210-211, 214-216, 218, 220, 221
Transport number, 120, 123-124, 182, 186, 203
Treblinka concentration camp, x, xii, 8
Trevor-Roper, H.R. (*The Last Days of Hitler*), 196, 200
Troller, Norbert (*Theresienstadt. Hitler's gift to the Jews*), 4, 180
Tylösand (Sea side hotel), vii, 204-205, 207-208

Viking Jews, vii, 11, 18, 28
Vanseløv, Heinrich Chr., 54-56, 217-
    218

Waffen SS, 64-65, 75
Wallach, Rachel, 188, 192
Wannsee Conference, 128
Warnemünde, 88, 112
Wartheland (Ship), 64
Weinmann, Dr. (SS-standartenführer),
    168

West barracks, 151, 155, 159, 175, 183
West Gasse, 175, 183
Westerbork (transit camp in Holland),
    190-191
Western prison, 49, 60-62, 89
White Buses, 27, 61, 161, 167, 183-184,
    187, 192, 194-197, 201-202, 208

Zucker, Otto (Deputy judenälteste),
    133